What I Found in a Thousand Towns

What I Found in a Thousand Towns

A Traveling Musician's Guide to Rebuilding
America's Communities—One Coffee Shop,
Dog Run, and Open-Mike Night at a Time

Dar Williams

BASIC BOOKS
New York

Basic Books
Hachette Book Group
1290 Avenue of the Americas, New York, NY 10104
www.basicbooks.com

Printed in the United States of America
First edition: September 2017
Published by Basic Books, an imprint of Perseus Books, LLC,
a subsidiary of Hachette Book Group, Inc.
The Hachette Speakers Bureau provides a wide range
of authors for speaking events. To find out more, go to
www.hachettespeakersbureau.com or call (866) 376-6591.

The publisher is not responsible for websites (or their content)
that are not owned by the publisher.

"Simply Love" lyrics by Holly Near, courtesy of Hereford Music (ASCAP)

"Snake Farm" lyrics written by Ray Wylie Hubbard,
courtesy of Snake Farm Publishing (SESAC)

"Sam Stone" Words and Music by John Prine, © 1971 (Renewed) Cotillion Music Inc.
All Rights Reserved. Used By Permission of Alfred Publishing, LLC

"Have You Been to Jail for Justice?" lyrics by Anne Feeney,
courtesy of Anne Feeney (BMI)

Print Book Interior Design by Cynthia Young

The Library of Congress has cataloged the hardcover edition as follows:
Names: Williams, Dar.
Title: What I found in a thousand towns / Dar Williams.
Description: New York : Basic Books, [2017] | Includes index.
Identifiers: LCCN 2017014725 (print) | LCCN 2017017215 (ebook)
| ISBN 9780465098972 (ebook) | ISBN 9780465098965 (hardcover)
Subjects: LCSH: Williams, Dar—Travel—United States. | Small cities—
United States. | Singers—United States.
Classification: LCC ML420.W544 (ebook) |
LCC ML420.W544 A5 2017 (print) | DDC 782.42164092—dc23
LC record available at https://lccn.loc.gov/2017014725
ISBNs: 978-0-465-09896-5 (hardcover); 978-0-465-09897-2 (e-book)

LSC-C

10 9 8 7 6 5 4 3 2 1

To My Parents and Sisters,
Gray, Marian, Julie, and Meredith,
who build bridges wherever they go
and have always inspired me to do the same.

Contents

"Find your place on the planet. Dig in, and take responsibility from there."

Gary Snyder

Introduction

Positive Proximity

IT DOESN'T START WITH LOVE. If you want to live in a great town, but you're not quite there yet, you don't just start to build that town with love, peace, civility, or morality. You start with a hill.

You say to yourself, *That hill, off the side of the high school, would be perfect for sledding. I know someone who could mow it with his riding mower.*

You call that guy and ask. He says, "Sure." On an early Saturday morning in late September when the streets are empty, he drives over on the main roads and mows the hill. You hand him a coffee and tell him your idea.

He says, pointing, "After it snows, you should get someone to just tamp it down, establish the track so the kids don't end up in the junk trees there."

You imagine thorny branches, kids with broken legs and stitches. Lawsuits, condemnation. Yes. Tamping. Tracks. Good idea.

"I know a guy with a plow," this guy says. "I'll get him to make a track when the first snow falls."

The snow falls, and the plow guy comes. He makes four parallel tracks and sends his niece over with a sled. You invite your kids and some of their friends to take a maiden run. All parties inform you that it's awesome. By afternoon there are twenty kids. The parents talk while the children sled.

A woman shyly approaches and says, "I'm on the PTA, and I was wondering if I could sell hot chocolate for a suggested donation. We're trying to fund some enrichment programs."

"Anyone can do anything," you say. "I have no claim on this. I just knew a couple of guys." Over the course of the winter, the PTA makes eight hundred dollars on hot chocolate and coffee sales. When people see it's for the PTA, they round up their donations as generously as they can. It's not a wealthy town, but still.

By the next year, the mowing guy knows a tree guy who's cleared away the junk trees to make more room for sledding.

The PTA woman who sold the hot chocolate has been talking about what the school is up to, what it could use. People offer to teach after-school programs and make school visits. One woman can come in to sing; would that be helpful? One woman has a python. Should she bring it? A librarian asks what the library can do.

By the next year, the sledding hill is the place to go. People bake for the PTA table, and a local farm is the milk sponsor. The PTA has accumulated a fleet of volunteers who tutor at the school. The woman from the PTA is dating the guy with the mower. The library and school are coordinating events. Someone has started a small concert and reading series at the base of the sledding hill in the summer because the slope of the hill is like a natural amphitheater.

Next year someone wants to run an outdoor film series. There's talk of a small community herb garden, and someone has approached the guy with a plow about starting a tool library. He says he'll talk to the gal at the VFW Hall. Maybe they could do it there.

That's when a father from another town, watching his kids speed down the hill, turns to you and says, "This is a great town. I wish we lived here."

What this town is building, aside from new trails and a better school, is positive proximity, or a state of being where living side by side with other people is experienced as beneficial. I have been seeing this phenomenon of town building for more than twenty years.

Someone starts something. Others join in. And then everything starts to shift into more clarity, more resilience, more goodwill, and more pride. Libraries find their way into the digital age. Schools improve. People actually sit and eat ice cream on the benches eerily empty for years.

I've seen the power of positive proximity firsthand in hundreds of towns such as Lowell, Massachusetts, hit with the twin degradations of industrial downturns and a crack epidemic in the 1990s. I saw it in Winston-Salem, North Carolina, where, after the R.J. Reynolds Tobacco Company left the state in 1995, the promoters of my near-empty concert were vowing that they would revive the city through the arts. *Good luck with that*, I thought. They did have very good luck with that.

I didn't understand the power of the positive proximity I had witnessed until I was having dinner at my friend Kate's house in Charlottesville, Virginia. Her husband, Hal Movius, who writes books about conflict resolution, filled my wineglass and asked, "What do you think determines the relationships we'll have in our towns?" Hal loves to pore through Harvard studies and explain them to dinner guests.

I said, "Values." No.

"Politics?" No again.

"Hobbies?" Wrong.

Hal said, "Proximity. That's all."

I disagreed. Into my mind came full-blown images, provided by news headlines, of neighbors fighting over parking spaces and fallen tree branches. I'd just heard the story of a company that could identify DNA in dog poop so people could know the genetic fingerprint, as it were, of the anonymous offenses in their courtyards. Early clients were co-op associations.

But then I realized with a jolt the study Hal was referring to was right. When people transcend the myth that proximity means conflict and invasion of privacy, they gravitate toward finding ways to integrate the talents and skills of their community members. Not only that, after people discover each other in the commons of town, more connections are made, and the next thing you know, you're Lowell, Massachusetts, that small city that had a terrible drug problem but now has five museums, a popular minor league stadium and team, and a free concert series that attracts thousands of families every summer.

I see towns and cities as being like people who build some framework of identity that allows them to assert themselves, do good work, and know where they stand. I find myself almost befriending them, wanting to introduce them to each other. Peoria, Illinois, have you met Cedar Rapids, Iowa? Seattle, Washington, you have some interesting things in common with Asheville, North Carolina. Gardiner, Maine, I think Dover, New Hampshire, could provide some helpful insights as you continue the winning streak you're on with your downtown.

Over time I have detected certain simple patterns that facilitate positive proximity. This book lays out three essential categories for building and growing it.

First, there are spaces, indoors and out, that naturally maximize the number of good interactions in a town. Generally these spaces have some individual character while still being open enough to accommodate the desires and interests of diverse citizens.

Second, there are projects that build a town's identity—socially, culturally, and/or historically—helping them become . . . themselves. These projects bring out the advantages of proximity by attracting the passions and skill sets of people who are like-minded in some ways but very different in others, cross-pollinating abilities and personalities. Citizens tend to see past their partisanship and biases when they're trying to accomplish something they can't do alone, such as plant a community garden or start a riverfront music series. These projects remind us, whether we're building the scaffolding, installing the floor joists, or attending events in the finished barn, that collective pursuits are achievable. Creating or discovering a town's identity can be the ongoing proof that positive proximity exists. You can feel it in the air.

Third, there is the abstract quality that I call translation. Translation is essential for positive proximity to take root and grow. Translation is all the acts of communication that open up a town to itself and to the world. Translation is not to be mistaken for civility. Translation includes a tacit commitment to facilitating all the variegated voices and personalities in our towns. Whether it's the shy math whiz student who has an uncanny technique for explaining algebra to struggling students; the eccentric obsessed with cleaning up the local cemetery; the commuting banker dad who wants to learn how to coach seven-year-olds in soccer (benevolent dictatorship all the way!); the neurotic, though brilliant, lawyer who steps in to talk her town through a zoning issue, translation is the ability of a place to incorporate every willing citizen's contributions, and in so doing, find ways to make life more interesting, welcome the outside world, and provide stability for those who need support, because strong positive proximity means that no one gets left behind.

When towns have any or all of these components of spaces, identity-building projects, and translation, they grow. They become more self-determining, and they thrive.

No one starts with the word "love," but in so many towns I've visited, particularly in the ones I've profiled in this book, something happens after the sledding hill, the playing fields, the concert series, and the local festival start opening up a world of local relationships. There is a warmth and wonder in the expressions of the residents. They say, "I love it here. I belong here. I can't imagine living anywhere else." Some people even go from saying, "I live here" to "I'm from here."

There is one preliminary question that will help you gauge the positive proximity in your town and your relationship to it. You probably know where you live, but where are you from, and where do you belong?

Part One

Spaces

How does the transition begin, the shift from having a place to live to having a sense of belonging in it? Often this kind of affinity begins with spaces where people can form loose networks of communication, where interactions occur but the conversations do not require us to bare our souls, defend our politics, or sign up to run a local festival as proof of community allegiance. These spaces can help us feel out the terrain and even assert, cautiously at first, our passions. At their best, they bring out something in us, some sense of engagement in the town, and we are happier for it.

When sociologist Mark Gransovetter came up with a theory called the "strength of weak ties" in the 1950s, he was seeing that the best place to find a job, or a new job, was in exploring one's "weak" ties, or acquaintances, not just in consulting a tight circle of friends whose interests overlapped with one's own.

The "strength of weak ties" also applies to the ways in which we find and sustain positive proximity. The information gleaned from outside our immediate world of connections is where we find out where and how to branch out in new directions. This network of acquaintances is invaluable to our community goals and for creating information webs that open up all the ways they/we can contribute to the collective life in our towns.

Ultimately, all these casual bridgings, clumpings, and cross sections of different people add up to familiarity with our surroundings. A roomful of strangers becomes a town of people we know, where someone knows someone who knows someone who can help you paint a field of flowers on an upright piano someone rescued from the dump to put out on Main Street, or to plan a school foundation talent show fund-raiser, or to bring in new playground equipment to replace the antiquated rust pile that has parents checking their kids' tetanus booster dates.

Out of the positive proximity that builds in spaces, we start to accumulate social capital. Social capital, like financial or political capital, is a kind of bank account. The community coffers of goodwill are filled up with the acts of people who sew costumes for school plays, weed out the broken tricycles at the local park, or donate a bench down by the river. There is a sense that people contribute to the common good and that we have the power to do the same.

Someone or a few someones have to make the first deposit. One imaginative example of the bank account analogy can be found in the Stone Soup fable, in which everyone is asked to help make a pot of soup. Townspeople believe they have nothing to bring to the table until a person says he'll make soup with just a stone and some water. Suddenly everyone has a single carrot, a couple of onions, or some salt. In my travels, I've noticed that after there are beginnings of collective contributions, most of the people head to their cupboards to see what they can offer. They understand that their personal resources can be a form of community currency.

Spending this currency helps to create a landscape defined by helpfulness, imagination, and collaboration. From that moment of recognition on, towns can draw from the bank account to create and maintain projects or refill the coffers as needed. Ideally, the investment of time and effort yields a high return of gratitude and generosity, and the store of social capital grows.

There are spaces that facilitate and help us organize our social capital. The right spaces can *also* inform us, from a safe distance, about who's a depressive buzzkill, which person is long-winded and should be avoided when you're rushing to work, and which yoga teacher has left a wake of casualties instead of clients. Putting ourselves into a space will always take a little personal effort, but hopefully our first forays will feel more promising than scary. Good spaces minimize the downside of potential argument and discomfort while quietly offering the dividends of knowing who's around us.

Generally, milling about in the great outdoors with some local touchstone for discussion is ideal for building positive proximity, whether the touchstone is in the form of local food (farmers' markets, gardening, community gardening), local sports (watching or participating at every level), or hikes with great views. But there is one condition: nonmotorized activity.

Nonmotorized means that sometimes you walk your dog without earbuds. You have occasions to walk instead of driving. You work in the garden without music or news (or have them on at a very low level). This is tricky. How often do you really venture out of doors without any sonic distractions? Mowing your lawn means you won't be having any interactions.

I remember weeding for three blissful hours while listening to an audiobook of Michael Lewis's *The Big Short*. My husband's podcasts blare while he is repainting old furniture. I'm not preaching that you aspire to Zen-like openness every time you're in town or on your porch. In fact, when we feel our privacy impinged upon, that's usually when we stop seeking out the spaces that get us talking to each other. A sense of positive proximity, at its best, is just the way a town breathes, with plenty of freedom to be introverted as well as extroverted.

The best spaces will meet us, and help us meet others, in a nonintrusive way, but they do help us have encounters. Interactions can feel like a risk, and modern life invites us to avoid that risk altogether. I was on comedian Pete Holmes's podcast, "You Made It Weird," and we talked about the existential challenges of simply walking out your door and talking with people. Maybe you don't want to take a chance, considering all we have if we stay indoors. As Pete said, "Your needs are met." This profound statement sums up decades of air-conditioning, subterranean rec rooms, big box stores, and Xbox entertainment. Meanwhile, we lose out on seeing ourselves defined by more than our four walls and possibly a telecommuting job.

There are unmistakable rewards of being part of something like one's town. Taking the plunge and experiencing ourselves as members of the community can be part of our primary identities. There is a plaque in my hometown library that shows the past board presidents. My father's name is there. Before the plaque, my grandfather was the president of the library. The library was once in a little brick building close to the local school. When my grandfather was president, he kept it up-to-date and made it a welcoming space for children and senior citizens alike. Over time, as the library filled up with more books (the Bay of Pigs, the Vietnam War, and Woodstock expanded the Dewey decimal codes), it became cramped and the towering stacks of books took over whatever community meeting space existed. That's when my father and his colleagues proposed building an ambitious, airy, inviting new library with an adjoining gallery and theater. My father personally fought for the theater to be built, despite heated arguments that the extra expense might sink the whole capital campaign.

My dad is a fabulous gardener whose pumpkins and tomatoes have won ribbons at the local grange fair. He thrives on privacy and in long, solitary pursuits. But he and his dad both chose to get out in the fray. My father grew up in Chappaqua and had three kids in the public school system. He had diverse interests, all of which generated conversations in the local deli and pizza parlor, on train platforms, at community day, and at three parent-teacher nights per year. We had lots of neighborhood parties, too. Even for him, a man who could happily sit and read about the Peloponnesian Wars and pore over seed catalogs, stepping out into a possibly contentious space of public service felt relatively safe. My father isn't an introvert, but his trust and familiarity with people in town kept him from retreating to his armchair or greenhouse. He rallied, he persuaded, and he prevailed. And in return for his efforts, Chappaqua has an outstanding library that one fan has called the "crossroads of culture and community."

So let's explore the spaces that build positive proximity for people like you and me and my dad. There is no requirement to be an active member of your community or to help improve it, but I will say that the Chappaqua Library was recently expanded, forty years after we attended its groundbreaking ceremony. My father is particularly pleased.

1

Beacon, New York: The Power of Created Spaces

I MET A MULTITUDE OF INTERESTING PEOPLE from Beacon when I moved to Cold Spring, New York, in 2003. These were neighboring towns about an hour and a half from New York City, too far for most when it came to a daily commute but perfect for those of us freelancer, gig-economy types who had to go into the city every few weeks. Both towns were filled with interesting thinkers and people who had chosen a quality of life that wasn't dependent on a high income bracket. I immediately found it strange that, although the towns had such a high demographic of creative minds, and although some people had lived there for decades, there wasn't more life on Beacon's Main Street or events that could engage more than a few subgroups of like-minded, audiovisual, artsy types.

Beacon was supposed to "happen" in 2004 or so. But it didn't. Its long Main Street was run-down, with all the boarded-up stores that many other American towns had. It was a small, struggling city. Despite the arrival of Dia:Beacon (*dia* is Greek for "through"), an internationally renowned museum, and the steady, patient work of resident Pete Seeger, a luminary in the music world, Beacon as a whole was not prospering.

The locals have all heard the story of Dia by now. Michael Govan, who worked at the Guggenheim Museum in New York City, and curator Lynne Cooke were flying over Beacon in a small, private plane. They saw an abandoned factory that once printed packaging for Nabisco Foods. Govan marked it on a map, drove to the site, and saw the future. This empty, light-filled space would become a museum that could house contemporary art installations with all the room they required. It would be accessible to New York City but just out of gossiping range from the New York scene. The space is the Dia we have today, as full of beautiful sunlight and airy, contemplative space as it is with outsized art, which includes Sol LeWitt's three rooms of *Wall Drawings*; Richard Serra's *Torqued Ellipses*, comprising four naturally lit, eight-foot-high distressed iron cylinders with entrances in which you walk and even spiral around; and Louise Bourgeois's eerily well-articulated *Spider*, which could fill a very big dining room.

I live eight miles down the road. I find peace and inspiration in this museum. I went so many times in 2007 that they started waving me through. I was writing lyrics there. One day, when I was still high from writing a single couplet (songwriting is slow), I walked down to the shores of the Hudson River, about a quarter mile away. What did I see but a tall man with a red knitted cap and a tiny chain saw. He was standing by the side of the river, ready to help a friend who was dragging up a tree branch that had floated ashore.

"Hello, Pete," I said loudly, because everyone in our neck of the woods knew that Pete Seeger was hard of hearing.

He turned around. "Hello, Dar!" he called. I knew what he and his friend were doing. They were finding good logs to cut up, dry out, and use for the Beacon Sloop Club fireplace. The otherwise unheated building was about twenty yards away, dank and unremarkable, with a long cement floor that could accommodate a line of card tables for big committee meetings.

No two buildings, Dia and the Beacon Sloop Club, could be more different, not to mention the icons they hosted on a regular basis. Dia brought the Merce Cunningham Dance Company into its space. Pete's sloop club members had a First Friday sing-along in theirs. Dia's visitors came from all over the world and spoke every language. Pete's group was from the region but gamely attempted to sing songs in many different languages. Dia is perfectly climate-controlled. The Beacon Sloop Club is heated by river logs.

Both Dia and Pete represented some pretty magnificent feathers in Beacon's cap. When Dia came along, it attracted high-profile visual artist Beacon residents in its wake. That's why everyone said that Beacon was about to "happen." Pete had been working and waiting fifty years for this. Where Dia and Pete's visions seemed to coincide (I won't presume to guess exactly what they were shooting for) was in believing their town could be a beacon of civilized coexistence—vibrant, spacious, affordable—and a haven for every kind of free-thinker, artistic or otherwise.

The new citizens of Beacon, and many of the old ones, too, were primed to live in a place with the freedom to roam in body and spirit. They didn't want to stagnate, nor did they want to gentrify the city and call it a day. Many of the new arrivals in town didn't have a lot of money themselves and respected the people who were already there. They had seen the downside of gentrification in Brooklyn and Manhattan. They truly wanted to do their own thing in a way that would ultimately add to the community.

But almost a decade passed with everyone waiting for Beacon to become what they had envisioned. It was like one of those logs Pete had dragged up that might still be too soggy to burn.

Beacon is flying now. The people who live there don't just like what they can do in their own cliques; they participate and collaborate in a cross section of projects. They do not live like satellites of New York City. They attend All Beacon Day, and they venture out on Second Saturday evenings, when the stores stay open, or they attend the dog parade or the annual lighting of the Bicycle Holiday Tree and the Bicycle Menorah. In other words, they don't just live in

Beacon; they are Beaconites. They even made a townie out of David Ross, former director of the Whitney Museum in New York City, and managed to snag his wife, Peggy, for the city council.

I met David at a music jam in 2010. He's a live wire. He jumps around from idea to idea with elegance and energy, quoting big names in the art world he counts as close friends. He's the first to say he's lived a charmed life. "I've lived in LA, Berkeley, San Francisco, Cambridge, New York. It doesn't get much better than that. I've been very lucky to live in all these great places, in beautiful homes surrounded by art." He made it clear that he is grateful, that in so many ways he "stumbled" into these great living situations. Then he said, "At the same time, Beacon is the first community I've lived in where I really feel at home. In my entire life, I'd never felt my neighborhood like this."

David didn't put up a sign that said, "I'm ready to see what it's like to live in a community." He went to Dogwood Bar, he went to Bank Square Café for coffee, he jammed with friends of Pete all over town, and he attended Dia functions. David and other newcomers were received into the spaces that existed in Beacon where they could find new frontiers of interest and engagement. And into these spaces he is now bringing his energies, quick mind, and goodwill. These are spaces that any town could have, some very traditional, some repurposed, and some temporary, but all of which are worth discussing.

CAFÉS

What are the most advantageous spaces for building positive proximity? First we've got to talk about cafés. Café culture is an expression that conjures up visions of Parisian boulevards, where people can reflect, converse, and dream their fantastical Parisian dreams. Café culture doesn't have to be a precious, rarified thing, however. It can be a powerful source of positive proximity in any town or city, specifically of the kinds of connections we make at the beginning of becoming a cohesive community.

Cafés are my office on the road. For the price of my American coffee, I can sit for more than an hour (unless it's crowded—I don't want to overstay my welcome) and write my thoughts, essays, and lyrics. A great café is part of the inspiration. There is something about the conversation at the counter, the community art and flyers pinned up on the walls, and the fragments of discussion unfolding around me that make their way into my psyche and onto the page. I've also noticed that some cafés are outposts for certain kinds of interesting people, extroverts who prefer to leave their houses and drink coffee around other people. They often like to talk about what they're up to and what their towns are up to. A good café is the ersatz salon of a person who likes to report and build upon all the interesting projects around her.

I've discerned four characteristics of cafés that increase the buzz of community-focused discussions.

1. **The two-roomer.** The main room is where the people at the counter take care of business, people go in and out, and a few people can sit for thirty minutes or so and leave. The second room is where the depressed teenager goes to write in her journal; where three people can have a long meeting; and where, if the occasion arises, there can be a larger meeting, a poetry reading, or a concert.

2. **The toy corner.** The toys are a boon to the children, sure, but the toy corner jump-starts some pretty potent community connections. Parenthood forces you out into many different territories, interacting with other parents you'd never dream of meeting otherwise. Parenthood is also very tedious. Think of all the good that can come when these parents, who are plugged into a cross section of the social scene and who are longing for grown-up engagement, can find each other.

3. **The friendly staff.** Ideally the people at the counter are open to the community. They know the news, they share the news, they know the people, and they are the ones who welcome you.

4. **The space that reflects the community.** That big, cluttered bulletin board where people put up little business cards and goldenrod-colored flyers for pancake breakfasts is, at its best, a big, beautiful mess. Then there's the local art up on the walls. You can find local publications in the deep windowsills. These are the surfaces with which people will interact on some level, and they show that there is a *there* there.

In Beacon, the Chthonic Clash, on Main Street, wasn't a two-roomer, but it was a sprawler, and there was a toy corner at one end. On the other end was a counter against the front window where you could turn your back and hunker down with a computer. In between were couches, small tables, and café chairs that let you decide how much space you wanted to take up.

Where the Chthonic Clash lacked that second room for planning insurrections and possibly keeping a young, ruminating girl hooked on caffeine instead of heroin, the friendly faces and the sense of Beacon's life more than compensated for the fact that we were all in one big space.

The art hung in the Chthonic ranged from student shows to professional exhibits that reminded me Beacon had lofts and work studios (that secretly doubled as apartments) filled with some very serious artists. The bulletin board was huge and right over the milk-and-sugar table, and I saw a disproportionate number of flyers for art shows and concerts posted there. It was like everywhere in Beacon, there was talent and creativity to be discovered. The bulletin board drew me in.

Chthonic is an ancient Greek word that roughly translates as "subterranean," but it is associated with mysterious ritual cults that existed before Christianity. How wonderful that Nell Ogorzaly, who opened the Chthonic Clash, named this café for what cafés do best, helping a town find a cohesive identity, sometimes in mysterious ways, through a critical mass of all these small, mutually curious conversations down at the roots. I watched something happening in 2007 and 2008 when I went there, but I couldn't put my finger on it. Later it became clear that I was watching all the underground activity necessary for Beacon to surface in the way it did a few years later.

I overheard lots of conversations about community-supported agriculture (CSA) shares and how to cook things that came in people's weekly boxes of food, like kohlrabi and kale. I joined a CSA. I heard other people talking about the secondhand clothing store across the street. I went there and found the perfect dress for my performance at a Simon and Garfunkel tribute concert. I introduced myself to parents whose kids went to my son's preschool. People introduced themselves to me, such as Greg Anderson, a great music producer in town with whom I now work, and a guy named Peter, I think, who sent me an e-mail about the American witch hunts because I was writing a song about them. As people stood in line to get coffee, I watched them introduce acquaintances to acquaintances. I had lived in Northampton, Massachusetts, which is a café capital, but I don't remember ever feeling that I was a part of what I was feeling in Beacon at the Clash.

Rick Price, who managed the café, embodied the community and invited you to be a part of it. He was young, in his late twenties, but he had already grown some roots and extended some tendrils into the town. He knew what was going on in Beacon at all times. But he was also good at taking you as you were. He went with the flow of the place. There were often one or two people who had walked down from a mental health facility a mile away. One of them would sit quietly with her coffee cup, long empty, watching everyone as he or she came in. Another was a man who would talk with you. He told me that I would do "great things one day," then cautioned, "But be careful." To Rick he confided that at some point he was going to mount a lawsuit "against all this Nothingness." Rick nodded and wished him luck.

When Rick and I spoke, he agreed that the five-year window of about 2004 to 2009 at the Clash was the Time That Was. What he might not know is that his open attitude and connections, along with those of other counter people who were also visual artists, served as a fulcrum and lever in moving the town forward. Given my attention span for writing lyrics (one minute in the zone, five minutes spacing out), I did a lot of spying and watching. The counter people were a catalyst of Beacon's social progress. Rick had created beautiful murals throughout Beacon, one on the library wall. There were postcards of them for sale at the front. He was part of an artist collective, and his compatriots wandered in and out. He loved good music and bucked the trend of turning on streaming music, instead putting in his own CDs or those of local musicians. When we spoke about this coming-together time in Beacon, he reminded me that we met because I asked him about a Radiohead CD he was playing.

He and the staff were good at filling a lot of orders, and they were never uptight about it. I heard them answering the same questions a million times. In all of these daily discussions, the people who worked there seemed to know that they were a part of something bigger.

The Chthonic Clash gave Beacon a starting point. Here was where you could feel connected and make connections. The coffee was great, and it was locally roasted, and all the pastries were baked onsite, which helped locate us in the local feel of the café, but it was also unpretentious and accommodating. The Clash closed in 2009, but other spaces such as the Bank Square Café and Homegrown absorbed the growing café culture, and now there are six or seven places to go.

BARS

Beacon also has some great bars. I want to reiterate what Jane Jacobs, a great urban theorist, warned: don't assume that a bar takes energy out of a city by filling it with deleterious social behaviors (that presumably come from drinking alcohol). A good bar can be the best place to tie up the loose ends of small, social subsets that, in turn, allow people to draw from diverse social resources and discover material ones as well.

When George Mansfield came to Beacon, he was known as a pioneer, or, more specifically, for the fact that he had "pioneered" places. He said, "As an artist you're always pioneering new neighborhoods and always setting the next boundary of where it's affordable to live." He had lived in the West Village, then in Williamsburg (a neighborhood in Brooklyn), and finally in Beacon.

As he made his way through these neighborhoods, he also evolved as an artist. He was a painter, and his friends were painters, but he said that despite his love of painting in general, "I started getting frustrated with that two-dimensional thing, that artifice of creating dimension or of creating space or light." So he got into three-dimensional art. "I started making sculpture because I wanted to enter space. I wanted something that you have a physical connection with, and I was also doing construction to support that, and I was constantly using my hands and tools, and I felt like I needed to integrate my art more into my everyday experience." And then sculpture turned into a next phase of designing and building art spaces, for which George was able to draw on his building and construction experience. And then came the challenge of the Beacon sewer pipes.

George was one of the first artists to move to Beacon. He moved into an apartment on Main Street with his wife, and it became clear that the sewer system was a mess. He started learning and thinking about all of the city's systems. There seemed to be an inevitable coming together of the artist, builder, and pioneer. "I started to understand the value of the infrastructure and how you can't build a community on a crumbling infrastructure, much like you can't build a building on a crumbling foundation. You have to build from the base up. So I got on the planning board."

When he was telling people he knew, a couple of years later, that he had given up art and that this community stuff had taken over, "That's when a friend said, 'You're making sculpture, you're living what Joseph Beuys talked about.'" Joseph Beuys coined the term "social sculpture."

Coincidently, Joseph Beuys has a room of his work at Dia:Beacon. I asked David Ross to describe, in broad strokes, Beuys's contribution to contemporary art, and David was kind enough to break it down by talking about the way Beuys brought art, politics, civic life, and the environment into the same arena.

David wrote, "Beuys wanted to ignore the seemingly disparate worlds addressed by his objects, performances, teaching, and political action, and it is generally acknowledged that his refusal to be boxed in by antique definitions of art is accepted even within conservative art world circles."

For George, social sculpture was a way to identify how his artistic sensibilities had expanded. "What more real space could you be involved in, what greater art can you make, than something tangible that you see each day and that will last for hundreds of years?" he asks. Now he's on the city council. And he owns Dogwood Bar. As spaces go, when the goal is to let the social sculpture of a community grow into its unique biomorphic identity, Dogwood is quite a work of art.

George used his creativity to build and shape the feeling of his space, and the result was everyone's favorite bar. It's a music venue; it's at the cutting edge of craft brews; it serves good food (but not too fancy); and it has wood floors, art-cluttered walls, no brass, no hanging plants, no judgment, no TV. He said, "It's a little rough around the edges, but I couldn't have a slick place. I couldn't have a place where someone felt that it was imposed upon the community as opposed to being organically from the community."

Dogwood also has one dynamic element that transforms community thoughts and wishes into discernible shapes and interlocking components, and that is George himself. He circulates throughout the bar during concerts and parties, listening to bar patrons who are often his constituents. He knows what's going on in the government pipeline. And if he's not around, Peggy Ross, a fellow city council member, is often there, as is Audrey Babcock, another city council member who is married to musician Bruce Molsky.

Many contemporary sculptures emphasize the qualities of the materials of which they're made, such as the serene earth-toned rust on Richard Serra's iron pieces or the sense of roughness in Michael Heizer's twenty-foot-high *Negative Megalith #5*, a boulder set into a bright, white gallery wall. These sculptures are down the road at Dia. Dogwood has a similar way of inviting its patrons, in all their textures and nuances, to fit harmoniously into the larger picture just as they are. George said that at its best, he envisions Dogwood "as an English or Irish pub. Little kids running around in the early evening. A plumber sitting next to a conceptual artist at the bar and having a conversation." I've been there at dinnertime. George has pulled this off beautifully.

Some bars are more social vortexes than community wellsprings, like the dark holes next to train stations in some suburban towns. Save for a friendly bartender (I hope he or she is friendly for the sake of the poor souls who patronize these gloomy shoeboxes), they don't aspire to build or manifest any kind of community endeavor. In fact these spaces just seem to soak up enough misery, through straight administration of alcohol, to allow their patrons to face the drill for one more day. They're more about maintenance than creation.

George wants his space to cocreate the Beacon he sees in the making, one that involves everyone's voice and energy. He said, "This community is really special. There's something really dynamic happening where there's this level of volunteerism. People are stepping up, going out of their way, bringing whatever experiences, resources they have to a problem or to a challenge. It's really phenomenal." He wanted to have a casual and authentic meeting place for people from all walks of life because Beacon has the potential to bridge old and new, worker and dreamer.

His bar is unpretentious, but for those who want to talk art and ideas, there is enough abstract art off of which to bounce their minds, such as a blue, tinsel crucifix with a small family of toy bears traversing the center, and the big, pop-art-style, primary-colored print that reads "FREE PAINKILLERS" over three tables by the stage. There are Dylan posters and vintage beer advertisements. The bar has music in only one of the rooms. I went there to see my friend Richard Shindell doing a pass-the-hat fund-raiser between two tours. He lives in Argentina, but he calls Dogwood a home away from home. The acoustics and the intimacy are what every musician looks for in his or her life on the open road.

George said that when he opened the bar, "I knew a really broad spectrum of people. I knew all the plumbers, the electricians, the laborers. I also knew the head of Dia:Beacon. I thought I could bring a lot of different elements of the community together. At the time we opened Dogwood, there really wasn't a place where you could walk in and get a sense of the spectrum of the community. That was the impetus to do this, not just as a business."

Dogwood is an example of how a perfect bar can be a space of gathering energy. Dogwood's function as a welcoming place at the community crossroads adds value because its owner was thinking about community over profits from the beginning. But considering how well the bar is doing, perhaps his priorities can guide a business model as well, although it's hard to advise a young entrepreneur to *be* a person like George, who said, "I'm still making art. I've just taken my creative energy and applied it to a community."

SPACES FOR MIXING AND MATCHING

Another kind of space can leaven the relationships in a town into a feeling of unity in which all the ingredients are both distinct and essential to a collective identity. These are free-form, amorphous spaces generic enough to accommodate people's ideas. They are there for you or your friends when you say, "There's this thing I want to do . . . ," and that thing involves more than ten people. These spaces don't define the people who congregate in them; they allow citizens to try out and find new relationships and definitions. Sometimes the spaces are temporarily constructed. Some are preexisting, but their owners and managers allow them to be reimagined for new purposes. Either way these spaces can be filled with social functions brought to us by community-minded people such as Rabbi Brent Spodek, who created the Beacon Hebrew Alliance. After you have a great idea that draws citizens into the public square, it's important to have a space, like an empty canvas, to receive them.

Rabbi Brent met with me in his office at the Beacon Hebrew Alliance, close to the corner of the central intersection of Main Street and Teller Avenue. For a synagogue, it seemed very similar to the churches I'd attended. I entered through a small kitchen with stacks and stacks of food and big garbage cans at the ready for any size of event, and I recognized the wide-open, linoleum-floored, multiuse basement space as I crossed to get to Brent's poster-and-postcard-filled office, where Hebrew inscriptions were juxtaposed with bicycling memorabilia. It was clear to see what Brent's passions were. He went to Wesleyan University a little later than I did, but he looked like the guys I met in college—lovely, young men on the short, friendly, intellectual side. He seemed energetic and engaged as I entered his office, but talking about ideas animated him even more.

The first thing I wanted to know about was a harvest holiday, Sukkot, I kept hearing about. Brent is famous for his celebration of this holiday as well as for lighting the Bicycle Menorah.

Brent smiled and explained that after Rosh Hashanah and Yom Kippur, the high holidays, which he saw as a time for "stripping away the narratives" about ourselves so we can be more open "to the experience of now," there is Sukkot. Following this stripping away, when we become more vulnerable to the present, Sukkot comes along. "At its core it's about ephemerality, of things passing."

The structural center of Sukkot, physically and symbolically, is called a Sukkah. The Sukkah is "this antihouse," as Brent described it to me. "It has to have a minimum of two and a half walls. It has to be open to the sky. It has to have a natural covering. And you have to be able to see the stars at night." The Sukkah is "pointing to what it's *not* in its flimsiness." Brent elaborates, "The structure is inherently transient. If it's too stable, it's not kosher. If it doesn't sway in the wind, it's not kosher." The Sukkah in Beacon is made of cotton and wood. If you lit a match, it would go up in a second.

Every year they put the Sukkah in the pocket park right at the west end of Main Street. People teach one-hour classes and give workshops in it. Anyone can teach. The parameters are purposefully loose. Brent tried to remember what they were. "Nothing flammable, that's a big one . . . nothing commercial . . . nothing hateful . . . I think that's it."

David Ross has led a class there, and so has my friend the science writer Andy Revkin. Book clubs have met there. Artists teach workshops. Brent asked if I wanted to talk about music and commodification as a spin-off of a course I teach at Wesleyan.

The openness and transience of the space relate back to a basic question: "What do you want to do with your limited time on Earth?" Brent understands that some religions offer answers to the big questions of mortality and the fact that "you get maximum one turn on this merry-go-round." But he has no interest in finding one right answer. "I don't want unity on the answer. I don't even want unity on the question, but I think the question is something relevant to everyone, everyone I know who is mortal." He invites other houses of faith to come and invites the arts associations, saying, "Diversity isn't just in religion, it's in types of making meaning."

Although the Sukkah provides an opportunity to deconstruct the clutter of our egos, paradoxically the space shows us how much community narrative can accumulate in even the most ephemeral and loosely defined structures in a few weeks' time. For all that these seminars inform a greater human experience, they can also be added to the dossier of what Beacon "is."

The location of the structure speaks to an emphasis on access and openness that one could interpret as community values. You can see everything going down if you're waiting at the traffic light on Route 9D. The Sukkah is right next to the visitors' center. There is no security force to guard it, yet no one has ever messed with it.

I have a feeling that the Sukkah is Brent's kind of structure. What he has "built" around Beacon follows the same guidelines of this lithe gathering place for the Sukkot: there is exploration; there is a 360-degree view of the stars; there are few, but essential, rules to guide interactions; and the heaviness of ideological footings can quickly make things . . . "unkosher."

Brent has found, and been invited into, a variety of spaces where Beaconites can combine and recombine their many voices. He and his friend Ben Larson-Wolbrink, the Presbyterian minister in town, started an interfaith Bible study they hold once a year. The first year was about Genesis and was called "Light, Dirt, and Longing." Leaders from four ministries participated, and at the end there was an art show of anything the theme or the study inspired. In the second year, when they studied Exodus, there were six religious leaders: Brent, Ben, an African Methodist Episcopal (AME) Zionist, a Spanish-speaking Pentecostal, an English-speaking Pentecostal, and a nondenominational black minister. Houses of worship and living rooms alike hosted these talks.

Certainly, distinct differences could be found among the ways people of different faiths viewed these books of the Bible. Brent's eyes

widened in recognition of the difference between Jewish and Pentecostal readings of a text: "Our relationships don't need to be predi-
cated on a false unity," he said. "There is a way to talk about things.
There's a guiding document that the groups use for interactions."
Brent points outside the room. "It's framed on the wall out there, a
Covenant for Communications. How to disagree, how to acknowledge that there might be multiple truths."

He said his favorite moment came after one of the Exodus groups
had met at the Presbyterian church. Afterward he walked two blocks
to Dogwood, as he often does with Ben (George said that at Dogwood,
it's a standing joke, "A rabbi and a minister walk into a bar . . . "), but
this time he noticed that a lot of other people had walked over from
the church to Dogwood, wanting to continue the discussion. One of
the things they do at these studies is to assign seating. This year they'd
assigned people to color-coded tables where one spouse went to the
green table, the other to the pink, and so forth. The people at Dogwood were in their new configurations. They chose to continue their
tables' conversations instead of heading straight for their spouses and
acquaintances.

Back at Brent's own synagogue, there is an exploration of personal
narrative and social landscape that parallels the community happen-
ings he helps initiate all over Beacon. I asked about programs the
synagogue runs, and Brent was at a loss. Where to start? But he talked
about the Melava Malka, a musical gathering on Saturday afternoons.
The program has theological roots in Sabbath traditions, but it also
sounds like the kind of community sings Pete Seeger organized. These
gatherings give everyone a chance to participate in new, and often
uncertain, configurations of music making.

Brent modeled the self-consciousness of nonprofessional musicians he led by giving me a small list of disclaimers about how he
didn't have a great voice and he didn't know how to read music. I
couldn't figure out why he was being so critical of himself until I
remembered my other hat as a professional musician. Yes, I am one,

but Pete Seeger, Peter Yarrow, Holly Near, and Tom Chapin are my heroes. The people who get other people to sing have a skill I have not mastered. Brent knows how to lead people in song. The Melava Malka is very popular here. He knows how important that is. It's hard to build a singing community, he said. That is true. So my hat is off to him.

These created spaces, such as the Sukkahs, the interfaith Bible studies, and the Melava Malka, allow for an incredible mix of interactions to occur as well as ways to experience and experiment with voice and therefore identity. Brent agreed that meeting a number of different people can lead to interesting networks of relationships. He called the encouragement to go out and find new relationships "accelerated serendipity."

Beacon had spaces, and Brent participated in creating them as well. Without them, citizens would not have had a chance to find each other despite any latent desire to do so, nor could they have spearheaded the opportunities to venture out into group activities. Brent has found spaces for events that celebrate outward-facing civic life, and his industry models the fact that we can all come up with mixers and matchers. More and more, up and down Main Street, there are one-offs and sustained programs that allow people to bounce their stories and ideas off of each other.

Brent went to his bookshelf and pulled out one of his favorite passages, from Adrienne Rich's essay, "Women and Honor: Some Notes on Lying": "The possibilities that exist between two people, or among a group of people, are a kind of alchemy. They are the most interesting thing in life. The liar is someone who keeps losing sight of these possibilities."

Any town could have a structure like a Sukkah, an open place of coming and going, one that paradoxically encourages a sense of place by getting people out from behind all the bricks and mortar of the town and into a better appreciation of the dynamic, human community around them. Or, if you don't want to do an impromptu

Sukkah-raising, citizens like Rabbi Brent have shown that many church, school, library, and even retail spaces might open themselves up to interesting new ideas. For Brent, the excitement of living in a place such as Beacon was to "come together, not despite our differences, but through our differences." I loved that Brent made use of so many different spaces where people could encounter each other and was always finding ways for his own congregation to encounter different parts of themselves as well.

Brent came to Beacon to help lighten the burden a town can suffer from getting overly identified with one crowd or even one way of seeing itself. He commandeered and crossed innovative thresholds into various spaces throughout Beacon and invited others to use his synagogue's space. In turn, he has influenced people to see more possibilities in spaces and more ways to offer the spaces they have.

I met Terry Nelson one frigid morning at the nice, warm Bank Square Café. We sat at a back table in the second room (helpful auxiliary space!) and spoke about the Beacon Independent Film Festival (BIFF), which he started in 2010. I'll admit, when I first saw signs for a film festival, I worried that Beacon was getting too hip too fast, leapfrogging its own organic growth and quickly morphing into a Brooklyn North. Terry, with his elegant, shaved head; small, neat, silver stud in his ear; and a short salt-and-pepper beard, smiled and acknowledged that he thought other people saw him "as one of those Brooklyn hipsters." But in truth, he had started a film society that sought to bring in new voices, both in the films it screened and the community it attracted.

Also, one of the main projects of BIFF is an eight-week film project for middle schoolers. With the help of BIFF volunteers and Spark-Media up in Poughkeepsie (we river people look out for each other), twelve or so ten- to thirteen-year-olds bring a movie from concept to execution. The adults bring in editors, writers, and even makeup professionals to guide the students while still giving them the lion's share of responsibility. There have been about five short films so far. They are shown at the film festival in September.

Before Terry could grow this collaboration, before the festival and the middle-school filmmaking, a number of venues opened doors to him for screenings. BIFF showed films at a collaborative workspace called Beahive, at Howland Cultural Center, and at the Beacon Hebrew Alliance, which Terry attends along with many other non-Jewish people. These spaces became springboards for diving deeper into the community and finding other potential common spaces.

The annual film festival now has a home at the University Settlement campus, which closed as a summer camp in 2007 and which the city bought in 2008. The festival always kicks off with a local band, making it a multimedia, community celebration. Terry and others were encouraged to use the campus so that citizens (and local government) could see its potential as a shared space instead of an opportunity for a sale to private developers.

"It's sort of a 'Fake it till you make it'?" I asked, to borrow a twelve-step phrase. Sometimes you fill a building with what you hope it will be before it's really there. BIFF brought in food trucks and tents, staging a festival in a way that showed the run-down camp's potential. Some of the attendees even came back to improve the space. Terry told me that one of the filmmakers returned to fix the stairs. Other community members helped with landscaping and painting. It's still rustic, but now it's up to speed. Terry and I both know people who have held their weddings there.

The success of the festival at University Settlement, among other events, did indeed catch the eye of the local government, and now Beacon has committed to keeping it as city space. In 2015 it reopened the Olympic-sized, indoor pool to the public with affordable membership prices.

WHEN SPACE IS OFFERED to try something new, like BIFF, that endeavor often grows and seeks its own space in the commons, such as

University Settlement, which then increases the amount of space designated for education, enrichment, and culture in the community. Terry seemed happy to play his role in the continuum of ideas that find temporary spaces on their way to inhabiting spaces that welcome others' ideas.

Others have been active members of the flow of imaginations and the rooms in which they can flourish. Gina Samridge, who piloted an arts program in the Howland Cultural Center, is now running her own affordable arts education space next to the diner on Main Street.

Beacon has also just renovated and expanded its public library. And because of the interfaith alliance Brent and Ben initiated, there are more church spaces bridging into the community space, available to host events.

The cafés and bars, with their community-minded owners, are going strong. The success of Dogwood as a popular music venue was one of the reasons my friend Phil Ciganer moved the Towne Crier, a three-hundred-seat music venue, from Pawling, New York, to right on Main Street, Beacon, finally connecting the east and west ends.

When people who manage properties in the commons of a town see that their townspeople actually like interacting with each other and use spaces to grow the commons, they will often reexamine their square footage to see what they have to offer.

THE LIVING SPACE OF SIDEWALKS

These days I'm having a harder time sensing who has been in Beacon a long time versus who's just arrived. There are people out on the sidewalks, and they stop to talk with each other. And that leads me to another beneficial space to explore and value in a community, the sidewalk itself. It is both a generator and proof of how spaces function to weave a community together. Urban planner Jeff Speck talks about the "fabric" of mixed architecture and storefronts along a main street. Beacon is starting to have a discernible fabric with many interesting textures. Main Street looks unified without uniformity and therefore incorporates many lifestyles.

Although the era of easily finding cheap, new space in Beacon has finally ended, there is already a critical mass of spaces in which people can meet and cross-pollinate, and there are also citizens who continue to share and find ways to expand whatever they have. These spaces allow for Beacon to reflect on itself and grow, socially and consciously, on its own terms. After that momentum starts and an interactive environment continues to run strong, a town will always (in my experience) find the space it needs for itself, for its own enlightenment and prosperity.

Almost all of these spaces exist on Main Street, bringing constant accompanying traffic into its stores, which means more profits go to local businesses. The developers have arrived from outside Beacon, of course. They will build; plans are in the works. But they will have to work within the form and definition of the social sculpture.

The architecture of the buildings is handsome, mostly from the mid-nineteenth century with its classic, Italianate, somewhat ornate, commercial facades. One by one, the building owners are renovating them. There are a few architectural gems restored specifically to retain their historic character, such as the former Howland Library, now the Howland Cultural Center, which retains its role as an open-feeling, cultural gathering space. Then there's the centrally located Beahive, which used to be the Bell Telephone Company building, and now as a shared workspace encourages collaboration as kinetic and tangled as the switchboard of telephone wires it originally housed.

Perhaps because so many people are paying attention to the history and historic detail of these buildings, Main Street is getting the approval of longtime residents. I also think the acceptance by some of the old guard is thanks to Beacon's magnanimous mayor, Randy Casale, who grew up here. He's in his sixties now and seems to have unlimited energy for juggling permits and personalities.

He said, "I make a simple analogy. You know people are afraid of change, and I get it, but in life, change is inevitable. And we all grew up and as clothing styles changed we never wanted to be out of style. We went with the new style! Well, guess what, the whole world changes. When new cars come out, we look to buy the new, trendier car; we don't want to buy an old Model T. I say, 'So why wouldn't we accept change in everything we do? If you don't change, you're going to fall behind.'" He told me that people who have lived in Beacon for a long time are happy to see new life in the downtown. I'm betting they will only admit this to Randy.

Thanks to all the buzzing and bustling originally generated in Beacon's spaces as it was becoming a more stable and cohesive city, the sidewalk's fabric has become social as well as architectural. The personalities within the walls of the downtown buildings spill into the streets. To walk down Main Street now is to experience the general glow from all the points of illumination generated by people like Brent, George, Rick, and others who recognize the social makeup of Beacon, including ones who seek to make a profit from the local economy.

Almost every merchant I've met there is trying to be a good neighbor, and most are community members themselves. And there is mixing of the commercial and noncommercial. When my friend Alice told me about how they launched the kids' art program at Howland Cultural Center, she made a special plug for Beacon Bagels across the street because of all its donations to events and workshops. Down the street David Bernz doesn't just want to sell you guitar strings at Main Street Music; he hopes you'll restring your guitar but also join one of the many song circles he runs with his son, Jacob.

In the middle of town is a newly painted, three-story, Italianate building with a couple of storefronts. In that building, another friend, Stacy, owns the Beacon Pantry with her husband, Steve. It sells lots of high-end, locally made foods, but the space itself, with its fresh coffee and sunlit tables, has a good, hospitable ambiance (I'm an expert at avoiding unaffordable and aloof cafés). I complimented Stacy on how nice the café felt, and she summed up the way a functional, sociable downtown can become part of our identities.

"The best memories of my life are doing errands with my dad when I was a kid," she said. "And after we went to the post office and places like that, we'd come to a place like this, and he would get his coffee, and I would get a cookie. And now I've been that place, and I've only been here two years, but I see kids coming back and growing up, and I think, 'They'll remember this. This will be their good memory.' And maybe they'll get a chocolate cookie or a butter cookie"— she points to the big jars on the counter—"and this will be that place. And I'll be that lady at the Beacon Pantry."

Mountain Tops, on the west end, is an outdoor outfitter shop proactively involved in getting people out to the Hudson River and up to our famous hiking trails. But I might just be mentioning it because Rabbi Brent is a big fan.

The owners of Hudson Beach Glass, a store that sells artisan-made glassware with onsite glassblowers (you can help blow your own ornament at Christmas), created an early anchor for craftspeople in Beacon. Upstairs the nonprofit arts organization Fovea Editions has ongoing, rotating, free exhibits of area artists' work. There's a small, open park next door with the Bicycle Holiday Tree and the Bicycle Menorah. People have also been experimenting with some vegetable beds. A few doors up is Riverwinds, an artisan craft store that features many of my friends' work. All of these spaces have retained the early pioneering spirit of nurturing talent by supporting the culture of local artists, even beyond selling their crafts.

Amy's African Braiding Salon, where I get my Ethiopian-born daughter's hair braided, takes walk-ins, and the chairs are always full. It is a busy scene and a social scene. I asked Amy if she liked living in Beacon, and she said, "Yes." She'd lived here for ten years and appreciated the fact that some of the African American families in town had been here for generations. I told her where I lived, and she noted that there were no black people there. I pointed to my daughter and said there was one, and she laughed. I said, "No, really, there were probably . . . twelve." Beacon has racial diversity. There is a legacy of many histories in Beacon's mix and an expectation that this diversity will remain and increase, with prosperity for all.

But there is an understandable, general anxiety about financial prosperity. Mayor Casale shook his head over a recent sale on Main Street. "When I was a kid in kindergarten, I used to have a crush on this girl, and her father was the local florist. I was going to write to her, 'Your father would roll over if he knew what his building was selling for!'"

Beaconites are worried about gentrification, and they should be. Housing costs have already priced out most of George's staff at Dogwood Bar. Mayor Casale said that he lives in Beacon and wants to stay. He pointed out that if it got too expensive, he couldn't afford to live there, and what good is it if the people who do their best work because they "buy in" to the city have to live somewhere else?

Gentrification is about financial displacement on two levels. One is pushing out residents who have created a sense of identity and cohesion in a town, event by event, layer by layer. The other level is abandoning the soul with which citizens created the eclectic, yet inclusive, feel of the town. Gentrification can create lack of affordability, and it can squash vitality when commodification and consumerism steamroll through the sense of positive proximity you can feel at Bank Square Café or Dogwood.

Unmitigated consumerism has a way of dictating to us, cheerfully but insistently, what we want to do and what we want to buy and that we always want to buy. Positive proximity, on the contrary, is the experience of valuing what we have and knowing that much of it is built by us and our neighbors, not bought and inhabited by pure profiteers. Gentrification "dons" the fabric that took decades for people to weave, ensuring through relationship-based transactions and some trial and error that histories, families, culture, and mutual respect guided the process. Buildings are for sale. And fabric can be bought. But at some point, the original material is all gone.

Some characteristics of Beacon could hedge the commodifying facelessness of gentrification. I say this, as many do, with my fingers crossed for this small city. Yes, there are gift stores with their baubles and trinkets. Some stores are more posh than others in a town where posh wouldn't have survived a decade ago. Overall, however, these stores arrived after a long ramp-up and many chthonic clashing interactions. This town has indeed finally "happened," and because this was relatively slow, it's happened in a way closely aligned with the original vision of art and freedom. There are still affordable grocery stores, drugstores, and coffee shops accompanied by the perks of rapidly improving public schools, more parks, the newly renovated library, and free days at Dia:Beacon.

Without affordable housing solutions, Beacon will still be challenged by a threat of displacing many of its most committed and creative residents. There are solutions, such as requiring that all new apartment buildings have a percentage of affordable housing. Over the next few years, about a hundred units of affordable housing will be built next to the municipal building. Mayor Casale hopes that new housing in general will even out the rapidly growing demand spiking the prices.

With city council members living in real time throughout the town (in the spaces that have functioned to keep these legislators out in the open), there is no looking away from the issue of gentrification or from seeking solutions. George said he researches housing affordability all the time. As an artist, he feels some obligation to mitigate gentrification. The creative, design-savvy pioneering of artists like him in downtrodden neighborhoods of New York City is what made them so desirable, after all. His colleague Audrey Babcock said she has faith that the current council is deeply rooted, thoughtful, and resilient. When it comes to cracking the nut of becoming a great town while staying affordable, she told me, "If anyone can figure it out, we can." Mayor Casale, meanwhile, was so excited about some new ideas from the council that he made me turn off my recorder to tell me about the affordable housing plan in the works.

People often shake their heads when I tell them about towns that have become at once unique, resilient, and prosperous. They just say, "Gentrification . . . ," as if inevitably the work at the commons only benefits a small segment of wealthy people. The people I know in Beacon actively discuss how they can grow in stability and prosperity without all the spoils going to those who came around after the town became more vibrant.

One way a town of many different incomes can share the wealth of the commons is through the work it puts into its collective strengths, like steadily improving schools. Terry Nelson told me about three hundred parents showing up in early January to protest what they considered the malfeasance of the school board (and many outsiders agreed). They had to stand outside in the cold and dark, and they did because they knew each other from a cross section of interactions, and they found opportunities to share information, identify a problem, and build enough trust to find solutions.

The other day a friend invited me to an organizational meeting about taking in Syrian refugee families. There had been a plan to receive them in a city up the river, but it fell through. Beacon citizens took on the plan, knowing that a critical mass of concerned residents would show up and also quickly knowing where to hold the meeting (Beahive).

So Beacon had three hundred people turn out on a bleak January night to rally for their school system, and its citizens were looking for ways to find room and board for strangers from the Middle East; these are achievable collective acts. But they require more than just organization; they require trust and some inherent sociopolitical understanding of what our towns are capable of accommodating.

We can look at Beacon as a hip city that's consequently drawing the attention of wealthy outsiders and developers, because it is, but

Beacon's process of self-discovery within its spaces, whether created, accidental, improvised, or highly orchestrated, earns the city a better distinction, I think. Its people know how to rally for each other; they know how to extend their resources beyond small, like-minded groups to people who are not like them, and they are capable of meeting "not despite their differences but through their differences," as Rabbi Brent says, to extend the common good.

In other words, Beacon is living up to a kind of sophisticated, multicultural identity that makes cities seem hip in the first place, complete with a multitiered economy poised to resist economic displacement. Mayor Casale speaks with friendly assurance when he tells me, "We are Beacon. A beacon is the light, and we're going to be the model for other cities."

2

Moab, Utah:
Natural Space

OUTDOOR SPACES CAN ALSO GALVANIZE an overall sense of positive proximity. Moab, Utah, a cornucopia of natural wonders, showed me the undeniable power of outdoor spaces. The town also manifests the inherent hazards of having so many natural assets, mainly because its outdoor spaces also draw a tourist crowd that is two hundred times larger than its population (1.5 million to 7,000) and because it's difficult to harmonize everyone's opinions about using the land versus leaving it alone.

At first glance, people seem thrilled that Moab has all that so-called unspoiled beauty. Whenever I mentioned writing about Moab, everyone—*everyone*—said, "I love Moab!" even if he or she had never been. They've seen the pictures. It is the poster town of a place that can, and does, capitalize on its treasure chest of accessible wonders. It sits between Canyonlands and Arches National Parks, two of Utah's highly touted "Mighty Five" parks in the lower half of the state. The parks are majestic and offer days of hiking. Thanks to its smooth and stunning slickrock trails, Moab is also considered a mountain biking mecca. And, to tie a green ribbon around the whole package, the wildly scenic Colorado River runs through town. Even the wide-open sky and clear desert air are things to experience. Moabites know the diverse beauty of their town.

If, in your town, all you have is a little creek and a grove of birch trees, there is much to learn from Moab as a place that grows as a proud community around its natural spaces, presenting those gifts to the world without exploiting them or being exploited by them. There is a balance between local life and selling T-shirts that depict Delicate Arch, one of the most recognizable symbols of Utah. Nature enriches Moab's identity as well as its coffers. Consequently, it is a town with strong positive proximity.

Would Moab denizens agree that it can handle its international popularity while still remaining an enviably cool, little community, with its own distinct character, that benefits from its variety of natural assets? Absolutely not. Most townspeople I spoke with were quick to tell me that Moab is starkly divided.

From all the feedback I got from residents, it's almost as if nature detracts from the ability to be a thriving community. Where there is undeveloped land, there will always be a tension between those who want to keep the land/water open and those who want to build on it or extract from under it.

And then there are the disagreements about what to do with all the motorized vehicles driving around and the complaints about road building, noise, and congestion. In the summer of 2015, cars were backed up for miles on Highway 191 as they waited to enter Arches National Park. There is talk of adding a third check-in booth, but everyone seems to know that you could build five more checkpoints and still have a huge traffic problem.

One can easily point out, as well, the enormous price tag of rescuing people who get lost or stuck in the bogs, riptides, backwoods, and mountain trails of any destination with rugged terrain. People can get really expensively stuck in the Mighty Five. In our Hudson Valley town of lesser-known trails, we finally placed trail stewards at the bottom of our hiking trails. When people showed up from Brooklyn in flip-flops to climb Breakneck Ridge, the guides sent them off to sea-level Little Stony Point instead. When people don't know the terrain, they can go flippity-floppity right into a crevasse.

And there is the financial imbalance that can develop in nature-based tourist destinations. Even in towns with fewer acres of trails and rivers, there is the question of what economic relationship can be had between the wonderland and the wallet. In towns like Moab, citizens' employment default is to become the bartenders, burger flippers, and room cleaners for an endless stream of visitors. Tourism alone, as an industry, will disproportionately fill up a town with zero-mobility jobs, and the service economy employment is somewhat cruelly coupled with a real-estate problem in which food servers can't afford a place to live while part-time residents think nothing of spending six figures or more for their second and third homes.

You might think that if you simply want to blaze a small trail to a waterfall on the outskirts of town, you will not encounter major tourism issues like this, but purposefully leaving land undeveloped can become controversial no matter how small the project. Anyone who wishes to protect and showcase natural sites must be prepared to point out that natural beauty can be a force that lifts our collective spirits every day, improves our communal health, and strengthens our local pride and sense of place. After those natural spaces are set aside for everyone to enjoy, it's hard for most towns to remember what they were without them. Moab, however, with its oil reserves and real-estate pressures, has to make the case for nature on an ongoing basis.

But here's the thing. The life that springs from all the outdoor interactions, that is, life beyond the doorways of people's houses, adds up to a strong civic identity. Moab has positive proximity. When you're coming from the outside, as I do, relying on strangers and the clarity of their signage to get around, you're looking at how well a town hangs together. My index of success is not based on how well people get along. I see how people get the job done. I can see how well Moab works, publicly and privately, almost at first glance, far beyond the basics of traffic lights and sidewalks. Moab couldn't be what it is without common goals, and, though natural beauty brings the overwhelming challenges of tourism, I think it adds to the harmony and sense of community Moab has.

Moab, for instance, has interesting institutions, such as a sliding-scale health clinic; a busy multicultural center; a recently renovated town hall and a mayor they love to love; a community radio station; and a secondhand clothing store, Wabi-Sabi, from which proceeds go to annually designated nonprofits. It has a Main Street full of independent businesses (though yes, plenty of chains, especially hotels). It is a Leadership in Energy and Environmental Design (LEED)–certified city, meaning that the whole city gets a stamp of approval for environmental conservation. And this is on top of a nice library and playing fields, recycling (even though my Moabite friend, Cosy, told me some people believe recycling is a "trend"), and a beautiful walking path along Mill Creek in the center of town. From all I see and hear, this town endeavors to take care of its own.

More than that, you can feel the spirit of Moab. I did one short house concert there in 1994. I loved it so much, I did what I never do: in 1998 I scheduled a vacation there in the middle of a tour.

My then-boyfriend, Doug, and I arrived at midnight from Salt Lake City. When I opened the car door and felt a wave of dry wind, sage-infused and still warm in the dark of night, I immediately remembered the romance of the desert. The next morning, we awoke to a small western town encircled by rocky cliffs that were deep red in the early sun. What was this enchanted place? Moab looked like fun, but it felt like magic.

We saw right away that we were in a town with its own culture and conversations. The townspeople, not just the tourists, were out in the streets and on the trails. At the local diner we sat at the counter, drank coffee from the excellent Moab Roasting Company, and listened to some men talking about a guy named Bob. Apparently, Bob was a guy who kept to himself out at the edge of town in his trailer. The men knew we were listening, so they elaborated even as they pretended they didn't see us. Bob was a burly man of mystery, something between a local and a legend, not so much misanthropic as wanting to drink his own water out of his own tin cup. There weren't interactions with Bob; they were more like sightings.

The conversation turned to a celebrity breakup in the news. The man had had an affair. The mistress was in hiding. The men at the diner were charitable toward all parties. Latest news was that she had completely disappeared, but one of the men said no, actually, he knew where she was. "She's out there with Bob."

Later that day we went tubing with fellow singer-songwriter Cosy Sheridan, who had fallen in love with Moab "because it looked like the floor of the Grand Canyon." I felt nervous as TR Richie, another talented folksinger and Cosy's boyfriend, drove us up along the jade-green waters of the Colorado River. What was this tubing? Was it one of those death-defying things naturally athletic people did? TR got out and plopped three truck inner tubes out on the red sand. I dreaded what would happen then.

But you know what tubing is? It's floating down a river in a giant black donut. And in this case, we were floating on a gentle current with the red rock cliffs rising up on either shore. Again, this wasn't just a tourist thing. It was just one beautiful, cheap way to spend an afternoon.

That was Moab. The coffee, the dudes, the simple pleasures in stunning locales, the town that let us happy tourists climb all over its rocks and float down its river. At every turn, there was someone to point out another arch and a bend in the river. They knew their town inside and out (mostly out) and took responsibility for it. That's positive proximity. In those three days, we went mountain biking, running, and hiking through town and in Arches National

Park. Moab welcomed us, warmly and hospitably, and we truly hoped we had been good guests. We didn't just want to visit again. We wanted to be welcomed back.

I returned to Moab with my family in 2010. I took a temperature reading, as I and kindred musicians tend to do. What was the feeling? Inviting? Happy? Depressed? Was this still a "locals first" town with guys talking about Bob and other characters, not just the enthusiastic park rangers who wanted to share their favorite trails? Just based on where we went, the answer was "Yes." The camaraderie among people working in these places and their discussions of local things, despite the peak season of travelers like us, were clearly there, as were their helpfulness and pride.

I played at the Moab Folk Festival in 2015. It still felt like the community I loved, but there was also some wariness this time around. The shutting down of Highway 191 at Arches had shaken the town. Not only had attendance records been broken every year since 2012, they'd been shattered, each year pushing the limits of what the town could handle. But Moab, the Moab I knew, was still holding strong.

Let's look at some of the ways in which incorporating nature has helped Moab build positive proximity. What I learned from my time in Moab, first and foremost, is that communities can carry out an effective kind of self-identifying conversation through the common experience of their terrain, but because nature doesn't necessarily generate solid living wages outside of government-paid park jobs (at Arches National Park, the weekly parking pass is twenty-five dollars; there is a very good gift shop; you can enjoy nature on the cheap, and most people do so because it is cheap), communities must always take care of their human needs and pay attention to their human economy as carefully as they facilitate the love of their landscapes and waterways.

Moab has an extra burden. Tourism brings in temporary populations. There is an inconsistent tidal flow of nonresidents. The town must find an axis of stability. When the human population and commerce are stable, towns can truly harness the ways in which nature can be experienced as shared wealth, and all those red rock and green piñon nooks and crannies can help perpetuate an abundance of face-to-face, often town-focused discussions.

TOURISTS AND TOWNS

In an increasingly postindustrial national economy, many towns have some sector of tourism in their economic portfolios. There is one thing towns have to do when it comes to people visiting from the outside. They must have places that are both visitor viable and resident relevant. I call this the V:R ratio. The ideal is to have businesses, spaces, and events that work for both the visitors and residents. Part of a V:R ratio's success, however, is to have some areas that don't overlap. At the end of the day, there will always be spaces for tourists only. And then townspeople must bolster their awareness of themselves, the devoted gatekeepers and stewards of their home, with places that they keep to themselves. Moab has the balance. It's fragile, but it's there.

Back of Beyond Books, owned by a friend to me and many musicians, Andy Nettell, has a perfect V:R ratio. There are books by a whole range of writers, such as Terry Tempest Williams, Edward Abbey, and Amy Irvine, who ennoble the southern Utah landscape with poetry, helpful histories, and absorbing prose. There are shelves full of trail maps. The literature is for all of us, both residents and visitors, who want to experience the poetry and prose of that landscape. It is a very tourist-friendly business. But Back of Beyond is also more than a bookstore. For residents it's also a place that offers itself as a local cultural hub close to the intersection of Main and Center Streets. It is a link between nature as a common experience and nature in the larger context of history and poetic reflection. It has book signings and readings every month, half of which feature local authors; it opens its doors during ArtWalk and generally holds a hearthlike space for information-sharing and local news.

Moab has a lot of quality hangouts the locals themselves can frequent before or after a morning hike. The importance of interactive spaces is specifically relevant to a place like Moab, where citizens have to continually make sense of their town apart from the traffic and noise of outsiders.

There are many restaurants in town, but the locals have their favorite cafés, such as the Eklecticafé, Wake and Bake, the Moab Diner, and the Lovin' Muffin, where they can have their discussions about what's going down in town. Travelers love them, too, and I'm sure that when the Eklecticafé's ten or so tables fill up at peak season, the tourists are seen as a major pain, but that doesn't mean they determine the personality of the restaurant. Eklecticafé, with its excellent but unfussy burritos and salads and a wind sculpture outside next to a giant, mosaic-tiled teapot, is pure Moab. The locals go to the same restaurants and bars the tourists do, too, such as Eddie McStiff's and the two or three Mexican restaurants, all near Back of Beyond.

As ordinary as it sounds, it's also important to the V:R ratio that Moab has a big drugstore on Main Street. You can find basic things like socks in the pedestrian center of the downtown. This seems obvious, but I remember being at the visitors' center in Franklin, Tennessee, asking where I could get an aspirin in this gorgeous little town (high positive proximity, too). The woman behind the counter shook her head sympathetically and said if there were one store she could bring here, it would be a plain drugstore. The closest one was a mile away.

The Moab high school auditorium is another space with a great V:R ratio. It's a state-of-the-art theater, with building materials such as sandstone that echo the immediate outdoors, that hosts events for out-of-towners. It's also a place where citizens can go en masse to celebrate or to agree or to argue. The night concerts for the Moab Folk Festival were there (as well as at another community space, Starr Hall). There are also many events for locals only. By having its main venue within its high school, Moab uses this resource year-round and students get more exposure to culture. There were teenage volunteers at the folk festival when I was there. They know it's very much their turf.

The multicultural center grew out of efforts by the local Episcopal church to recognize the large and mostly silent Hispanic population that staffs many of the restaurants and hotels in town. One very successful event has been Día de los Muertos (Day of the Dead) in early November. The spaces and events, created to recognize the cultures and contributions of the sometimes non-English-speaking citizens, new and old, have incorporated valuable perspectives into the community as a whole. One woman described how meaningful it was for people in town to reflect on the loss of its members not just once, when they died, but again on a day of recognition during which the departed were seen in the context of an interwoven community. She talked about an eighteen-year-old boy who was dearly missed by the many who knew him, and she stressed how important it was to memorialize him in this larger town ceremony, months after the acute shock of his death.

Andy Nettell told me about another event put on by the multicultural center. It held a *Dancing with the Stars* fund-raiser at which six Hispanic women taught six "gringo guys" their dances (not traditional ones), while other Hispanic local citizens cooked all the food. They held it at the high school, and it was a hot ticket, drawing six hundred fifty people.

It's an important survival tool to find the value of every resource in a desert. The high school and the multicultural center have multiuse spaces to incorporate the best of the community's intergenerational, multiethnic identity. I noticed that whereas in Beacon, all the permutations of indoor conversations spilled out into its streets, Moab's myriad outdoor conversations seemed to find traction in its interior spaces.

There are many highly athletic events for visitors, such as the marathons, half-marathons, and Ironman runs that pass through town, and then there are those that cater to out-of-towners and locals alike, such as the Moab Folk Festival, which had about a 50:50 ratio of residents and visitors. Again, although some events bring outside revenue into the town, a strong V:R ratio allows the town to enjoy the bounty that exists outside of commerce and taxes as well. For example, everyone admits that the supermarket in Moab, City Market, wouldn't offer as much if it weren't for the influx of traffic, though no one is a fan of the long checkout lines in the summer.

The tourists themselves, in their limited interactions with Moabites, have their charms as well. When I went hiking with Jessie Walsh, a hospice nurse in town, she said, "After a long winter of seeing all the same people, I have to admit, I really like seeing some new faces." The V:R ratio works for Jessie. There are wide-open spaces, but socially things can get claustrophobic. She appreciates the tourists that come into Moab from all over the world. The tourists bring the world with them. I'm sure Jessie noticed, as I did, the seven or eight languages you hear out on the trails. She enjoys this diversity, but this is still her town.

STEWARDSHIP AND PRIDE

Moabites have lots of ways of getting you out on their land and into their river because they are enthusiasts themselves. Another way Moab resists getting swallowed up by the tourist trade is that its residents put themselves out there with their expertise and guidance. Moabites know how to do it. These are people who fell in love with this town, and, like romantics, they followed their love.

There's an ethos that this town has fostered. The locals are not snobbish. When you meet them face-to-face, they are not resentful. Yes, I was brought to one park where I had to swear not to tell "non-Moabites" where I'd been, but in knowing that there are some places that are secretly their own, in retaining a little of their own mystery, Moabites are more generous with tourists in their exploration of the remaining turf. They are the stewards. They know what the land can take. They know why you're here because they came for the same reason. There is fun to be had, and they are experts at it. And if you just stay on the trails, you're golden, though it's even better if you carpool and come in the off season.

The mutual enjoyment of the river and the rocks is another great builder of positive proximity. People are out and about, sharing information all the time with each other as well as with new people. Everyone seems to have a favorite trail or path, and the well-traveled terrain keeps continual, though complicated, geocultural oral history alive. We've heard of Edward Abbey. Moabites I met referred to him as Ed.

I spoke with one of the first people to introduce mountain bikes to Moab, Robin Groff. Robin was one of the citizens who set the tone of generously sharing the land. People were dubious when he and his brother, Bill, opened a bike store, Rim Cyclery, in town just after the uranium business tanked. Uranium had been the main industry of Moab all the way into the mid-1980s.

Robin lives near the center of town in a long, one-story bungalow with a nice, big shade tree. He's in his sixties now, with white hair and a flowing white beard. He looks a little more like a motorcycle guy than a mountain cycle guy.

Robin, whose whole family worked in mining-related professions, remembered when the price of uranium dropped by two-thirds almost overnight and everything went belly-up. He sat there all winter wondering what he was going to do, when he had a revelation. "Moab was sitting in a very unique situation and that is we sit at the entrance to two national parks. No other community in the US except Jackson Hole, Wyoming, is in that same position."

Biking was a popular sport at the time, but it was somewhat effete, more of a thin-wheeled, European-based business. But then "mountain bikes came out, and we could see the significance of that right away. And so we invested heavily in promoting mountain biking here."

At trade shows, the brothers found people who were game for a trip to Moab to test the slickrock trails. "Almost all of the people in the mountain biking industry were young and rebellious." The Groffs were, too.

Robin said, "Adventurers like to hang around with other adventurers. It doesn't matter if you're a mountain biker or a climber or a river runner, you all have basically the same perspective." It's all about taking risks because "adrenaline is too big a high." Moab is a land of many highs.

Robin and Bill brought a new kind of pioneer to Moab and never lost the pioneering spirit themselves. "When we first started out and right after mountain bikes came in, there was nothing in town. So we also started the first touring company in town. We put in climbing gear. We had outdoor gear. We had river-running gear because none of those things were available."

But soon things started to roll, so to speak, and as other touring companies and stores started popping up, the Groffs went back to bikes. Robin and Bill had done their part in re-creating Moab's outdoor profile, showing how this expanse of ancient natural monuments, including those with dramatic names like Devil's Garden in Arches National Park, could also be a Playground of the Divine.

So, there's another secret: Moab has created an economic structure, outside of the hospitality service sector, that benefits from nature. And its citizens participate in it. People come to play. The citizens play, too. They engage in their own local conversations, accumulating wisdom and weighing in on conserving resources so that everyone can continue to have the same high they experience.

And perhaps because Moabites have such an interactive experience of the land itself, they are not shy about giving feedback to their popular mayor, Dave Sakrison. They get right in with him throughout the decision-making process. He, in turn, offers leadership that leans toward his constituents instead of bending over backward for the tourists.

PUTTING THE CITIZENS FIRST

The mayor is another hedge Moab has against being overrun by outsiders. No matter how diverse and divided the backgrounds and priorities of Moab's citizens might be, Mayor Dave is receptive to the town first and foremost—its buildings, its services, and its citizens. Dave used to own Dave's Corner Market. Cosy told me, "There is a picture of him by the coffee machine—he's about thirteen years old, standing in the doorway of one of the local motels with John Wayne." The older men in town would hang out on the bench outside and have coffee. Dave put pictures of them on the wall when they passed on. He is a respectful witness to his town, so everyone likes Dave even though he drives a Prius and wants to bring wind power to Moab. And when he became mayor, he watched out for everyone. The citizens have an ethos of stewardship, and local government has shown a sense of stewardship for the citizens.

Mayor Dave said, "We made a conscious effort when we decided to go down the tourist path that we're only going to do things for the people that live here. And the people that come benefit from some of the things that we've done. We thought outside the box, and I think it's worked pretty well."

And that's exactly how things look in town. The playing fields, library, city hall, and other public spaces surpass those of many towns I've seen. Obviously there are tax revenues from tourism, but the leadership is focused on the quality of the commons, shared by all but starting with the citizens.

Town-first attention to affordable housing, for instance, has been a major issue. The government of Moab has initiated building affordable housing units close to town. Another big solution Mayor Dave and many others have presented to Moab is to diversify the economy away from service-sector jobs by creating a regional campus for Utah State University. Land has been set aside for it at the southern end of town.

Regarding the added benefits a college can bring to a nature-based and nature-loving economy such as Moab's, Dave said, "It's not going to be your typical liberal arts college or what have you. What they're going to concentrate on is tailoring it to the community itself. We'll have land management, we'll have ecology, and we'll have the College of the Colorado River, basically, which is going to look at all the environmental impacts to the river."

A campus could absorb a lot of visitors when school is out of session and keep a couple of hotels from being built. Mayor Dave said this extra source of accommodation was a consideration. However, there's a traffic concern about the college. There's an argument that a campus will bring in even more polarizing fast-food jobs via the kinds of all-night chains college students often patronize. There's a ridiculous Tea Party–type question about whether county money should be spent on education. The project has been held up. Whether or not the campus gets built, Moabites know they could use a business or institution that draws on the same love of nature but is not related to tourism. A university could alleviate some of the frustration people have about employment opportunity.

There is also a tourist-friendly (and economically advantageous) reason to put the town first. Mayor Dave's priorities allow Moab to retain its own personality. Travelers value a town with character and, at their best, add their vacation dollars to the growing good, not the leeching bad. People love the feel and character of this town. They want to support the woman with the long braid at Back of Beyond Books who knows the best picture book about the desert for kids. They want to know that as they come through en masse, there's still room in the canyon for a recluse named Bob in his trailer. They want to see locals such as Robin Groff riding past them on his way to his next adventure. They want to know that the nurse at the hospital came here because this is where she felt like she could be herself. Tourists can get a bad reputation, but in truth, many travelers seek out towns with a personality like Moab's and will endeavor to respect and experience the town on its own terms.

I live in a tourist town. I don't feel trampled by our visitors. I like it when they buy things from our merchants, and I feel proud when young couples pass our house, looking at each other with the silent question, "Could we live here someday?" For now they want to kayak and hike here, but they understand that we live here, too.

THE WONDER OF OUTDOOR SPACES

It's time to appreciate the positive proximity that comes from beauty itself. Although Moabites are excellent stewards, leading the way for visitors, they are also *led*. When you've got the power of nature as your common denominator, as Moab does, you've got an opportunity to be influenced by its beauty, letting it guide a shared sense of wonder, abundance, and generosity. Perhaps that is why I see Moab as a community as well. The people have let themselves be moved—influenced—by the splendor that surrounds them.

Throughout the town, people describe their connection to the town through the landscape. Chuck runs a block-long store that specializes in Native American art. He was originally part of an oil speculation team making its way down from Montana. When they reached Moab, he quit the oil job and stayed. He told me he never tires of the way the light changes across the cliffs over the course of the day.

When I asked Jessie Walsh what brought her here initially, she made a circle in the air with her hand: "All of this," she said. I realized that many people I met had made a similar hand gesture when I asked what brought them to Moab: "This." Moab offers a somewhat pure example of the power that nature can have over a community. Natural beauty can be a transcendent community tie. Not everyone has the luminous optimism I found in Jessie Walsh, but I think we might all admit that nature can give us a little metaphysical boost that we can, in turn, transfer into our communities.

For anyone who assumes "nature" doesn't exist in his or her town, that the surroundings are too drab and unattractive to be reveled in, it's instructive to note that in the mid-1980s Moab resisted seeing itself as a paradise defined by nature itself. Moab was a uranium-mining town. Arches National Park was already in existence (Edward Abbey was a ranger there when he wrote *Desert Solitaire*), but the roads had barely been built, and national park visitation was not as big as it is now.

Joe Knightley, a real-estate broker who has served on the travel council and chamber of commerce for almost forty years, asked if I knew where Moab was in the Bible. I didn't know. "See, the locals know," he said, with a little smile. "This is Mormon territory, and there is a place in the Bible that is Hell's Hole. It's the closest to hell you can be on earth. And in the Bible it's Moab."

So from the start, Moab had associations that didn't automatically connect it with the way we can discover ourselves and each other out on the land, let alone with keychains and camper vans. It was, in fact, a fun town, but in a rough-and-tumble, "work hard, play hard," mining community way. Then in about one day, the price of uranium plummeted, the uranium mines and mills shut down, and half the people, three thousand of them, left. Joe said he would look out the window of his downtown office. "I could sit there and watch deer and geese cross the street. So that kind of gives you a visual of where we were at that time."

The five-member Moab Chamber of Commerce met at what is now Jeffrey's Steakhouse in the very room in which Joe and I were sitting when I met him. Together they decided to hold two nights of town meetings at Starr Hall for people to say what they thought should happen next. "And we had both nights standing room only. The place was packed. We're talking about people whose families were born and raised here. I mean true locals. And so the conversation was very open, sincere, because they could feel the dying of the community with all these boarded-up houses; they knew that their neighbors were moving out."

One man from Workforce Services, an agency that helps people find jobs, stood up. Joe recalled that "he said, 'You know, this is a unique destination place that people just would come to if they knew it existed.'" He was suggesting an economy based on tourism. "Everybody laughed," Joe said. But the Workforce Services guy added one more thing just to reinforce his argument. According to Joe, he said, "You know, our place is so beautiful, even our dump is beautiful."

Back at the steakhouse, Joe Knightley and his fellow chamber members sagaciously adopted the dump comment. If tourism had any potential, the chamber and its small travel council of which Joe was part would have to shoulder the effort themselves. At the time, Utah's distant state government had all but forgotten about them. Joe said, "I am not exaggerating. I could go to Salt Lake for a state meeting in the early 1980s and tell my peers 'I'm from Moab.' They would look at me straight in the face and say, 'Is that in Utah?'"

What happened next is particularly instructive because it shows how a small group of people managed to build the positive proximity to make a peaceful shift from mining to rock climbing. Members of the chamber came up with an idea to drum up a little press for a natural paradise once deemed the last bus stop on the route to hell. They decided to have a "Most Beautiful Dump" contest, pitting themselves primarily against Grand Junction, Colorado, about two hours east of Moab. Grand Junction residents had bonded with Moab over the fact that they, too, felt neglected by their state legislators in Denver.

A freelance journalist named Vicky Barker put together a press release that threw down the garbage gauntlet and sent it off to Grand Junction. The *Daily Sentinel*, in Grand Junction, printed it, and then the story really broke.

Joe said, "The *Denver Post* the very next day saw it, and they posted it as a front page that those hippies in Moab and rednecks in Grand Junction are creating this competition and is Denver up to the challenge? Within a week it got picked up by the Associated Press and all the print media were printing it and doing it. And I started getting phone calls. I wasn't prepared for this."

But Joe and his friends rose to the occasion. "I wrote a little ditty, a proclamation, that Moab is challenging the world on who has the most scenic dump. I'm the judge. I'm the president of the Chamber of Commerce. I already know who won. So what I'm doing is looking for who wins second place. Everybody laughs. I got interviewed three times by Larry King. I got interviewed by Dan Rather twice. We were on the front page of the *Wall Street Journal* twice and once on the *Wall Street Journal* in Europe, front page. We were literally on television, all three networks. We estimate we got eighteen million dollars' worth of advertising. John Fogg and I were on the cover of *Outside* magazine."

Then came the biggest call. Charles Kuralt wanted to feature Moab for his travelogue segment, "On the Road." The idea was that Kuralt would help Joe "judge" the contest. "We had eighty-some-odd applicants for second place. We had Paris, Zurich, Geneva, Amsterdam, London, some people in South America, and then lots of cities in the United States."

The Moab Chamber of Commerce brought the contest to Main Street. Joe explained, "Each downtown store would sponsor a city or a town and would have all the pictures of that town's dump in their front window, and if you liked Scarsdale, New York, you could go in and sign. And if you liked everybody and just wanted to put your name on everybody, no problem; this was very loosey-goosey."

The camera trucks came rolling into town for this chaotic, fun contest, but the most important moment, from how Joe describes it, was the opening shot for the show. The La Sal Mountains, just beyond the southern end of town, had received their first snowfall the night before. This would be the backdrop of Kuralt's interview with Joe and John.

"They went early in the morning; the wind was blowing. It was powder, it was perfect, it was just a plume blowing off the mountain, and the camera is coming down on the mountain, and you see the snow blowing, and it's a crisply clear blue sky. It is absolutely gorgeous. And it goes down the mountain, and the camera zooms in a little bit, so you see that there's forest, and *it's* just absolutely gorgeous. And it comes down to him talking to me, and then it goes down a little farther . . . and there's the dump."

I was sitting on the edge of my chair to find out who'd won. "In the end we selected Kodiak, Alaska. Their dump had the trees, the ocean, and a bear walking across, and it was gorgeous. We had over sixty reporters and television cameras at Pack Creek Ranch announcing who won, and the mayor of Kodiak was so excited about it he flew from Kodiak, Alaska, to get the award and the trophy, which was, by the way, donated to us by Tonka Toys. And what it was, was a highly polished chrome . . . garbage truck. Highly polished chrome, large garbage truck on a mahogany panel as the winner of the Moab Scenic Dump Contest."

In an insecure moment of town transition, the dump contest was clever, confident, and inclusive. The great thing about natural beauty is that if you find a way to focus the cameras on it, nature can take you the rest of the way, and in this case, it did.

I've heard about a lot of painful transitions coming out of steel mill closings, mines shutting down, and the displacement of manufacturing. Moab's was one of the quickest and most disorienting collapses, but its turnaround moment seems to have been the most dynamic and even fun. It's not every day that you attract the attention of the Parisian garbage department.

Moab is at a serious crossroad. There is a surfeit of attention now, and from it comes the affordability question, with unsustainably expensive housing, health care, and everyday expenses, which can feel like a slap in the face when you and your forebears have built and fostered all the good that brought your town into the spotlight.

Melissa Schmaedick, who runs the Moab Folk Festival, also works with the US Department of Agriculture and speaks with farmers all the time. She talks about their deep love of the land, very much like that of the newer residents. She knows that farmers can be just as annoyed as nature lovers by loud and lawless all-terrain vehicles (ATVs). For all the respect shown for different kinds of tourism, there is a shared irritation about ATVs.

There are two issues when divisions occur. One is the feeling of being unrepresented. That is a political divide. But the other is being unheard, and that is a community issue, and that can be addressed. And bridging the divide could come from the land itself, just as the land has provided so many other ways for people to connect. Melissa said she's met many families "who have lived here and made this their home for many, many generations and have a really strong attachment to their roots and to the beauty of the community and this common story of survival."

Andy Nettell told me about a reading at Back of Beyond Books by a rancher. Other ranchers came for that, and he said he started thinking: How could the bookstore host more stories about the hard work on the land as well as about the land itself? Melissa said she can see a wish for newcomers and visitors to honor the "struggle that the community had in the past and the fact that it was really their work that created the space for these folks to come in."

Maybe the land itself can be the calmer of disputes. The land holds time differently than we do. It doesn't have to get from Point A to Point B, cursing the coffee that spills in its lap on the rush to work or speeding to harvest a crop before a hailstorm. The land shows us all our rich histories, of the native peoples in Utah, the generations of ranchers, and the modern, radical, environmentalist devotees of Edward Abbey who encourage us to listen to the land itself and experience its mysteries. These stories are both as stratified and united as layers of a sandstone cliff. Moabites have a bond to share and locate themselves in a way very particular to their specific geography. They tell me they are divided on many issues, but from what I've seen, their connection to the land expresses this bond.

OTHER PLACES, OTHER SPACES

Let's leave Moab now and go up the Cascade Trail, through mossy rainforests and into Seattle, where we can look at the way a city has incorporated nature into its urban identity. Many other cities have done the same. None have done it better.

When I asked my friend Bellamy to meet me at Benaroya Hall in 2013, she said, "Meet me under the Chihuly." The what?

I had to meet a reporter later that day. He also said, "I'm just downstairs from the Chihuly." It was a given that I'd know the Chihuly, a ten-foot-long, hourglass-shaped chandelier of handblown glass that's teeming with white and beige serpentine cylinders spilling through a tower of ornate glass spheres.

Technically Dale Chihuly's sculptures are "cultural" icons in Seattle, not "natural" ones, but I recognize his work—and that of many glass and textile artists—as emblematic of Seattle's natural identity. The chandeliers at Benaroya Hall, despite their name, *Crystal Cascade*, suggest a parallel world of marine life that exists in the bordering Puget Sound. Like much of Chihuly's work, the *Crystal Cascade* chandeliers have glass that flows outward and upward as if it is underwater. There is a modern, aquatic elegance in his pieces that underscores Seattle's identity as a city on a body of water, reminding us that beyond the wide, paved plazas and cement staircases at the Puget's shores, there are undulating sea grasses, kelp, octopi, and anemones.

Seattle is famous for Microsoft, tech millionaires, and a gadget-savvy populace. It is also home to a ferociously independent music scene that began in the 1980s through the 1990s, not just the presenting stage of Nirvana and Pearl Jam but also of the media-skeptical and extremely innovative riot grrrl bands such as Sleater-Kinney, L7, and Bikini Kill.

But the sense of the sea is everywhere in its public spaces, inside and out, especially thanks to the monumental, biomorphic pieces by Puget Sound glassblowers and weavers who have staked out a unique, artisanal identity in their region. Seattle has a culture that's set within a very specific and dynamic landscape, and it's all woven together.

On a big loom, the "warp" consists of vertical strings through which the "weft," the horizontal strings, are woven. In Seattle, there's a metaphoric, electronic warp of smartphones, piercings, overdriven amps, and architecture like the silver, cacophonous, Frank Gehry–designed Experience Music Project. But this highly charged warp is woven through an even deeper weft of Dungeness crab legs in the markets, educational signs with depictions of limpets and eelgrass, and the constant, misty sheets of salty air. Where deep grunge and sci-fi tech ideas could turn into dystopic isolation, Seattle is instead deeply sensitive to its identity as an ecosystem to be protected and respected. Seattle is filled with indoor spaces advantageous to building positive proximity, but it is the mix of the outdoors and indoors that makes every conversation a little more unique, with a bit more sense of shared place. Strong, emblematic, natural representation gives Seattle a feel, a palette (neutral browns, greens, blues, and a dash of neon-orange starfish), and a dialectic counter to all the wires and conduits in one of this country's most dynamic urban centers.

Another region that has made the most of its unique natural flora and fauna runs along the Eno River near Durham, North Carolina, where the homegrown Festival for the Eno takes place every July. I love this festival for the music, but I'm really in it for the T-shirts. They don't have anemones. These T-shirts have illustrations of Eno River life, such as the little brown bat and the red flying squirrel. The Eno T-shirts show us the animal kingdom's equivalent of "so square they're hip." You don't need to be an orca to make the grade. You can be proud to be an eastern crayfish in the shallows of the Eno River.

These creative ways of integrating natural surroundings into the public art and architecture of cities can anchor our appreciation of our overall, unique regions. Whether you're inside or outside, these natural identities silently express themselves in public life. An hour after I'd landed in Fairbanks, Alaska, I was walking along the river walk and encountered the dramatic and somewhat austere Antler Arch, made of moose and elk antlers. That's when I knew I had arrived, not when I passed all the airport and highway signs welcoming me to the city. The Antler Arch had grandeur as well as an almost spooky sense of epic natural history: I could sense the grand-scale life cycles of this utterly unique place.

Large creatures stalk the Alaskan terrain. Everything that walks, swims, or grows in Alaska is large, as I'd learned from taxi drivers who told me the size and weight of salmon they'd caught and from tours where it seemed that even the daisies along the road were the diameter of dessert plates. The Antler Arch was there to remind me that this somewhat remote college city sits in the valley of a majestic and magical state.

Same goes for the entire sperm whale skeleton that hangs above the lobby of Homer, Alaska's elementary school (where Jewel went!). Homer has a renowned school system partially funded by oil subsidies. Homer had the perspicacity and positive proximity to allocate subsidies for the schools and for regionally specific signifiers of the nearby Cook Inlet (e.g., a whale skeleton—not something you see in Connecticut).

The Echoing Green

When I first saw signs of interconnectedness in Beacon, I thought I knew their exact source. Not a café or a bar, but instead that place where the weirdest, weakest ties occur because they are not determined by humans but instead by another mammal. Beacon seemed to come together at about the time it built a dog run.

Where do these completely different worlds collide so productively? At the dog run. I asked a friend who goes to the dog run if this were true, that this is where Beacon's disparate populations came together. "No, it's not true," she said. So much for my theories. Then she said, matter-of-factly, "Well, it was the dog run. But it was also the playing fields."

Ah, yes. I knew this from my own experience in my town. There is something magical about the "echoing green," as William Blake describes it, where we watch our family members, usually children, playing with unbridled joy, determination, and encouraging signs of new skills. In a prosaic, but no less important, way it's where people, usually parents, of very different backgrounds stand side by side for even longer periods of time watching their families play sports. Do they become bosom buddies there? No. But these are the open fields where, like players in a game with subtle and complicated rules, we come to understand our social terrain.

I will repeat the pleas of many urban theorists, starting with Jane Jacobs, who argued for parks with many uses at all times of the day. Author Peter Owen goes so far as to question the wisdom of Central Park, arguing that the same square footage, broken up into fields for pickup games throughout New York City, would better serve the metropolitan population. Jane Jacobs drew a picture of Rittenhouse Square, in Philadelphia, where she credited all the comings and goings of businesspeople, parents, and retail traffic from bordering stores for the success of the park. For those who think uninterrupted, wideopen space provides a metaphoric breath of life to the city, she scoffs at the "science-fiction nonsense that parks are the 'lungs of the city.'"

Bringing residences and businesses right up to the edge of green spaces keeps them alive. I won't go so far as to criticize Central Park. It has functioned as many parks have for New Yorkers. But an underused park is an energy draw and often a dangerous place as well. And worse than that, it wonders where all the children are. A neglected park is a lonely park.

Outside Looking In

Other towns and cities have walking or hiking parks that extend outside the city limits. These parks are natural assets that can build positive proximity in that they create a space for perspective and contemplation. They are unexpectedly powerful additions to any cityscape (and possibly easier to zone because they're not in the middle of town). Congress Street, the main strip in Portland, Maine, becomes, almost seamlessly, the Eastern Promenade, which curves around to a bluff over the ocean and then slowly descends back into the downtown area of the waterfront. Portland has high positive proximity. Its citizens have long been ahead of the curve when it comes to "buying local," supporting local artists, and infilling their urban center. The promenade connects the city with its maritime history, not to mention its maritime present. Anyone who walks in Portland can see a real city and have a real hike in the space of an hour as well, providing a natural and historical context.

Likewise, at the end of Baseline Road in Boulder, Colorado, is the entrance to the Flatirons, a mountainous park named for the heavy clothing irons you'd heat on a stove back in the day. It's crowded enough that I've always felt safe when I've gone there, but it's also off to the side so you can have a quiet moment as the wind blows through the aspen leaves. It's the kind of place where you wonder if you might actually run into a bear or a mountain lion. And that is important to a place. Cities are natural places repurposed into human habitats. The trails that grow out and around the city create a relationship between the natural environment and the places we have built upon it.

I appreciate these extension-of-city trails for many reasons: they are sprawl buffers; they are day-trip diversifiers that still allow the inner city to keep its compact, urban allure; and they are one more thing that can be shared by all people, as opposed to parks that can be reached only by car. But I think the existential argument for a walking park on the edge of town is very strong, too. Like a good waterfront, a natural place just outside of town creates a vantage point, a place to have a contemplative conversation, and an experience that combines our observation of nature and human-made habitation. It is a good place to press the pause button, look into the city, and appreciate what we have, both by admiring the city's vision as represented in its skyline and by recognizing the surrounding natural formations that also make it unique.

A town can also embrace bordering iconic landscapes as a way to wake up the streets and downtowns of our cities. Poughkeepsie, New York, converted an old railroad bridge into the Walkway over the Hudson. It has become a major attraction. Poughkeepsie has had its problems, but this city has enlisted a powerful ally, the mighty Hudson, to raise its profile. Poughkeepsie maps show walking and biking routes through historic districts that lead to and through the river walk, interweaving Poughkeepsie culture with the stunning views.

The Walkway over the Hudson would qualify simply as an extension of the city, but the city of Poughkeepsie worked hard to incorporate it into the city itself, thus emphasizing the city's Hudson Valley charm and river-town history, both of which can get lost in an urban center.

About two hundred miles west of Poughkeepsie, the Cascadilla Waterfall in Ithaca, New York, connects Cornell University above to the city below. A long staircase runs alongside it. The natural equivalent of a monumental vertical sculpture, Cascadilla graces the city and connects the feel of Ithaca to the many gorges in the Finger Lakes area.

Both cities, Poughkeepsie and Ithaca, created a way to access natural wonders not only for their own sake but also to highlight their urban connections to all their natural beauty. As in Moab, there is the elegance of something being left alone, unbuilt, to identify a city. The only structural work is in the walkways, signs, and stairways leading along them. They all let people have time to themselves and with each other focusing on nature, not commerce, and seeing the beauty of public space, not just private property.

No matter what your town has to offer, even a little natural beauty defines our sense of place, and that is fertile ground for positive proximity. Clearing a small trail, planting some flowers, preferably specific native flowers, in or around public places, and otherwise finding natural spaces for gatherings or solitude can remind us why we live where we do, even if one neighbor has a National Rifle Association bumper sticker and another keeps a dog-eared copy of *The Monkey Wrench Gang* on the nightstand at all times (yes, Moab, I'm talking about you). Our natural surroundings, especially those we work together to preserve and celebrate, remind us of why we stay and how our common ground allows us to transcend differences with our neighbors.

3

Wilmington, Delaware: Waterfronts

The Piñata Problem

Some cities have what I call a piñata problem: there is great wealth, but it's hanging from a high place, far away from the city commons. There are mansions on the outskirts of town filled with famous citizens, high-paid executives, and even a scattering of multinational CEOs. Meanwhile, the downtown could desperately use a capital influx but does not get one despite the opulence that encircles it. In 1995, I decided that Wilmington, Delaware, had a big piñata problem.

I was opening for Holly Near at the Grand Opera House on Market Street, in the center of town. I took a long walk after sound check. The streets were run-down, and the people looked down on their luck, which seemed strange for a city with the headquarters of both the Dow Chemical Company and DuPont USA. However, Wilmington has been nicknamed both Chemical City and Murder Town. DuPont was a major supporter of the opera house. But what was its relationship to the daily life of the city? A Forbes 500–sized piñata seemed to be waving over our heads, bound by ideology or isolationism to stay so far out of reach that it would never be broken open and spill its bounty into the streets.

In striking contrast to the depressing scene outside the opera house, Holly's concert was a lovefest. I got swept up with the rest of the audience into her insightful, bighearted performance. Holly talked about how she'd told a friend that she was dating a woman and how the friend had excused herself to throw up. Years later, she told another friend that she was dating a man, at which point that friend excused herself to throw up. Holly said, "We have to stop making each other sick!" And then she sang one of her best-loved songs, "Simply Love":

> Why does my love make you shift restless in your chair
> And leave you in despair
> It's simply love—my love for a woman.

We were crying, we were singing, and we were imagining all the bridges we could build in the world with love, simply love. But Wilmington? Couldn't imagine it. It seemed like a lost cause to me. I couldn't see what would bridge the wealthy and low-income worlds. Of course, at the time, I was not the seasoned traveler I am today. I always thought love was the answer. And it's not.

Luckily, Wilmington wasn't asking me for any solutions. Wilmington knew that love is an outcome, not a plan. Developing the waterfront was the plan, though I don't think even Wilmington realized what a difference a waterfront could make.

START AT THE WATER

Making the most of a city's waterfront could technically be seen as just using another advantageous, outdoor space for building positive proximity, but I have seen so many transformative water-connected projects, I've decided they deserve to be broken out and examined on their own. They have their own specific advantages. Wilmington,

Delaware, provides an excellent example of how a waterfront can bring life back into a city. I saw that new life in Wilmington when I returned seventeen years later.

In 2012, I played at WXPN's Queen Theater, a new venue in Wilmington owned by the same people who run the WXPN World Café in Philadelphia. I brought my family and hoped there was a decent place to walk and eat after sound check, but I wasn't holding my breath. The only hint I had that something had shifted since 1995 was an e-mail message from a high school friend saying I would love the city. Lo and behold, I looked on a map and saw that the Delaware Children's Museum was within walking distance, with Harry's Seafood Grill on the way. That's when we found Riverfront Wilmington and a new way to see the city.

We weren't an easy family. My son was eight and wary of "fun" plans, and that day my three-year-old daughter didn't want to go anywhere that the tall and charming Joey Ryan of the Milk Carton Kids, also on the bill that night, wasn't going. But we pried her off his leg, and off we went.

Harry's Seafood Grill, right on the river, was, to my relief, a family-friendly restaurant. No fear of resentful staff or comments from a neighboring table, even though it was one of those fancy, soft-shell crab, craft beer kind of places. We sat outside. ING Direct, whose American Internet-banking headquarters was nearby, had its own small pirate ship serenely patrolling the waters. If I were a financial institution whose name came up a lot during the recession, I might avoid the symbolism of piracy, but it was pleasantly old-fashioned, and my kids loved it.

Along the water's edge was a line of outsized birdhouses modeled after houses in famous paintings. We sat outside in front of Christina's House, from the best-known Andrew Wyeth painting. After lunch, we followed the river past flowers and pampas grass to the children's museum, whose sponsors included all of the Fortune 500 businesses I knew in Wilmington.

This city will always have wealth extremes, but now there was a gathering force, a public space into which community wealth, public and private, could be poured. The Christina River creates a conversational and physical focal point, a magnet for new businesses, and an energetic center for Wilmington's new life. A stable, human-scale, pedestrian path was running through Wilmington. It seemed that Riverfront Wilmington could be a catalyst for the city's ongoing transformation, considering that the rest of the city seemed more stable than when I'd been there in 1995.

I got to test my theory that the waterfront was spurring Wilmington's progress when I was at a whiskey- and beer-tasting fund-raiser for Philadelphia's WXPN. I'd had a couple, as they say, and apparently that's all it took. I lost all of my inhibitions and revealed my passion for urban planning to anyone who'd listen. Fortunately, I met David Fiorenza, a professor of urban economics at Villanova College, and we started talking about Wilmington, Delaware. It turns out David teaches about Wilmington in one of his classes.

"What *happened* here?" I asked, referring to the new life I was seeing in Wilmington. "Seriously, what *happened*? It's that waterfront. I know it. I can tell."

"The waterfront, yes," David said, but he indicated there was a longer story to tell. He gave me his card.

I called David, and he told me about how the waterfront had come to be. I'd assumed that someone with the last name Dow or DuPont had written a big check to clear away the brush on the Christina River and get it all started. "Astonishingly, it was the government," David said, and then he gave me a short, impressive history that included people's desire to clean up parts of the river for a nature preserve, followed by a fact-finding trip to Baltimore, which was completing its own large-scale, harbor-front project, and finally a river-based revitalization that seemed to be continuing all the way into the city.

It's hard to pinpoint two or three characters who were the most responsible for the waterfront project, though I noted in the movie

Ten Short Years, about the development, that the project was conversation-driven from the start and facilitated by a one-on-one conversation. Note how small things can be the start of everything. Former governor Russ Peterson said, "[State Senator] Bob Marshall and I met at a little parade, and there was pouring rain, and we stood under an umbrella and talked about what we could do to save this riverfront."

To walk along the Christina River now, it's hard to imagine how it could remain obscure given how busy and beautiful it is. But all too often, bodies of water like this will remain hidden, often because of the industrial history that unfolded along their shores. Like many American rivers, the Christina was simply lost in time. It had been the city's booming industrial center for more than a century, where military ships were built and launched from the Civil War through World War II, after which the shipyards were changed to paper mills. There were always tanneries there as well.

When the factories closed, their properties wildered into scrub brush that camouflaged decades of dumped refuse. Given all the years of its industrial heyday, there was understandable trepidation about what people would find if they tried to bring a waterway back. But two men sharing an umbrella started the conversation, and slowly but surely they brought their dream to fruition.

A new governor, Tom Carper, was soon pressed into service in developing the river. He became a believer, and, after a helpful visit from the governor of Maryland, he and a few other early supporters got the Delaware General Assembly to establish the Riverfront Development Corporation (RDC). Through this corporation, the government continued to play a formative role in a mixed-use waterway while also opening the area to private businesses.

Executive Director Michael Purzycki has been at the RDC from the start. He said that the government gave the corporation an enormous amount of freedom. This was his baby. Halfway through our talk, he brought me over to his computer to see before and after pictures, pointing out a number of pivot points that occurred when they brought in various businesses, pocket parks, and museums.

The first project was to clean up a marsh that became the Russell W. Peterson Wildlife Refuge, named for the former governor who had first come up with the idea and who had spent time bird-watching there with his sons in the 1950s. From there, a walkway extended east, transforming the riverbank from a wasteland, as they called it, to a destination for families and businesses alike.

Here are some things Riverfront Wilmington gives its city:

1. **An excellent investment in public spaces.** As the RDC grew its mission to develop the waterfront, the river and land became like matching grants for each other. Cleaning the water and riparian marshes allowed Wilmington officials to "match" their progress on land, clearing away the rusty detritus and old tires to pursue new projects.

   And whenever they added a new path along a hundred yards of riverbank, there were a hundred nice yards of river to "match" it. Mixed-use projects started to pop up along the water, like restaurants and apartments, in a series of public-private relationships. The water effortlessly mirrored every real-estate and infrastructure investment while also calming any impulse to overdevelop.

2. **Safety.** Riverfront Wilmington is more than a mile long, and it feels safe. Riverfronts are usually safe places to run and walk. I know this particularly well as a traveler. More than a few of my bandmates have gotten off the tour bus in their running shoes. They ask the promoter to point out a river-, lake-, or oceanfront nearby because paths along the water tend to be attractive and flat. Also, coming into unfamiliar terrain, I know that whenever I'm walking on a planned waterfront, I can be seen from some combination

of boats, the opposite bank, open exposure along my bank, a nearby parallel road, and other people on the path. Riverfront Wilmington has two gyms on it, and when people go there at night after work, they combine their workouts with running, so you'll find plenty of people there after dark.

3. **Orientation.** Rivers also help travelers orient themselves. The Christina and Brandywine Rivers wrap around Wilmington from the north and south. It's hard to get lost along a body of water, and it will often help you get found. As a traveler or a citizen, it's easier to dig into discovering a city if it has some sort of "wayfinding" anchors of this kind. Signs are great, and landmark buildings do the job, but a body of water that runs through or beside a city will serve as a constant compass.

4. **Collaboration.** No one entity can take on a waterfront project alone. One of Wilmington's proudest claims is that many public-private-nonprofit collaborations have gone smoothly, combining apartments, businesses, and entities such as the Delaware Theater and Children's Museum. These relationships have facilitated other partnerships throughout the city.

5. **Perspective.** A waterfront provides a helpful, continual view into a city. As I walked along Riverfront Wilmington, I could see the different neighborhoods and buildings more clearly. People can see how the city is put together and how it is connected, which helps them connect to the city as well. Whenever I've walked along a riverfront with a friend, we end up talking about the city we're in. No coincidence, I say. Wilmington's waterfront is especially good for understanding how this small city is built and how it's growing.

Wilmington stands to gain most from this waterfront because Riverfront Wilmington builds the positive proximity this city will require as it moves forward. It attracts visitors of many backgrounds, instills confidence in civic engagement by being a good example of collective action, and creates a different narrative than the awful Murder Town label bestowed by a national magazine, which sticks to Wilmington only too well in Facebook headline culture.

The financial district was being revitalized at the same time as the waterfront. And to give credit to a multipronged effort, Market Street, the cultural strip of town where I opened for Holly Near at the opera house, was already keeping more doors open after dark by the time the riverfront plans were under way. Whenever I talked about Riverfront Wilmington, people were quick to point out that these areas of town were changing at the same time. Michael said that whenever the city was trying to bring new businesses into the financial district, "the first place they would take them was the river walk."

If all goes well, the financial district will look to the waterfront as more than just a way to attract business talent. River walks are made for the people, and when they're done well, people are there all day, every day and into the night. But when I went for my long walk after sound check at the Queen in 2015, there weren't a lot of people on Market Street, and I was struck by how empty the financial district (which I call the FD) is at night. The buildings are impressive, a mix of clean, modern architecture and old, colonnaded, federal-style offices. But clearly the FD is dead after work hours. Likewise, when I stayed in the FD the year before, a big Starbucks seemed to be the only option for breakfast outside the hotel. That's not a sign of bustling street-corner life. Around the FD were some very sweet neighborhoods, but from what I saw at 6:00 p.m. on a Saturday night and 10:00 a.m. on a Sunday morning, the FD didn't fit into the fabric.

The FD itself still has to "get a life," namely a nightlife and a weekend life. It's a neighborhood just like any other. For it to lie empty for so many hours a day leaves a dark space in the middle of the city. Without opportunities for people to congregate in the ways they do at Riverfront Wilmington, the FD is going to slip backward into negative proximity, giving us "proof" that you can dress up a neighborhood with all that generous capital from corporations, but you can't trust the people in it. If the FD can't get it together, Wilmington will have to get more and more security guards to do what a social scene would do for free.

By contrast, near the end of one of my visits to Wilmington, I returned to Joe's Crab Shack and asked if Riverfront Wilmington was safe at night, and the server told me it was well lit but "just keep your head on a swivel." I could have left my swivel at home. It was very well lit. There were overhead lamps and bollards (they look like thin pillars) that curved along with the path, lighting up the walkway and the foliage. Very pretty. Very peaceful. I bade good evening to a drunk man on a bench.

I saw diverse groupings of people. They were all coming out of the back entrance of CrossFit Riverfront, very busy at 7:00 p.m. on an autumn Tuesday. Business colleagues, still in uniforms and suits, strolled along. I saw them all: runners, lovers, families, friends, drunkards, and me, a tourist.

I saw the logic in the intelligent coexistence of the public path and private businesses. The CrossFit gym was next to a "trampoline park" called Stratosphere that still had some business, and they were both next to the Delaware Children's Museum, at which the miniature golf course is open nightly for about five months of the year.

Michael was a strong advocate for the miniature golf course, and he was particularly pleased to point it out to me in one of his pictures. They did it well. I'd want to go there on a balmy summer night after dinner and ice cream. That's what I love about the whole Riverfront Wilmington. It's as if the RDC said, "Aw heck, as long as we're doing all this, why don't we do it really well?"

FROM THE WATER TO THE REST OF THE CITY

Riverfront Wilmington connects history, nature, recreation, and commerce in a breezy, accessible way.

As I watched people all using Riverfront Wilmington for different purposes, I realized that I had completely changed my impression of Wilmington from a piñata city to a city that welcomes people from all walks of life, with all they have to offer.

When I walk down it past Joe's Crab Shack, which is where I'll take my kids the next time I go, I see the multiplex theater, the Delaware Contemporary Art Museum and Theater Company, and the fresh-faced, young people rowing by as well as the signage that explains the river's natural life, its shipbuilding history, and the role of Wilmington in the Underground Railroad. I notice that the convenient, clean, and pretty Amtrak station (one of my favorites) is right there next to the river. I see all this and think, *This city would be perfect for a person who wants to live in an eastern city that connects to all the major cities around it. It's the perfect size and location.*

Riverfront Wilmington models and builds positive proximity in the way so many people can access it from so many points and have the space and beauty for good conversations. However, Wilmington still recognizes itself as a work in progress. The reflection of the sun on the water can only bounce so far, and there is an oft-repeated fear, quietly expressed by some citizens, that success will merely allow developers to displace and replace whole populations.

But if Wilmington wants to keep its deeply historical and cultural character and grow the stability and prosperity of more neighborhoods, places like the FD can take Riverfront Wilmington's cue and incentivize ways to mix and match the way people use its ten blocks, which is to say, if the businesses in this district facilitate more retail and community space (i.e., don't just build a cement plaza) at street level to match the high finance going on upstairs, they'll be surprised by all the creative, culture-building, hand-in-hand, private-public relationships that come out of it. Like Riverfront Wilmington, the FD was a massive undertaking. It is a short walk to Riverfront Wilmington and could easily be an extension of its positive-proximity building success.

Another important section of town, next to the FD and even closer to Riverfront Wilmington, is North Market Street. After visiting Michael at the RDC, I headed over to visit David Bromberg at his violin shop there. As I headed up the street, I realized I was close to the Grand Opera House, where I had first opened for Holly Near. How did the street look now? It looked better. It looked busy. There were no boarded-up shops. It was not gentrified; it was just working.

At Bromberg's Fine Violins, centrally located on Market Street, David was already walking out to greet me as I entered. Tall and affable, with a big beard and rimless glasses, David is a soft-spoken but very charismatic musician. He is truly beloved among his many performing friends and certainly his audiences. He's also a badass onstage, but in between songs he tells stories about young love and encounters on the road that show his kindness and hard-earned wisdom. At his store, he led me down past violins and cellos in the corridor to his office, which had just enough clutter to show how busy he and his partners were despite David's other job as a touring musician. He is known for his guitar playing, but he learned about violin making during a long hiatus from the road.

David told me that the city of Wilmington gave him a good deal on his store. The mayor himself told David that he remembered hearing music up and down Market Street back in the day and hoped it could happen again. It was as if the mayor were looking to turn Market Street into a river walk of culture, which would complement Riverfront Wilmington, four blocks away.

It hasn't proven to be an easy task. David set up some jams at a local restaurant that started to get more and more successful, but after the restaurant closed there wasn't a good place for it. The Queen Theater, where I played in 2012, was a block from David's store, but so far it hadn't been receptive to a regular jam session. I commented that the neighborhood looked more alive than the last time I was here in 1996. David acknowledged this but also said his favorite pizza place still wouldn't deliver to his address.

David added that Market Street was revitalizing before the Riverfront Wilmington project began, but I worry that its cultural venues are still adhering to the old piñata problem formula, catering to people from outside the city who attend concerts and drive away. The Queen has food—good food, in fact—in house. The opera house doesn't, and I don't know what people do for dinner. Unlike many venues, it offers no suggestions on its website. There are very few ways the cultural venues connect with the street that "flows" alongside them.

INCLUSIVITY

Wilmington is 60 percent African American, and so is a majority of the people on Market Street. Walking up and down the street, I saw the All 4 One Barber Shop, with a hand drawing of Barack Obama and a poster with a picture of a small girl imploring us to stop the violence. I was trying to find out what kind of cultural programming would best connect with this area. What was at the opera house? *Swan Lake* and *Annie*. There were upcoming performances, such as *Freedom Train* and *I Have a Dream*, that addressed black history (for Martin Luther King Day), and there were a few African American performers, but a review of upcoming acts showed the roster to be about 90 percent white. However, there was a diverse roster of children's shows: black, white, and brown faces were all represented for young audiences—as well as purple and green faces when you included puppets.

Next to the opera house I found a lovely bookstore, but I noticed only two African American faces among the authors of about thirty books in the window. One was the story of a little girl. The other was by Michelle Obama. There were three books about *Downton Abbey*, the public television series about an English baron, his family, and their fleet of servants, set in the early twentieth century. I went down a few blocks to see the calendar at the Queen. I actually counted the artists, many of whom are my friends. Again, the lineup was about 90 percent white in a neighborhood that looked 90 percent black. I recognized the name of one white woman who was coming at the end of December. It was me.

Given the ambitions of Riverfront Wilmington to be a beneficial space for all, it seemed like a lost opportunity for cultural venues to neglect creating a point of integration between the performance arts venues and the neighborhoods where they are located. Even if Riverfront Wilmington is a gateway for further development in the city, strong, integrated neighborhoods can be in dialogue with developers to determine the course of building.

Two festivals in the city do represent diverse cultures, with a special tip of the hat to African American history. There is the Clifford Brown Jazzfest, which is free and near the top of North Market Street, and there is the People's Festival for Peace Tribute to Bob Marley at the Tubman-Garrett Riverfront Park, on the corner of the Christina River and North Market Street. Bob Marley lived in Wilmington for a short but critical moment in his career, and the city embraces his legacy.

I don't want to disparage Wilmington's journey into a more integrated, harmonious, twenty-first century; I just want to flag it and say that for now, Riverfront Wilmington looks like the most instructive example for harmonizing the whole city, just as all of Wilmington's street festivals (Greek, Italian, and African American, to name a few) allow the city to celebrate its diverse populations.

Riverfronts and river walks also provide cities some good metaphors. There is mandatory open space when water is the border of a public commons. Usually, the undeveloped real estate (the water) belongs to everyone. I think, too, of water metaphors: connection, depth, waves and ripples, common resources, and things that are liquid and that flow in the same direction. I've watched how well-loved waterways provide quiet reinforcement to the momentum of a city's shared prosperity.

OTHER WATERFRONTS, OTHER TOWNS

In *Ten Short Years*, Peggy Strine, who became the chair of Wilmington's RDC, said, "I didn't even really know there was a river back there because all I had ever seen were these old, abandoned buildings."

I still see many cities with brush-covered, hidden waterfronts, and I wonder what their potential might be. So many of our waterfronts have been forgotten or covered over. There is a reason for their neglect. At the peak of the industrial buildup of American rivers, many cities like Wilmington had combustible river syndrome (CRS). This is my term for what happens to rivers when their industrial uses overshadow all others. The river becomes a body of water that henceforth cannot be considered for fishing, swimming, sailing, riverside dining, parks, or coveted waterfront housing.

CRS happens when you build factories all along the banks, understandable because rivers are the optimal place to pull in engine-cooling river water. They are also good for dumping waste in a semidiscreet, semilegal fashion. Finally, rivers court big, cargo-bearing boats that burn fuel and sometimes release a ballast tank full of Lord knows what.

CRS occurs after a critical mass of effluents have saturated a waterway, and one day the scale tips. The water isn't quite water anymore. A person lights a match, the American version of the River Styx makes headlines, and a city is embarrassed. At least this is what happened to the Cuyahoga River in Cleveland in 1969. Cleveland was embarrassed, which isn't fair to Cleveland. The Cuyahoga was far from an isolated case of CRS. There were plenty of other rivers going up in flames, too, like the Schuylkill out of Philadelphia and the Buffalo River. The Rouge River in Dearborn, Michigan, caught on fire all the time.

To give Cleveland its due, in 1968, the year before its river fire, Cleveland had actually passed a one-hundred-million-dollar bond to clean up the Cuyahoga. Adding insult to injury, in fact, the famous *New York Times* photo of the blazing river was from another fire there in 1952 (but in fairness to the *New York Times*, the river had caught on fire thirteen times since 1868). Meanwhile, the city's mayor, Carl Stokes, along with his brother, Louis, consequently testified to Congress in support of the Clean Water Act, which passed in 1972. I hope that Cleveland can redeem its river history in 2019 when the city celebrates the fiftieth anniversary of the river fire by capping off five years of environmental cleanups around the city.

Wilmington's waterways technically never had CRS, even though the Christina River was where many famous ships were built. Tanneries also release a prodigious amount of toxic chemicals over time. Given the nonexistent environmental standards of the time and the multiple chemicals required to build ships and to tan hides, I'm guessing that Wilmington was one flicked cigarette away from disaster.

Other American rivers, including parts of the mighty Hudson River, which I see out my window every morning, were close to this incendiary threshold in the 1960s and 1970s. I think this is why so many cities, like Wilmington, got a case of abandoned-building-and-poison-ivy-riverbank syndrome (yes, I made that one up, too). Their waters were polluted and probably dangerous, so their riverbanks became disused corridors of free-for-all garbage dumping. Hiding a polluted river is a way to prevent illness or injury. And you can't torch a river if you can't get to it.

Today, riverbanks are still the ideal place to put energy companies. Unlike manufacturing plants, many of which have moved overseas, today's natural gas, coal, and nuclear plants are still next to rivers. And just as utility plants love river water, lumber and paper mills do, too, and they will often compete with the public when it comes to taking up river real estate.

But where the rivers have simply been neglected and hidden from sight, I would advocate that they be uncovered and rediscovered. If you're Detroit, you might even take a factory away! Detroit removed a cement factory to complete its river walk.

CULTURAL CONVERGENCE AT THE WATERFRONT

There are a couple of other ways in which waterfronts can enhance the identity of a city and bring more wealth and goodwill to the commons. By the end of the 1990s, I noticed that I was playing at more and more concerts and festivals by the water. In 1998, I played at the Three Rivers Festival at Point State Park in Pittsburgh, taken by eminent domain in 1974. The Ohio, Monongahela, and Allegheny Rivers converge there. The park is also the site for the scenic ruins of Fort Pitt. The ruins as well as the park's iconic big fountain and the three rivers were behind me as I played. I couldn't have asked for a better stage set.

Here are some other great waterfront festivals I've gotten to play:

In Maryland, my band was at the end of a pier in a nature sanctuary. People talked about that concert series for years.

Clearwater Revival, started by Toshi and Pete Seeger, has found its home for more than a decade at Croton-on-Hudson, connecting the music to the river Pete and Toshi loved so much. The sloop *Clearwater* and the *Woody Guthrie* sail back and forth throughout the festival.

Louisville, Kentucky's Forecastle Park, once an industrial site on the Ohio River, has massive green lawns where multistage festivals are held, adding to Kentucky's many homegrown assets like bourbon, horses, and very successful farms. Forecastle Park, which presently stretches for more than a mile along the Ohio River, allows Louisville to have big events that bring the world to the city on a large scale, often for free. There, they fill you up with Kentucky favorites such as derby pie, and you are hooked. At least that's what they did with me.

Waterfronts also hold some of the best stories of a town's history. Rivers and ocean ports were the highways and industrial centers in our country. I've visited some cities where the combination of rivers and history bring that interesting fourth dimension of time to their pedestrians. Richmond, Virginia's canal walk is a work in progress that combines the easier and more difficult parts of its past, touting the history of commerce, acknowledging the horrors of the slave trade, and drawing attention to the often underappreciated accomplishments of African Americans over three centuries.

The ruins of the Gold Medal Flour factory in Minneapolis combine learning about history with extensive walking and biking. Mill Ruins Park shows enough crumbling walls and infrastructure to inspire the imagination, and there are signs to tell you about what you are seeing. The Mill Museum is close by and offers more hands-on information, but Mill Ruins Park is a very evocative walk through nature and time. You sort of feel like Lord Byron walking through the ruins, but with a twist because it's more industrial and it's the history of flour.

RECREATION FOR EVERYONE

Waterfronts also let you get to the water, and because the waterways we're looking at are collectively owned and maintained, participation in water activities adds one more way to get out of our houses and appreciate our towns. With cleaner waterways that you can actually reach, you also have the option of putting yourself, and other stuff like boats, into the water.

When I was last in Eau Claire, Wisconsin, I walked over to the Chippewa River and saw a flotilla of inflatable donuts, loungers, and rafts heading downstream. Not only was Eau Claire creating more park space along its rivers but also it was getting people into the water and offering many more things people could do with their time there. I called a bike rental store to ask where people could rent things to put in the water, and the manager said there wasn't much of anything but that when he was crossing the bridge on the way home at 5:00 or 6:00 p.m. on a summer afternoon, he would see two or three hundred people floating his way on whatever they had.

You can rent kayaks and paddleboards for about twenty dollars an hour along the Willamette River in Portland, Oregon, which isn't cheap, but again, it creates more ways to get around and enjoy the river. And you can put your own boat, paddleboard, or inflatable floaty in for free.

As my friend Anne Weiss brought me along the river walk in Portland, she pointed to a large square fountain where tons of kids hang out in the summer. She said that the fountain was a great way to let people who couldn't swim still get wet.

Hiding behind the good idea of the fountain, of course, was a bigger thought: when I see people floating and paddling around the river, I wonder if someone might start a low-cost swimming instruction program, too. Where I live, we spent a mint on our kids' swim lessons, telling ourselves that they were worth every penny. My husband spent countless hours making sure our kids were strong swimmers. It's a survival skill. It's another way to explore the world.

But with the time and expense of swim lessons comes the income divide of swimmers and nonswimmers, and nonswimmers are much less likely to become boaters and paddleboarders. As towns and cities are offering more ways to get in the water, they could narrow opportunity gaps and enrich many lives if they facilitated ways for people to learn to swim.

IF IT CAN WORK IN DETROIT . . .

In looking at ways in which a waterfront can create more egalitarianism in cities, I set my sights on the impressive Detroit RiverWalk and what was happening there. Detroit, a city in which socioeconomic stability has been more precarious than in Wilmington, declared bankruptcy in 2011. It also had an arsonist, or perhaps a group of firebugs, who added the final touch to blighted, abandoned buildings by igniting them. Walking along the Detroit River, I could look right into the city and see nearby blocks of charred, even skeletal, buildings with no glass in the windows, no roofs. But I also saw single buildings and blocks being rehabbed. In Detroit, the rehabilitated waterfront allows its citizens to re-envision the city itself.

I spoke with Mark Wallace, president of the Detroit Riverfront Conservancy, about the story of the Detroit RiverWalk. There are many similarities to that of Riverfront Wilmington. For example, it was a public-private relationship from the start. Mark said, "It taught our civic community how to work together. It was a partnership that really required a broad coalition of public, private, corporate, and philanthropic and civic sectors. In 2002, 'community' and 'engagement' weren't two words you'd find together in a sentence."

Three partners launched and sustained the conservancy. The first was General Motors. The company had already committed to staying in the Renaissance Center on the waterfront. Company leaders felt that Detroit had turned its back on the river as a civic space, and they wanted to change that identity, so General Motors built an atrium facing out to the water and kicked in twenty-five million dollars for a river walk. Then the Kresge Foundation wrote its biggest check ever, for fifty million dollars, and finally, the city of Detroit became the third largest contributor, in dollars and gifts in kind, including payment to raze two cement factories and promising to cancel its plan to locate casinos on the river.

The Detroit Riverfront Conservancy was formed in 2002, and one of its first tasks was to find out what the community wanted. More than a hundred meetings were held in places such as church basements and schools. Mark said the citizens were feeling a bit hopeless at the time, and many of them had a "depression of expectations." "They would ask for things like 'pretty flowers along the waterfront.'" But bigger themes started to emerge, such as the desire for a space for kids and families. Another request was for a design with a connection to Detroit's cultural history, specifically to its African American residents. Mark said it's a detail, really, but one of the things the conservancy did was to imprint many of the bricks and paving materials with Kinta patterns from African fabrics.

There was a call for informal gathering places. The conservancy discovered that the "most flexible were the ones that were used the most," so it made communal space as open-ended as possible.

The conservancy also got very specific requests. A person in a wheelchair said that every interaction with a friend in a park had to be face-to-face because it was hard to have a wheelchair on the grass. The wheelchair had to stay on the pavement facing away from the water. The Detroit RiverWalk has little cement pads next to benches so that friends can sit side by side looking at the boats and the river together.

At the end of the day, one hundred forty million dollars were raised for an endowment to build and maintain the Detroit River-Walk. It is 3.5 miles long, which makes it the perfect location for fifty runs and walks per year sponsored by the conservancy. The Detroit RiverWalk also hosts the Reading and Rhythm Festival for children, with music, a celebrity reading a children's book, and a donation of thousands of kids' books. One man said his daughter had collected six books over the years, and that they constituted "her library."

The outdoor festival River Days has an outside sponsor, Soaring Eagle Casino, that is not on the river but works with the conservancy to present guest luminaries, such as the Tuskegee Airmen, and music from artists such as Gladys Knight, Bell Biv Devoe, and Dave Hollister. There is also an ongoing schedule of yoga and tai chi groups, and there are cultural exhibitions in partnership with local arts organizations.

Having just come from Wilmington, I was thinking about what a river walk can actively do to bridge social schisms. Detroit has a long history of racial division, and the bankruptcy left many people pointing fingers and making generalizations that didn't help racial tensions. Water is, almost by definition, neutral territory. You pour water on a fire. Water calms. Could a walkway along the waterfront function to ease the tensions of a city and even set it on a better path going forward?

Mark was fully aware that with its beauty, serenity, and all of its cultural offerings, the Detroit RiverWalk also presented an opportunity for social stewardship and even for peacemaking. He said that the Detroit RiverWalk had come up with three increasingly ambitious goals "since day one." The first was to be "clean, safe, and pretty." The second was to be a "world-class gathering place, and this was more aspirational." The third was to be a "gathering place for all."

Mark pointed out that every great city, be it London, Paris, or Detroit, started with a celebrated waterway and a city's enlightened relationship to it. He added, "Every great city also has someplace where everybody feels welcome. Think of New York City. You don't go there to see a bunch of businessmen all in suits, where everyone looks the same. You want to see the guy walking down the road with a dead chicken, and someone with a Mohawk, and someone with piercings in places you never would have imagined." The success of a city is not in the achievement of homogeneity, it's in the peaceful coexistence of its heterogeneous groups.

So how did the Detroit Riverfront Conservancy succeed in extending an invitation to all of the citizens and beyond to feel at home there? For starters, in all of its press and publicity materials, the conservancy consciously represents people from many backgrounds and walks of life. Its leaders also didn't want to displace previous uses of the river, such as fishing, so there is a place to fish.

The conservancy is particularly intentional about its staffing, specifically security. Members of the security staff are trained not only to de-escalate conflict but also to see themselves as "ambassadors" of the

Detroit RiverWalk. "They are the eyes and ears" and answer questions about where to get coffee and what time the carousel closes. Then, and only then, they provide security, including the sense of security.

Though there are pushbuttons and callboxes to bring help all along the Detroit RiverWalk, there are also two or three security staffers on bicycles at all times just to be visible and helpful. From what I've heard, all good community policing includes people on foot and on bicycles engaging the populace at eye level. Residents of Detroit make up 95 percent of the security force. They understand the city. "They know they'll see executives walking around at lunchtime or a mother with four kids, and she doesn't even have five dollars in her pocket. What's going on is familiar to them," said Mark. In order for the Detroit RiverWalk to function as a builder of positive proximity for all, the keepers of the peace must respond to diverse visitors. The "safety" must feel truly safe.

I revisited Wilmington after I'd spoken with Mark Wallace. At about eight o'clock at night, I walked the length of Riverfront Wilmington. I saw a tall man slowly walking as his two small children ran in figure eights around his legs. One kid would run to the fence and look out at the river. And then the two kids were rolling around. I will mention, because I have brought up the issue of racial division in Wilmington, that this father was African American. He looked exhausted, as many parents do at 8:00 p.m., but his kids were entertained. He didn't have to bend over. He didn't have to look over his shoulder. He had the airspace above all that crazy activity to think his thoughts. It was a reflective space. It was a safe space. To me Riverfront Wilmington seemed like a commitment, however limited, to some peace of mind for its citizens. Michael Purzycki, who championed Riverfront Wilmington from end to end, is now the mayor of Wilmington. Thanks to Riverfront Wilmington, and some parts of the city growing around it, the city now has a stronger claim that it is growing in prosperity for all, not just a small segment of its population that holds the moneybags. I hope its development continues to grow in tandem with a city that helps everyone feel more proud of where they live, high income as well as low income. A rich legacy of safe and healthy kids, beautiful parks, and contented citizens is, after all, the true wealth of a city.

Part Two

Identity Building

"FLOWERS ARE NEUTRAL." My friend Denise Frangiapani was telling me about how her county revitalization group, Sullivan Renaissance, in the beleaguered Catskill region of New York, had been planting colorful flower- and tree beds at the off-ramps on Route 17. This planting was the result of a group of people stepping back to see what might raise the visibility and morale of the beautiful but struggling Borscht Belt, as that region is sometimes known, named for the predominantly Jewish summer vacationland of the mid-twentieth century.

But it was about more than the plants. This project demonstrated that citizens could create their own beauty and attract other people like themselves who would be willing to put in time for the public good. It drew people onto common ground and introduced them to other people who might have had no more in common than their interest in gardening and being involved with their town in some way. And the planting provided an opportunity for a community conversation: identity-building projects are by nature more proximally oriented than partisan divided.

Towns cannot create civic engagement from scratch. Without positive proximity, there can be no grist for civic connections, and there are all too many opportunities for us to withdraw from the commons before properly examining what we might find there. We can easily prefer a relationship with the smooth-riding, electronic highway of online communities that can be navigated from one's couch. But when there is a project afoot, even out on the bumpiest of social surfaces, citizens can leave their houses, acting in their own interests at first but often pushing past the known frontiers into new relationships and challenges. Then they can experience positive proximity firsthand.

As these people bring their skill sets and varying social comfort levels out into the commons, they also help to make their towns unique. The more unique a town is, the more identity-building projects there will continue to be and the more real chances people will have to leave their homes, and their computers, and get involved.

There are many components of identity. Every town has its own culture, natural features, and history. What are your town's origins: nineteenth-century, modern, colonial, and precolonial? What is its unique topography? What is grown in your area? How can you tap your local talents or invite the world of ideas into your town? All of these questions direct us toward tangible, up-from-the-ground identity building that involves the give-and-take of different personalities and interests.

Enhancing the identities of our towns through a range of projects humanizes them by bringing together names, faces, and skill sets. With these projects, "local government" becomes a recognizable part of local experience, too, and the idea of local office is less daunting. Self-government is part of the organism that is community. We the People means people like *us*. That guy who stands up and calls the mayor a fascist every month or so? That's just Bill. He volunteered for the community pancake breakfast in March. He's a good man who maybe dropped a little too much acid a few decades ago. Bill rants. Bill taps our maple trees without asking permission and gives us a bottle of syrup from them every March. Bill's okay. Oh, and that council member? We planted flowers together.

I will warn that when citizens read articles (especially online) about the importance of "community" and decide it's time to "engage" in the name of certain abstract values, they can wander into some murky territory. I spoke with a class at Vassar College about positive proximity, and one student told me about how in his Northern California home, there was some vague agreement that the city should identify itself as "green," meaning that it would be a model of sustainable living practices. The last this student heard, however, the city had been locked in a battle over the best green use of a public space: Should it be the location of a groundbreaking, efficient incinerator or a park?

I've been to this city more than fifty times over the past thirty years. I won't reveal its identity but it has recently built a community arts center that will hopefully focus some of the enormous wealth and big egos of residents toward the common good. For now it has low positive proximity. It's not negative; it's just . . . impersonal. If a town has low positive proximity, a principle such as peace, love, or green can turn into a nine-headed Hydra of possibilities: Which love? Which green?

Better to aspire to having a sense of each other outside the village hall first. My friend Jill Stratton, a social psychologist at Washington University, calls the civic deliberation process at its best "grappling." Grappling doesn't mean an easy path in decision making, and yet Jill encourages us to enjoy the ride. She said, cheerfully, "I love the grappling."

And for the outsider like me, projects themselves, apart from the positive proximity they build, hold my fascination. I probably won't remember a town with the credo "We Love to Be Civil," but I'll always have a soft spot for Orange, Massachusetts, with its Garlic and Arts Festival.

4

Phoenixville, Pennsylvania: History

HOW DO YOU REACH into the past to find your present and future? To answer that, we must follow the sound of slightly ominous chanting in the distance. It's early December in Phoenixville, Pennsylvania. Thousands of people stand at the edge of town shouting in unison, "Burn that bird! Burn that bird!" Above them a phoenix looms with archaic, graceful severity, eighteen feet high, constructed out of wooden pallets.

Every year more people take part in the spectacle of the Firebird Festival. Dancers writhe with lit torches as the excitement grows. And then, suddenly, the dancers charge to their positions at the base of the firebird, tip their torches, and touch their fire to tall, angular legs and feet with foot-long talons. The flames climb. The cheering erupts. Soon the whole bird is engulfed. There is a moment when the phoenix stands, her beak, wings, and prow-like chest clearly defined against the night sky in pure fire. Soon enough, slats of wood start to fall like burning feathers. Then the body, consumed, starts to collapse. By morning, the phoenix is a wide, shallow pit of ash.

A small group of people then returns and starts digging in a slurry of mud and ash to pull out small clay birds made by people in town.

The birds have been fired once in a kiln and a second time in the heat of the burning phoenix. Everyone makes two birds, one to keep and one to sell to raise money for the next year. After they are retrieved, the birds are brushed off to reveal the charred and iodized designs that the fire has imprinted on them.

This digging out, on a very grand scale, is what Phoenixville did over a twenty-year period. It dug into the ashes of its past to pull out its fragile, fire-mottled treasures. More than two hundred years of history found their way into the plans that invigorated the prosperous, highly functioning downtown we see today. Phoenixville has risen carefully and creatively, and it provides a wonderful model for towns and cities everywhere. After all, everyone has a history.

Death of a Way of Life

In 2007, I played a gig in Phoenixville. I recognized it as one of many Pennsylvania towns struggling to find its twenty-first-century identity. A true revitalization of mid-Atlantic Rust Belt towns had many obstacles to overcome as those places soldiered along to the end of the twentieth century. Stretching from New York to Ohio, steel mills and coal mines went from boom to bust almost all at once, so it was difficult for any town to hitch its wagon to a nearby star. When motivated citizens would propose a project such as a coffeehouse concert series, there weren't many regional resources to kick everything into gear, let alone audience members who could afford to attend.

Meanwhile, big box stores lurked around the edges of every struggling town. In fact, the big box strategy was to find Main Streets with disappearing businesses and weak political will. They moved in, undercutting and capturing most remaining local business.

When Phoenix Iron and Steel downsized to almost nothing in the 1980s, Phoenixville fell very hard. The King of Prussia Mall provided another fatal reason for everyone to abandon its demoralized downtown.

Borough Manager Jean Krack told me what he saw when he first passed through, years before he worked in Phoenixville: "You have people that were doing less than stellar things for profit or income, and it was readily apparent; it was, 'Okay, can I find a different road to drive through to get where I'm going?' And that was in '98." Eli Wenger, co-owner of the Steel City Coffeehouse, gives a less elliptical account of what those "less than stellar" businesses were: "When I was growing up, Phoenixville is where you went to get drugs."

Jean Krack said, "The steel mill had long since been closed, and so, like many steel towns throughout Pennsylvania, this town was just folding onto itself. Having been in other communities nearby with other steel mills that have gone down, when that occurs, and that traffic begins to come in, quality of life goes to heck in a hand-cart." But at the turn of the twenty-first century Phoenixville, almost like a person on the other side of a death or divorce, started to come back into the world. Specifically, some determined people stabilized the town with unique, history-based projects.

I saw the early efforts to revive the town when I played at Phoenixville's Colonial Theatre in 2007. The Colonial, a historic theater, was a big part of the effort to bring the town back. Renovating a building and bringing life back into it is a great way to honor local history and make the most of what is left. But I worried. Part of playing in towns is that I worry about them. Could this midsized town support an old six-hundred-thirty-seat theater? Wasn't that a little big? Could they afford to heat it? Could they find an audience?

The theater was still a little rough around the edges, but that was part of its charm, and I could see how excited the volunteers were to have music in their downtown. The staff members introduced themselves, and the promoters sent flowers backstage to me and to Lucy Wainwright Roche, who was also playing that night. These were all good signs.

There was a straight-up beer-and-burgers restaurant nearby. Like the Colonial, it was serviceable and friendly. People could go there before the show, and that would help the town: keeping an audience on your main strip before and after concerts is key for compounding the value of the concert venue. The coffee place down from the Colonial was another music venue, the Steel City Coffeehouse. It was a funky, sprawling café, a highly beneficial space for gathering up all the eclectic conversations and energies of this town and helping its residents imagine new steps for going forward. And it had excellent coffee. The ducks were lining up. *Still*, I thought, *this town could go either way.* The work of a few can only go so far.

When I returned in 2011, there were lots of restaurants, there was plenty of great coffee, and I saw further improvements to the Colonial, which now had a nicer dressing room and was open three hundred sixty days a year.

How did the town that had faced such a complete shutdown come back in force? There was strong leadership for sure. Large, ungainly, wire-tangling trees were chopped down, new trees were planted, lampposts were painted blue, benches were installed, and sidewalks were repaired. But something has to precede good governance. Otherwise, why bother governing at all?

Everywhere I looked, I saw Phoenixville's use of history as its strongest life-giving force. It was in the architecture, the murals, the signs, and even in the majority of my discussions with people. They restored the structural integrity of the town's old buildings while also delving into their social history to locate themselves in the present. This town was growing from its roots.

SAVING THE BUILDINGS

How did it start? About twenty years before, a forward-thinking group called Phoenixville Area Economic Development Corporation (PAEDCo) worked with the historic preservation office of Chester County to secure historic district status for Phoenixville. Barbara Cohen, a petite and extremely energetic woman in her sixties, with a love of history and a degree in design, was part of PAEDCo and had sat on many boards since the 1970s. "There are twelve hundred properties in Phoenixville's historic district. You can't just do or take down whatever you'd like, okay? It has to go along with that fabric."

Absolutely. I had seen the thematic unity in the town's architecture right from the get-go. Historic district status creates a blanket standard of preservation that adds up to the overall feel of a town, not to mention a better opportunity for history to reveal its charms and keep its good stories. Old buildings also provide great bones for revitalization, even though sometimes preservation can be a high-maintenance investment. Barbara confessed that when some of the stonework in the Foundry Building had to be fixed, for instance, it took them six months to track down the right mortar recipe. And the building's slate roof required extra studies of its load-bearing capacity.

But the dividend is that Phoenixville's preservation efforts allowed its citizens to dream within its historic district architectural code. They walked into these historic buildings and brought back elements of the town's past as a way to define its unique identity, spark imaginations, inspire community involvement, and bring people in from the Schuylkill watershed and beyond. History-related projects have boosted morale and kept everyone involved. Phoenixville has a wonderful personality and a sense of ever-growing, if variously defined, prosperity. And it's just a lot of fun to be there.

In addition to the Colonial Theatre, there is another landmark, the Foundry Building, that has incorporated historic elements and themes into its labor-intensive renovation. It also went on to become a physical anchor in the community as well as a bridge to a rich history.

Just down the hill from the Colonial on Bridge Street, French Creek winds for half a mile around the outlines of the former Phoenix Iron and Steel Company's buildings. It's all empty space, a clear absence of what was there before. Only the original Foundry Building remains, and that's because a development company planned to make the fourteen-thousand-square-foot space into a gym for its proposed townhouses.

The developers ended up walking away from the deal, which jeopardized the future of the Foundry Building. Even though the building was designed by Henry Hobson Richardson, who came out of the same architecture firm as Frank Lloyd Wright, and even though the building combines the gravitas of stone walls with the elegant simplicity of early twentieth-century design, and even though one could argue that at least one structure should commemorate the foundry that made iron columns for the Washington Monument, well, you know, the foundry could have gone, too.

Luckily, heading into the 1990s, the concerned citizens of PAEDCo, including Barbara, all hundred pounds of her, stood between the foundry and anyone who wanted to take it down. It was one of the first buildings protected by the historic district designation. "The first thing you need to share with anyone who wants to do something with a town that is in mourning because it has lost its manufacturing base," Barbara said, "is you need to create a reason for people to come to that place, whatever it may be, whether it is history, or geography, or some combination thereof." The region's richly varied manufacturing history, along with its impressive historic architecture and the natural beauty of the Schuylkill River, converges at the Foundry Building.

PAEDCo secured a three-hundred-thousand-dollar grant to buy the building. A new developer came, but then withdrew. Then, at a gala event unrelated to PAEDCo, an enthusiastic supporter of renovations like this, a developer himself, happened to speak with the head of the PAEDCo board and ask how the project was going. Upon learning that it had stalled, Bernard Hankin and the Hankin Group took the lead with an investment of five million dollars.

Before this propitious conversation with Bernard Hankin, there had already been a crisscrossing of community connections, grants, and historic designations to put the building on everyone's radar.

Already the positive proximity of like-minded people in town had blossomed into the purchase of the building. And then, with a strong community to welcome them, the Hankin Group arrived.

A crowning moment was when Pennsylvania governor Tom Ridge named the Foundry Building the main location for the interpretation of the Schuylkill River's industrial history. Barbara got in deep with design and content. About a quarter of the Foundry Building presently houses the Schuylkill River Heritage Center.

Barbara also wanted to create a memorial to Phoenix Iron and Steel workers. This is a concept that has helped many former mill towns of the Northeast: if you want to memorialize an industrial past effectively, include the workers. Acknowledge their hardworking legacy, not just the owners whose names are still on the street signs. Barbara drew a rough design on yellow tracing paper and showed it around. It was a semicircle of upright phoenix columns, the support structures that had made Phoenixville famous not only for the Washington Monument but also for the raised platforms of the elevated trains in New York City and for bridges throughout the eastern United States. The plan was to erect the columns and then to pave the surrounding space with bricks inscribed with the names of both heritage center donors and past foundry workers.

Barbara got to see her tracing paper plan come to fruition. "I got a call from Cagley Harman engineers about six months later: 'Barb, we've got twelve or sixteen phoenix columns going to the scrapyard.' They were taking down the Stegmaier Brewery up in Wilkes-Barre." That was in 1996. They hadn't yet finished the paperwork to buy the Foundry Building itself, but that didn't stop Barbara's pursuit of the irreplaceable columns.

One of the PAEDCo board members, Joe Mooney, "sent a truck and went and got them. And they laid on his property until 2003, until we had raised the money to create the sculpture garden." Every story Barbara told had a reference to a friend or acquaintance called upon or simply charmed into service, building an alliance of support for the foundry and for Phoenixville's revitalization by proxy.

A Space Where the Present Meets the Past

Now it was time to bring in the right business to fill up the building. Because the heritage center wasn't meant to take up the entire foundry space, PAEDCo brought in advisors to suggest more uses for it. There is a massive main hall with an overlooking mezzanine. After long deliberation, everyone decided that the best use of them was as a "flexible event space." So now, along with the heritage center on the east side of the building and the memorial that curves around the plaza at the main entrance, the large, light-filled Foundry Hall hosts weddings, conventions, and even dance performances.

There is something extremely effective in mixing the past and present. The way the Schuylkill River Heritage Center planners and designers have incorporated iron columns, shafts, cogs, and commemorative bricks into the Foundry Building makes it much more interesting than a generic space for events. In addition to the memorial garden and the heritage center, which connects to the main space through glass doors, selected pieces of big machinery have remained in the larger room, such as two Cupola furnaces you can see through the front entrance.

Barbara said many people choose the Foundry Building for weddings because they want some resonance of the region that holds their families' histories. Weddings and memorial services are opportunities, after all, to trace one's family roots and to feel their connection to the past. The staff told me one of the favorite wedding photo locations is in front of the giant cantilevered crane on the main floor.

The Foundry Hall event space also helps the crowd circulation in the heritage center. It's hard to get people through the door of historical societies. The heritage center is there for any visitor to learn more about where they are. Even I, a history lover, don't get my family over to our local history museum enough. However, I can think of plenty of weddings at which I would have liked to escape to a well-curated history room with an inlay of the Schuylkill River on the floor and an interactive map of the river's past industries on the wall, designed by Barbara Cohen herself.

It's the feel of past and present and the invitation for the imagination to wander between the two that gives this space its appeal. History echoes in the walls of the Foundry Building, much as it does, poetically, within our psyches, especially at life-defining events.

ARCHITECTURE THAT HOLDS THE CULTURE OF THE DOWNTOWN, THEN AND NOW

The Colonial Theatre feels so connected to its colorful history that I wouldn't be surprised to hear it had a resident ghost. And yet it is very much a part of Phoenixville's present life. Physically, it's just like it was a century before as a vaudeville theater. It is at once grand and unpretentious, a stylistic and functional connection from the past to the present. Its lobby has a high ceiling and staircases on either side leading up to the balconies and offices, but it's a little darker than the lobbies of some old opera houses. Nothing is tattered, but nothing seems particularly new. There is no chandelier. It is not ornate, just very comfortable, with a pleasantly pervasive smell of popcorn.

One of the guiding forces of this extremely popular venue is Executive Director Mary Foote, who has a genial, unflappable air about her. She is tall, with short, gray hair and a gentle, patient smile. Her style is streamlined and low maintenance. The Colonial Theatre has lucked out in having Mary at the helm because she and the staff, to whom she often gives credit, have been fulfilling the historic vaudeville mission statement. It is a theater of the people for the fun of the people.

Mary did not start her career in arts management. She got her master's degree from Temple University in community organizing.

But she said that when the theater went up for sale around the year 2000, "It was really good timing." She had built up enough trust in Phoenixville to recommend that the Colonial become a nonprofit. She successfully floated the idea "that the community would own it and really use the theater—as a colleague said in New York—as the living room of Phoenixville, to come and just be together and celebrate."

Vaudeville theaters were very much like the living rooms of their small cities. They were there to provide low- to middlebrow, not highbrow, performances. Today the Colonial has movies with as much variety and even campiness as its former vaudeville shows. There's a relaxed spirit of fun, there's plenty of room, and if people are feeling really fancy, sometimes they'll have a TED Talk.

A community-representative kaleidoscope of events and audiences passes through every day. The staff has been receptive to people's ideas and wish lists, so there are first-run movies, a classic film on Sundays, children's movies on Saturdays during the school year, and then there's the weird stuff.

The theater hosts the First Friday Fright Night. Mary said, "A group of young men who love that kind of film came to us, and now they program it for us. They come up with the ideas. Also, after they realized First Friday Fright Night was about one kind of cult film, and there were other kinds of cult films they wanted, we added a third Friday, which is Cult Night." She sounded a bit like a mother who affably mixes up fake blood for her son's zombie costume and helps him construct the cardboard-and-foil axe to plant in his head.

Chuck Francisco, a dedicated volunteer who does social media programming at Villanova University as his day job, is one of those young men to whom Mary referred. He said, "I was coming for horror shows because I love horror films, and I said, 'Why can't we show *Mystery Science Theater* episodes?' So they're like, 'All right, just pick one. And host it.' So I started down that path, and it's been a while."

He said, "We do marathon movies, like all night sometimes, just for fun. So it's really just a matter of, I asked, and came in."

In the age before television and highways, towns were laid out for a pedestrian culture, with their chief entertainment centers on Main Street. Today the theater continues to exist at street level, at once feeding and responding to a downtown culture. When Mary and the Colonial Theatre Association brought the place back with a spirit similar to how it had existed in the past, it finally thrived as it had a century before. Prior to the association's arrival, the Colonial had been opened and shuttered many times.

Another reason the Colonial thrived was that the staff seized upon an opportunity to feature, and truly celebrate, one of the lead actors from Phoenixville. Not only that, the actor had a famous movie scene that took place in the Colonial itself. Mary and friends took those bona fides and ran with them.

In the 1950s, there was a Christian film company just outside of town called Good News Productions. The members were a tight-knit community who ate together, worshipped together, and made low-budget, sci-fi movies together. One film, directed by Irvin Yeaworth, did better than the others did. This one had a young Steve McQueen in it. This one had a theme song cowritten by Burt Bacharach. This film, *The Blob*, created an international film star, the Blob itself, born in Chester County, Pennsylvania.

When the Colonial reopened in 2000, newly owned by its nonprofit community group, its members were given a copy of *The Blob* by the son of the director. Soon after, Mary got a call from the local National Public Radio (NPR) affiliate asking how they might celebrate Steve McQueen's upcoming birthday. The staff members turned the screening into an event with the seductive title Blobfest.

After selling out two screenings of the movie the first year, the staff members knew they had something special on their hands. Audiences loved being in the theater where a famous scene was shot, even staking out the seats where the characters sat. Blobfest grew like . . . the Blob, becoming a weekend-long, multimedia celebration every July.

When I got to Blobfest in 2014, Chuck Francisco was holding down the fort, but he talked me through Friday night as they were setting up the stage with a game-show spinning wheel, drums, and mikes. One of the female performers was already in her taffeta skirt and bouffant wig as she directed stagehands with the props. Chuck said, "We have an entire evening of stage show. It's camp, it's whimsy, it's a variety show basically, so we have musical numbers, we have a band, we have set pieces, skits, prizes. This place will just fill up with people who are all going to have a good time. And then it culminates at nine o'clock with the run out."

At 9:00 p.m. it's time for the audience to flee. In the movie, there's a scene where the Blob oozes through the air vents like a giant, melting, red, Naugahyde couch. Reenacting the sci-fi teen terror of being absorbed into the Blob's quivering corpulence, the present-day audience streams through the lobby in a frenzied panic. The heavy, glass doors burst open. Outside, thousands of people await, cell phone cameras rising in the air to greet seven hundred people as they run screaming from the building en masse.

Some people scream persuasively; some could use a little practice. Other people have a special thing they do. "There's this big older guy who has the largest popcorn bucket," Chuck said, "and his thing is to run confused, turn around and throw popcorn in the air, and then go in the other direction. And he does it every year."

After the variety show and reenactment on Friday, there are panels, speakers, and screenings on Saturday. Sunday offers the more laid-back screenings for families and people who want to enjoy *The Blob* without the hubbub.

Blobfest changes from year to year, with its own planning and marketing committees. For instance, first there was a tinfoil-hat parade (foil hats are supposed to protect us from alien mind invasion), with more than three hundred hats worn the first year. Then the Village

Art Center took it over with a juried contest. The businesses in town welcome Blobfest on their sidewalk signs. Mid-Century Modern, a great atomic-age antique store down the street, lends whatever the Colonial needs for its displays. Every year there's a variation on the theme as well. When I visited, the theme was Godzilla and other Japanese monsters.

Mary Foote goes to conferences at the League of Historic American Theaters every year. "Everybody there wants to identify what makes their theater special. They're all beautiful, we know that. But if something unusual happened, then you're very lucky. That's where I think *The Blob* and Blobfest are so crucial to the bigger picture of what we're doing here. Not everybody gets that when you're revitalizing your town. You have to find that idea that will really spark something unusual."

When you choose to capitalize on your history, you are creating something exciting and irreplaceable. Phoenixville has a unique story, spirit, and historic theater that will always belong to them alone.

REBIRTH WITHOUT GENTRIFICATION

The texture of Phoenixville's history offers some resistance to faceless gentrification. There is a message that underpins the prettiness of its nineteenth- and early twentieth-century facades: its residents don't forget how these buildings and streets came to be. It has been meaningful for Phoenixville citizens to resurrect both their structures and the stories behind them.

A genuine nineteenth-century, interior, brick wall might make perfect product placement surface for an Urban Outfitters or Diesel Jeans store. But Barbara is clear that revitalization is not just about bringing buildings up to snuff. She refers to the preservation efforts as "packaging history for economic development." And, she points out, with more than twelve hundred structures to choose from, the buildings are collectively a departure point of discovery. They don't work if they're taken too far out of their historical context.

Another element of history-minded towns is that they attract the interest and engagement of history-minded people. People who are serious about history, whether amateurs or professionals, have great respect for their towns. They are never dismissive of their regions, aesthetically or otherwise. They're much too busy exploring all the cornices, belfries, old letters, and other metaphoric time passages in the places around them. They provide valuable witnesses in any community. These are the people who find elaborate Victorian details hiding under aluminum siding or the hidden history of an old neon sign. They're ready to take any town at more than face value. If an outside entity comes in to erase or efface the historic identity of a town, it will find knowledgeable resistance.

I remember saying from the stage of a small New York state theater that I thought its city was beautiful. It was. The audience just laughed. Their city had been so mired in official corruption and employment downturns that they no longer experienced that magical dimension of history in their streets. History lovers never laugh at their own towns. They learn about them, and often they spend a considerable amount of time translating the value of their towns to others.

People who are interested in things like saving old buildings are also not shy about finding preservation grants, advisors, and helpful agencies or just tracking down the precedents set by other towns. In Phoenixville's case, the townspeople's efforts brought in a whole community of people who loved and respected all the rich details of Phoenixville's industrial and preindustrial past, and that's another important reason history-based projects can generate so much positive proximity. Phoenixville attracts these enthusiasts, who, in turn, bring out the history buff in others.

Here's another way in which Phoenixville's strong sense of historic identity adds to its overall independence and prosperity: the downtown appears to have no chain stores. I asked Borough Manager Jean Krack if the town had a formula business restriction. A formula business restriction means you can't have a business that also has more than two or three establishments in other towns. Existing restaurants that expand into other towns are grandfathered in; it's a restriction with some breathing room. But Jean said Phoenixville didn't need it because people just wanted to patronize local businesses. I found his bemused answer stunning. I pressed him, saying that chain stores have a way of adding more sugar, salt, and marketing so that people will choose them over local businesses.

Jean just shook his head. Somehow it didn't even compute that people would want a chain frozen yogurt store when they had Brown's Cow, Warren Brown's ice cream parlor, which has served Philadelphia's Bassett's Ice Cream (made by the oldest ice cream company in the United States, founded in 1861) on Main Street for the past ten years. Everyone loves that ice cream, not to mention Warren himself. And why go to a franchised café when Steel City is better and its name reminds you of the town's claim to fame? Across the street from the Colonial Theatre, the Artisan Café has equally good coffee, provides a peaceful ambiance, and sells local pottery, recognizing that many ceramic artists have chosen to settle in the area over the past few decades. These places use the historical context of the region to promote their businesses. They identify with the identity of the town. Why would you go anywhere else?

These questions will be put to the test when Phoenixville adds three hundred fifty residential units to fill in the ghost space along the French Creek.

SOCIAL HISTORY AS A KEY TO IDENTITY

For Barbara Cohen, the relevance of Phoenixville's past goes way beyond the buildings. When she talks about Phoenixville's social history, she is just as animated about the town's uniquely egalitarian legacy as she is when she talks about the light from the Foundry Building's clerestory windows or the bridge built with elements from Phoenix Iron and Steel that she herself photographed while she attended a medical convention with her husband in Iowa. "The Reeves family, David Reeves, purchased the millworks in 1829, and they established a school in 1834 for the workers' children. But he sent his own children to that school as well," she said.

The modern mind can embrace the importance of what David Reeves did: he used his resources to build an entire public school to compete with the kind of private school to which he could have sent his children. There were almost a hundred private academies along the East Coast by 1834, many of them around Philadelphia, but Reeves made an unusual decision to raise young minds equally and locally.

Barbara catalogued a history of religious and social tolerance. Pointing to a picture of nearby mountains, she said,

> The Irish were Catholic. During the potato famine in Ireland, 1841, they poured in here and literally dug their way through for the original Reading Railroad. A little bit later, you had all these revolutions going on in Germany and Eastern Europe, so you had immigrants coming from all over. In the nineteenth century, Phoenixville was a terminus on the Underground Railroad. When did the Grimes [African Methodist Episcopal] Church begin? 1889. Is it still in existence? Yes. Bethel Baptist Church? 1912. Same year as the synagogue. Everybody gets along. So, whether Dad had a job at the steel mill or at the textile mill up on the hill, everyone was a community participant.

To Barbara, there is a strong connection between the environment of inclusivity from the past and the Phoenixville we see today. "To give you the backdrop of Phoenixville, what sets it apart, I think, from other communities, is the fact that it was a place where if you were Irish, Polish, Hungarian, German, African American, or Jewish, everybody could get a job at the mill." And bringing this aspect of history closer to the present, she adds, "My mentor was an

African American lady named Debbie Mitchell. And she's pictured on the Phoenixville mural with a yellow blouse and a green skirt. She got us young doctors' wives involved in the 1970s. In 1972, Debbie Mitchell was on the Board of Directors of Phoenixville Hospital. Doesn't that tell you something?"

There are plenty of stories that cast Phoenixville in a less favorable light. Phoenix Iron and Steel, partly owned by civic-minded school opener David Reeves, paid notoriously low wages. The Heritage Society dutifully tells the story of low labor standards and noncompetitive pay, but the stories it chooses to feature in town mirror the principles important today. Iron-fisted managers are not on the Phoenixville mural. Debbie Mitchell is.

The inclusiveness of Phoenixville in the past is also a major component of positive proximity in the present. This community functions for everyone in it. A town can revitalize its main streets and boast a network of locally owned businesses, but some wealthy and very cold-to-the-touch towns are full of boutiques and frilly, independent shops. Traveling minstrels like me avoid them, and, interestingly, they often have no performance venue. These are not exciting communities. They are exclusive enclaves.

Phoenixville's past helps inspire its inclusive present. Its all-local downtown mirrors a whole town of diverse incomes, ethnicities, and sensibilities. When I spoke to the young owners of Mid-Century Modern about Phoenixville, they said they were always trying to convince their friends to live there, too. Their neighborhood is low rent but not low safety or low appeal. They love their neighbors, and they say there's a block party almost every month. Their part of town is across the train tracks, a quarter mile past the Foundry Building. In my travels, usually "the other side of the tracks" is where you don't want to be after dark, but this is not the case in Phoenixville.

Up the block from the mural that features Debbie Mitchell, Steve Manning opened Philly Fadez, an old-fashioned barbershop. His clientele is mostly African American, and, from what I saw when I spoke with him, mostly teenaged boys. He echoed Barbara's description of who was welcome in Phoenixville going back centuries. "I've said my door is open for everybody. I have a lot of different nationalities coming here, and we all sit here and we talk about things going on in the world. And we talk about things going on in relationships. And things going on with the kids, and we all come to a conclusion together pretty much in here."

He said he wanted to open a barbershop in town because there wasn't one, "and by that I mean a traditional barbershop." At Philly Fadez, the traditional expectation of a lot of "talk about things going on" still holds. Steve said, "There're not a lot of African Americans around." He chose the most visible corner in town to have a place where kids could congregate inside and outside, and they do, whether they need a haircut or not. "This is the fish tank," he said, "and it's the best place, you're on the corner, you can't beat it. And I just love family-oriented places, so that's it." He is a single dad, as are the other two barbers who work there. All their kids grew up around the shop and the backrooms that Steve renovated.

American towns can be very self-segregating. The decision to put a traditional African American barbershop at the main intersection of a town that is predominantly white calls on a history in which "everyone was a community participant," as Barbara puts it. And there might be a more direct connection between Steve's inclusive message and the town's inclusive philosophy of yore. His mother grew up in Phoenixville, and knowing of her experiences, he knew he wanted to raise his kids there.

Not everything has been rosy, of course. Steve encountered "negativity" when he first came to the space. "A lot of people thought I couldn't do it down here. But I got a lot of support from the community and kept on thriving, and it's here." He emphasized that he didn't want to dwell on any resistance he had experienced. He had better things to do. There was a crowd of teenaged boys waiting for their haircuts when I first visited Steve. There was a proud veteran who wasn't "quite able to pay today" whose hair Steve was cutting the second time I visited (I had to come by twice that morning because he'd been giving free haircuts at the nursing home). Steve seemed very busy including everyone; he didn't have time to think about exclusion.

Across the street from Philly Fadez is the Steel City Coffeehouse, where I spoke with Eli Wenger. Eli, like Mary Foote at the Colonial, is what I call a community character builder. He and Mary are good at providing a place for people who don't necessarily paint inside the lines or even want to. These two community character builders welcome many different skill sets and, let's say, a range of mental frequencies.

Eli is particularly open to the "range of mental frequencies" part. This openness is yet another way of respecting Phoenixville's past. "We call them Phoenixville crazies, lovingly, and they're not crazy; it's just there are eccentric people," Eli said, referring to some of his customers. "And it can be frustrating at times as a business owner because you do have to deal with things where it's like, 'Look, I just need five minutes to do my job,' and you have to have conversations with people who are in some cases . . . trying to hold it together."

The "crazies" are a part of Phoenixville's history that, much to the town's credit, has not been swept under the rug. When a facility called the Pennhurst State School and Hospital closed its doors in 1987, many of the former patients came to Phoenixville and found their way into group homes or assisted-living situations. Like many so-called mental asylums, Pennhurst was a living nightmare. Its claim to fame today is that it's haunted. So providing a friendly ear and an understanding nod is not only a way to acknowledge the diversity of the town but also pushes past a tragic history that ended with a diaspora in Phoenixville.

Another crucial aspect of respecting a town's past is to recognize and include its older citizens. Jean Krack and every other town leader I met said they depended on the contributions of time and care that engaged, retired citizens give the community. Towns need their senior citizens for their knowledge about where they live as well as their volunteer work and their expertise. They provide a valuable bridge to the history of a town.

Phoenixville's senior center is two blocks from the center of town and is very active. I find that there is a relationship between senior civic engagement and the closeness of senior centers to pedestrian town centers. Another town that has a very engaged senior population, also with a senior center right in the downtown, is Stoughton, Wisconsin. Stoughton has a long Main Street with independent stores, a renovated opera house, a busy craft center, and bulletin boards filled with upcoming events, all of which I associate with high positive proximity. The senior population plays an active role. Stoughton's Norwegian history is well preserved, with a Syttende Mai (Norwegian founding day) festival every year and rosemaling, a traditional Norwegian style of panel painting, gracing the corridors of its town hall, painted by its oldest citizens.

Many senior centers are between two and ten miles from the heart of town, not exactly walking distance. My suggestion is to follow the lead of Phoenixville and Stoughton and keep senior centers, with all they have to offer, close to Main Street. Another suggestion I'd make based on community centers I've visited (and played in) is that even when a center is technically a senior center, it's helpful to have other traffic coming through in the space itself. Even a name like Seniors and Friends Center welcomes younger people, particularly kids.

The active presence of senior residents is particularly important to a town's youngest citizens. When I taught a music history course at Wesleyan University, I noticed one aspect of the students' upbringing that seemed to give them an edge: students who had a strong relationship with their grandparents, or grandparental figures, had the most interesting comments and showed the most breadth of insight in their discussions and writing. There was just enough distance in time for students to feel the otherness of history, while there was enough proximity in time to feel the effects of historical events. From the student who said, "My grandma said everything was better made in the 1950s" to the one whose left-leaning, government-worker grandparents were exiled to Alaska during the McCarthy era, those familiar with the perspectives of people fifty years their elder did the best in the class.

If we look at a roster of populations that have traditionally experienced vulnerability in the United States—low-income people, minorities, and senior citizens—we see that Phoenixville invites everyone's participation, and the town itself is better for it. Respect for history has strengthened Phoenixville's buildings and grounds and what is put into them. Locating inclusive community values in the past has strengthened the town's narrative. Barbara is there to tell you that a civic-minded interdependence has existed for more than a century. She calls it the "DNA" of Phoenixville. As if to sum it all up, she takes me to a retrieved sign that hung for years at the entrance of David Reeves's school: "In Phoenixville, the People Make the Difference."

OTHER TOWNS, OTHER HISTORIES

Phoenixville gives us a helpful list of ways in which the historic infrastructure and social wiring of a town can draw in the energy (and dollars) of visitors and citizens alike. It's immediately apparent when a town has chosen to identify itself by polishing up and clearly identifying how its past has brought it to its current status. Here are a few more examples of towns that have illuminated their histories in ways that bring positive proximity into the present.

Lowell, Massachusetts

Like Phoenixville, Lowell survived a very difficult period by salvaging gems from its history. I got to see the bad old days firsthand. In the summer of 1995, I made my way to a small stage at the edge of the woods for my concert. I passed a volunteer on the way. "So, uh, did you lock your car?" she asked. When I plugged in my guitar and started sound check, the sound guy introduced himself and said, "You locked your car, right?" A young volunteer later told me, "You probably shouldn't lock your car, because then they'll break the windows." They, the suspected car thieves, were most likely the people who got swept up in a notoriously awful crack epidemic in Lowell.

I'd been in downtown Lowell earlier that day with my manager, Charlie, visiting the Lowell National Historical Park, which told the history of the town's famous textile mills. We saw the short documentary. We walked along the Pawtucket Canal. Lowell's cotton mills not only defined the Industrial Revolution in the United States but also formed the crucible of its labor movement: teenaged girls, many of them from Ireland, mounted a successful strike there for higher wages and better working conditions. Lowell was also the home of Beat writer/icon Jack Kerouac and painter James Abbott McNeill Whistler.

Charlie and I stood in the lobby of the National Park Service building and remarked how sad it was that Walmart was coming for Lowell. We tended to see Walmart as the grim reaper of ailing downtowns, maybe even lowering the scythe before those towns had died. We assumed the staff would appreciate our condolences. They were angry. They told us not to disparage Walmart. Lowell needed the jobs.

Maybe they thought Walmart was a wonderful store and were defending its honor, but I couldn't help thinking that they were angry because they knew Lowell shouldn't have needed a big box store to help its economy. There was so much history and beauty there. So much space. So much potential. If you encounter a historically rich town that's not living up to its potential, inevitably the feeling in the streets will be one of frustration and anger. You can't help but feel there's a voice of history—a proud voice—in all of those brick walls and ruins of watermills. It's like a story that deserves to be told but has been unjustly stifled. Lowell was one of those towns.

It was true that Lowell needed jobs. An economic downturn, not a loss of historical context, fueled the drug epidemic and sapped the spirit of the city. But Charlie and I felt that if Lowell could dig in and return to some part of itself, a town that defined the course of American history in so many ways, rather than grasp at jobs that would take more life out of its downtown commerce, it could attract businesses with its unique identity.

Today, playing music in Lowell is a completely different experience than it was in 1995. The Lowell outdoor concert series in Boarding House Park is a coveted gig: the stage is huge, the sound guys are great, and it's free to the public. The dressing room is in the actual former boardinghouse of the Lowell Mill girls. The building is now the Mogan Cultural Center, which is across from the Boott Cotton Mills Museum, which is down the street from the American Textile History Museum and New England Quilt Museum, which are around the corner from the Whistler House Museum of Art and the Jack Kerouac house. And on the other side of a main drag of Mexican, Thai, and Italian restaurants is the National Park Service site, which abuts a new apartment building.

History is the heart of Lowell and one of the main drivers of its economy. There are galleries and maker spaces that host the arts and crafts that build on the traditions that first put Lowell on the map. And the closest Walmart is two miles from downtown.

History as a Wayfinder

Sometimes the small things set the wheels of inquiry in motion. Throughout North America, I've seen signs, symbols, and motifs of history that give towns an instant historical context. They enlighten my experience as a traveler, but they're also touchstones of common experience for a community. It's good to understand how a town came to be. Was it a paper city like Holyoke, Massachusetts? Was it a turn-of-the-century, hot springs spa like Eureka Springs, Arkansas?

History can serve our communities without too much effort, but it does take a little work. Putting our histories side by side with the present, even symbolically, gives us an instant burst of perspective and our towns an extra distinction.

In my town, there's a sign that reads:

> ### SUGAR LOAF
> #### ON THE NORTH SLOPE OF THIS HILL WAS
> #### ONE OF THE FORTS BUILT, 1776–1777
> #### TO DEFEND THE HIGHLANDS,
> #### FROM CONNECTICUT TO NEW JERSEY.

This is one of many Revolutionary War sites on my town's bend of the Hudson River. The commemorative sign was placed there in the early twentieth century in a font size that was appropriate for pedestrians, equestrians, and early motorists. But today there is no shoulder on the road, and the speed limit is forty miles per hour, so it is a sign for no one.

When I stopped in Dover, New Hampshire, I parked right next to a kiosk with an enlarged old photograph showing the exact three blocks in front of me but from the year 1920. I looked down at the photo and then up at the city today. I looked down, I looked up. I loved it. I loved all of the photographs I found around Dover.

I walked into a long former textile mill. The mill complex, including buildings, a waterwheel, and a pedestrian bridge, takes up more than ten acres. One mill has apartments; the others have businesses and a restaurant, Blue Latitudes. In the mill, the windows are set deep into the original brick walls, and their sills are lined with antique industrial spools and spindles. Original pulleys hang from the ceilings. Little wheels (spur wheels, crown wheels, etc.) hang like artwork in the expanses of high-ceilinged walls. Again, as with the "back then" photos, you can imagine how the space was used and, by extension, who used it.

Outside, near the mill's clock tower, is a sign that commemorates the first women's strike in the United States. Unlike the mill girls of Lowell, these young women were crushingly unsuccessful. They suffered humiliation on top of defeat because the local newspaper sympathized with their employers and came out with a blistering, smackdown editorial against their even daring to strike. Still, Dover chooses to remember this first strike, which was followed by more successful ones in another mill town decades later, not many miles away, in Lowell.

I asked Bethany, my server at Blue Latitudes, why she thought there were so many signs and symbols of Dover's history around us. She said without hesitation that there were many independent businesses around Dover, and they wanted to keep it that way. The businesses in town sponsored all the signs. The interest in and curation of history out on the streets galvanized the network of people who loved going into Dover's past when it came time to decide how to populate its extensive campus of historic buildings. The industry of the past is now matched by postindustrial freelancers, small businesses, and local stores throughout the town.

THE LIVING EDGE OF HISTORY

Then there are towns and places that take history one step further. They have introduced me to an important historical issue and then invited me to see how that same issue is alive today. Have we come far? How much further do we have to go?

On a sweltering August morning, my son and I took a tour of a third-floor tenement apartment in New York City's Tenement Museum. The space was about six hundred square feet, and it held a family of five plus an entire tailoring operation. Our guide seemed to feel personally connected to this extended family, and by the end of the tour, so did we. She passed around a photo of the daughters in the 1970s, proof that this immigrant couple had provided a stable foundation for the next generation.

We took the afternoon tour out on the sidewalk. We saw local businesses that had survived, such as Muscot glasses and Russ and Daughters, the beloved seller of all things bagel and smoked fish. And then our tour guide said something, almost sotto voce, that confirmed my sense that the Tenement Museum's commitment to the neighborhood's future was as strong as it was to its past. The museum employs a full-time, pro bono immigration lawyer.

When I went to visit the Civil Rights Memorial in Montgomery, Alabama, I went through a labyrinth that featured familiar heroes such as Julian Bond, Ella Baker, Martin Luther King Jr., John Lewis, and Pete Seeger. I see the voting rights victory as one of the proudest moments in American history. The civil rights movement was about justice and dignity, galvanized in song and poetry. When I went through the gift shop on my way out the door, I spoke with Lecia Brooks. It turns out that Lecia is the outreach director for the Southern Poverty Law Center (SPLC), which is right next to the memorial.

Both of these institutions, the Civil Rights Memorial and the Tenement Museum, drew me in and reminded me of the histories that define the inclusive, democratic society we struggle to be. But woven into the museum experience in New York City and right outside the door in Montgomery (via the SPLC) was the reminder that we have plenty of opportunities to engage in the present and pay respect to the people who work hard for a more equitable society today.

I love nothing more than grabbing a cup of coffee in Salem, Massachusetts, in the summer. The smell of beeswax candles and essential oils rolls out of stores into a maze of colonial streets. In some stores, I can hear a psychic consultation from behind a folding screen in the back. Salem is a great place to find modern Wiccans.

Salem went to war against witches in the eighteenth century. Today there are many who challenge and seek to rectify the injustices of the past through their museums, shops, and annual conferences. The voice of modern Salem rings true and clear: the witches won.

Did your town have a notable turning point? Did your community take on the responsibility to heal and evolve from tragedy? Chances are, then, it still participates in addressing the questions its history posed. Living-edge institutions in New York, Montgomery, and Salem say, "Important things happened here, and we honor their importance by endeavoring to build a stronger democracy."

I lived in Northampton, Massachusetts, for eight years. I was always proud to live there. *60 Minutes* did a segment about it called Lesbianville, and Leslie Stahl was the interviewer. I think she wore a black, leather blazer. Go Leslie! Soon after, someone addressed a letter to the town of Lesbianville instead of Northampton, and the letter got there. Jordi Herold put the envelope in the window of his club, the Iron Horse.

Northampton was a place for members of the LGBTQ community to settle down and grow their families with confidence and community support. Northampton was also a place for students to explore gender and sexuality. I watched very young women holding hands, wearing matching backpacks with pink triangles they'd cut out and sewn on them. And when it came to pride, our Pride March was as proud as San Francisco's.

Northampton is also the home of Smith College, where Sylvia Plath, Gloria Steinem, Barbara Bush, and Nancy Reagan all went to school. Abolitionist and suffragist Sojourner Truth lived in the neighboring town, Florence, for more than a decade in the nineteenth century. There's a statue of Sojourner Truth there.

But I have to be honest. I wish for more in Northampton. I wish it had a building that was an archive, museum, and resource center. I wish for a center that might have the kind of pro bono lawyer the Tenement Museum employs. Smith stays at the frontier of women's and gender issues, including a strong commitment to examining race and class within the gender movement. But how far can an elite, private college go with these topics beyond books and discussion?

Tucked inside their offices, the health-clinic workers and therapists of Northampton offer Eastern and Western medicine, wellness, and empowerment-based women's (including trans-women's) health practices. But out on the streets, the downtown does not reflect the radical work the many women, on and off Smith's campus, have done to break repressive molds in education, legislation, health care, and leadership. The way you know you're in a women's college town should not be the presence of seven chocolate stores and an Eileen Fisher boutique. One building would be perfect for a living-edge institution such as an archive/museum/resource center in the middle of town, but I doubt the owners, Urban Outfitters, are planning to leave anytime soon.

Finding the living edge of history means that we enlist the past to press us into seeking solutions for the future. Could this be true where you are? Are the Dust Bowl ballads still eerily relevant? Can the victorious movement to clean up a river raise morale to face new waterfront challenges such as invasive species and pollution?

BACK IN PHOENIXVILLE, WHERE THE PAST MEETS THE FUTURE

Phoenixville appears to know exactly how its present prosperity contrasts with that of its recent past. One of the ways in which this town goes forward is in remembering its sudden slide backward not long ago. Jean Krack told me that basically you've got seven years to make and hold on to something good that you can create. That's the rule. And yet Phoenixville is on about year twelve.

History requires upkeep, as do celebrations, like First Friday nights, Restaurant Week, and the Firebird Festival, that spring from the successful return of a downtown. The firebird itself requires three weeks of building, and volunteers come from all corners of the town to work on it. In view of what this town has accomplished, there is understandable excitement about what is yet to come and a sense that with every plan will come the citizens who have had enough good experiences in the town commons to want to find the next adventure and work to realize it.

With a solid base of supportive citizens and tools such as the historic district protection in their tool kit, Phoenixville's civic leaders have been in discussions with the developers of the new housing units. They don't feel steamrolled by the arrival of outside builders or new people.

The Colonial is expanding into an old bank building next door and counting on new pedestrian residents to attend midweek readings and once-a-month concerts.

Barbara Cohen is talking with the developers because she has plans to grace the hillside near the former steel mill with the very first Ferris wheel, which she has procured, piece by piece, over many years. Its structural elements came from Phoenix Iron and Steel, and she foresees its presence as a crowning jewel "like the Hollywood sign."

When I first saw the finished clay birds dug out from under the fire-consumed phoenix of the Firebird Festival, I assumed that each person's first bird symbolized the present while the second was the future. But Phoenixville is more than a town with any old future. Phoenixville has a strong identity emerging from a well-preserved past, embedded in its buildings and embodied in its population. This town presents a time-traveled, wonderfully variegated beauty like one of the clay birds buried in the ashes of the firebird and marked, cracked, and filigreed by fire, ember, and smoke. So to me the second bird is something else. It is the bird of possibility.

5

Carrboro, North Carolina: Culture

COMMUNITY ART SPACE

"Let's see the boards here . . . looks like there are thirteen concerts, eight theater pieces, one children's show, Transactors Improv for families, the community photo show exhibit, and four special events. . . . The Tibetan monks'll be back in two weeks to do a sand mandala in the gallery. They'll work all week and then wipe it away in a few moments." Art Menius, former director of the ArtsCenter in Carrboro, was showing me around this community art space in North Carolina's Triangle Cities region, which also includes Chapel Hill, Raleigh, Durham, and Cary.

I've always loved Carrboro, and to me, the ArtsCenter is at the heart of it. It presents all kinds of events, inviting artists from around the globe. But classes and local performances allow the townspeople's own creative impulses to flourish. Residents participate. The town has an economy in which artists and artisans can work alone and interdependently. Ultimately, the cultural environment influences the way the people of Carrboro live their lives. Overstatement? I don't think so.

As Art Menius and I continued around the corner and into the main room, he nodded in the direction of another smaller theater, the West End, in back, "which right now is full of kids in the after-school arts immersion program. They get to explore arts in a very nurturing environment for them. And that's a small model of the summer camp programs, which bring in hundreds of kids."

Art has worn many hats, working as executive director of the International Bluegrass Association and manager of what is now the Folk Alliance International. But the ArtsCenter seemed like a perfect fit because there was a daily commitment to connecting art to the community, and that was Art's thing. He also has a topical song show at a small radio station, WCOM, that sits right at the entrance of the ArtsCenter. The location of the station is a new development that Art and the founder of the ArtsCenter have made happen. Every time I have returned, in fact, there is something new happening there.

We continued walking toward three or four classrooms (depending on how you used them) with foldable tables and stackable chairs. "Are the art programs here affordable?" I asked. "Yes they are," he replied. "And we also have scholarships for families in need."

Art said that the after-school program, offered one hundred eighty days a year, presents the biggest challenge to the ArtsCenter's fund-raising efforts. "What we've got on my immediate right here is the painting studio, and next to you there is the dance studio, which is a little, uh, small, but still it gets a lot of use, including by the Carrboro Modern Dance Company. We still have people who use the art center's darkroom, amazingly enough."

A state-of-the-art jewelry and metallurgy studio is upstairs. Ahead of us was the clay center, with its three kilns. On our way there, we passed a few tiny ballerinas lining up at the water fountain. Other children fluttered by. Art smiled at all of them benignly, as if he was letting some goslings cross his path. Finally, we got to the small dressing room, which Art called the "green room that was cobbled together while Joan and Dar were en route in 1996."

"Did they make a green room just for Joan Baez?" I asked. "That they did," Art said.

Unlike some of the other towns described in this book, Carrboro, by the time I arrived in 1996, was already a highly functioning little town. I had discovered it in the New York City Public Library when I was compiling a book called *The Tofu Tollbooth*, a directory of natural food stores for travelers. Carrboro residents were some of the friendliest people I'd spoken with, and they were very proud of their food co-op. I'd always promised myself that if I could make a living as a musician, I'd find my way there on tour.

Sure enough, Carrboro was a wonderful find for a young traveler like me. The Weaver Street Market had a feel similar to the unpretentious neighborhood theater in which we were playing. The town itself seemed to have a friendly personality. I felt comfortable there, perhaps the way you feel welcome in a happy home. The ArtsCenter was the smallest venue on Joan's tour, but certainly one of the most hospitable.

I've been to Carrboro more than ten times since then because I've also played at the rock club Cat's Cradle, about five doors down in the same building. In the early 2000s I came with my family and wandered all around town, observing how strongly the local jewelry, brewery, and band scene were all part of the town's cultural geography. Creative forces permeated Carrboro, and they encompassed music, crafts, food, and drink.

I also got a sense of the area's overall cultural participation from the audiences I met after shows. They had stories to tell and poetry folios to share. They praised my show with an addendum of "and this is what I do," which is a very healthy audience attitude. Whenever I play there, I leave with a few books, cards, and sometimes a beautiful necklace (thank you). Behind the signing table where one signs autographs was the gallery of local art exhibits. I was an artist in their art space. The ArtsCenter is a stimulating, synergizing, little-but-mighty place that provides the trellis on which positive proximity can grow in years to come, extending way past the concerts and art shows themselves.

Venues like the ArtsCenter bring new life to a town before a performer like me arrives for a show, because an enormous range of dovetailing skill sets is needed to put on a concert. There are the sound person, the lighting person, the coffee maker, the coffee server, the volunteer coordinator, the person who designs the posters—you get the idea. If all of this culture-building activity is happening within a community art center where classes and workshops are also held, as they are in Carrboro, even more opportunities exist for artists, art lovers, and art amateurs to find common passions and complementing talents. At the ArtsCenter, these organizers and managers work in an environment with a buzz you can feel as soon as you walk in the building.

As a space that allows citizens to widen their net of loose ties for their mutual benefit, the ArtsCenter is as good as it gets. You can see the mix and match of community members who might not have any other reason to know each other. These relationships can be unusual in a very useful way, exposing people to each other's hidden abilities, such as silk-screening and making complicated spreadsheets. Not only that, people really get to shine in the roles they choose, even with less specialized jobs. Shy people can bake, gregarious people can sell merchandise, temperamental people can file things in the backroom, and all are important.

When the graphic designer wants to help her son start an open mike at his high school (and by the way, every high school should have an open mike), she knows who can organize the space and who can emcee with confidence. If the librarian wants to host a performance gala for a capital campaign, he knows the detail-oriented person who can budget the event down to the last penny as long as she and her prickly personality are cordoned off from audiences and donors. There is a diverse gathering of abilities united under the wide-ranging interest in culture. All of these positions make up a living address book of community contacts.

At the ArtsCenter, almost every position is paid (the ushers are volunteers). This is admirable but atypical, and it still has a very "little engine that could" feeling to it. There are specific jobs in teaching, running the box office, and taking care of the backstage needs, but there is also friendly flexibility throughout the space, showing that an arts center can also be a place where people stretch themselves in different ways. Any community space might offer a chance to strengthen one's abilities, but an arts center will often demand an unexpected range of them. The last time I was at the ArtsCenter, I heard the box office people fielding every kind of question with great breadth and diplomacy, and the young man who set up the green room for us excused himself to deal with a kiln crisis.

Obviously, you don't start a venue as a way to identify skill sets, but the community-building potential that comes out of this kind of intrepid, organized (mostly) force, with all of its varied interactions, might be the most effective identity-building project I've encountered. Certainly at the ArtsCenter, I've met people who welcome the crossover from arts talk to community talk. Art Menius's latest role, for instance, is as the economic development representative to the county transportation board.

Knowing the beneficial social outcomes of collaborating in the arts, communities also can, and often do, consciously enlist people who might otherwise feel undervalued and overlooked. At the ArtsCenter as well as many other venues I've played, there is an understanding that for many citizens, this job is their primary social connection to the town, and adjustments are made to facilitate them. Some retired people have more stamina than three people combined, but they can't drive at night and need a ride. Some teenagers can work very hard as long as you don't paralyze them with judgment and instead quietly supervise them from the sidelines.

The biggest advantage I've seen in these fleets of staff/volunteers is a basic—and strong—incentive to work together harmoniously. When there's a show to be put on, there really isn't an opportunity to dig into political differences or harbor strong resentments. The eyes of the community, and of the visiting artists, are upon the show's pre-senters in real time. I've heard plenty of volunteers complaining about each other, but I've rarely seen a community-run venue close. Staff and volunteers know, or learn pretty fast, that if the sound guy is uptight, then you just stick to your own turf. You cut the brownies into squares, put them on plates to sell at intermission, and don't hang out with the sound guy.

And then, of course, when you pull off a show that both the audi-ence and the performers have enjoyed, there are reasons to be proud and the inspiration to do it all over again. That kind of collaborative spirit infuses the community at large.

BRINGING IN THE ARTS BRINGS IN MORE

I'm biased, of course, but I believe that performances by different traveling artists serve as cultural trade winds blowing through a town that help to keep the dust of complacency or ennui from settling.

Traveling artists and creative guests bring in colorful, eccentric, poetic ways of seeing the world. Their performances are like the man-dala the monks created at the ArtsCenter. A sand mandala is an or-nate, painstakingly created tableau made on a floor with colored sand, and no trace of it remains after a mandala is swept away. Its beauty, its cultural geography, and its spiritual impact are preserved in memory.

With new ideas come new conversations. I came through towns in the 1990s singing songs such as "The Christians and the Pagans," with lyrics like this:

> The Christians and the Pagans sat together at the table.
> Finding faith and common ground the best that they were able.

And just before the meal was served, hands were held,
and prayers were said,
Sending hope for Peace on Earth to all their gods and goddesses.

I hoped these songs, like dispatches from the frontiers of a new social landscape, might allow audiences to recognize themselves as part of a new American narrative in which the paradigm of a stern, rigid pater or mater familias presiding over a table of silent relatives was giving way to grandchildren who dared to keep in their nose rings and even show up with a same-sex partner here and there (and at our house). I have been told, every day I've ever been on tour, that my friends' songs and concerts—and yes, my own as well—have been icebreakers for families and communities.

And then there are the very strange inspirations and role models we might find, like Ray Wylie Hubbard. Ray looks like he sprang fully formed from the parched, cracked earth of Texas: roughout boots with Cuban heels, hair a combination of rock star shag and weather-beaten longhorn, roguishly charming smile, and cobalt-blue glasses. He has songs like "Snake Farm." Here's a verse and chorus from "Snake Farm":

Well Ramona's got a keen sense of humor
She got a tattoo down her arm
It's of a python eatin' a little mouse
Wearin' a sailor hat that said snake farm.
Snake Farm—it just sounds nasty.
Snake Farm—well it pretty much is.
Snake Farm—it's a reptile house.
Snake Farm—Uuuggghhhhh.

Don't you want Ray in your town? Wouldn't you like your kids to see how many ways there are to see and be in the world? This snake farm actually exists, by the way.

Perhaps because the ArtsCenter has all ages passing through every day for classes and after-school programs, many people bring their kids to my shows. The presence of any kind of art venue invites young people to be involved with presenting and attending performances, but even better than that, they get to see adults talking about music, and they get to see how their town responds to poetry and heretofore unmentioned subjects. It's one thing to tell your kids to stay off drugs. It's another to sit with them, along with your neighbors, listening to John Prine sing "Sam Stone":

> There's a hole in Daddy's arm where all the money goes.
> And Jesus Christ died for nothing I suppose.
> Little pitchers have big ears,
> Don't stop to count the years,
> Sweet songs never last too long on broken radios.
> Hmm-mm-mm-mm.

Art centers are also a great way to give your town a global education. A storyteller from South Africa, Poland, or Japan can put her country on the map, especially for young listeners. International performers know they are ambassadors and find ways to educate audiences about their countries. Another dividend of bringing in international artists is that audiences often step up to be ambassadors of their town, too. Both the witnessing and being witnessed bring vitality to our everyday proximity.

THE REWARDS OF WELCOMING THE ARTISTS

Towns can also get a financial boost from artists who come through. I know many performers who consider about twenty different towns their homes away from home (for me it's more like a hundred). Traveling artists talk to each other about where they travel, the food, shopping, and people as much as they talk about music, gear, and tech stuff.

Traveling performers tend to be exceedingly grateful to people who help them through their melancholic loneliness, a common side effect of time on the road. Depressive loneliness is: "Who am I, and what the hell am I doing here?" Melancholy is more like: "That copper beech tree on the town green is beautiful; that tree will change; that tree will die; we will die, but we will be loved, like the copper beech tree, and yet, etc., etc." Melancholy responds to beauty and kindness. I'll always remember that when I played at a club in Manchester, United Kingdom, the dressing room was spare and dimly lit, but there was a vase of daffodils to welcome me. I started to cry. We travelers are grateful when we can experience ourselves in places, not just know about them.

So if you start a venue, remember that bands are tourists, too! I recommend kick-starting these relationships with artists by putting lists or maps in dressing rooms that show where you can get new guitar strings, good food, a toothbrush, coffee, and presents for your kids. If nothing else, we minstrels usually want to support local economies; after all, they support us. We want to support towns like Carrboro with its Weaver Street Market, garden patio restaurants, laundromats within walking distance of the venue, and sunny, spacious cafés.

Carrboro has held the door open for me every time I've come through. At this point, no matter where I'm playing in the area, I always make an effort to swing by Weaver Street the next day, like I'm visiting a friend. Musicians talk about Carrboro. Many of us know and love Art Menius. All of us love the food co-op and the Open Eye Café down the street, but we also love the general feeling of the town. With its hospitality, Carrboro has created bonds with artists that have gone far past the stage itself.

Carrboro values its own artists, too. Art Menius told me about the regional bands as well as the places where people could play music together. There are open mikes and song circles (the ArtsCenter has one on Monday nights) that foster local talent. There are colleges in the area where a band can gain some experience and traction, but a college band can only stretch its wings so far if it is confined to the campus.

Carrboro has venues that support new artists and venues where bands can have regular gigs. Both kinds of spaces, apart from being places where communities can form new and different ties, allow regional bands to grow their talents and their draw. Local bands are great gifts to their communities; they rock all night, and then you get to talk to the bass player at the grocery store. Local bands help a community in many ways. For one, local musicians and their audiences add eyes and ears to the downtown scene, keeping the streets more populated and arguably more safe after hours.

But aside from adding to the community's nightlife, local musicians contribute around the clock. They often lend out their sound and recording equipment, play benefits, visit schools, lead jams, and collaborate with other musicians (including students) in the area. Carrboro has this kind of musical population.

ROADMAP OF CULTURAL LIFE

The other thing I love, right in the heart of Carrboro, is Vespertine, a two-room, local artisan shop owned by Danish native Olivia Hjermitslev. I've always found things to buy for my friends and family there. Olivia says of Carrboro, "Here, we do buy local, and when you buy local, people can produce more, keep the prices down, and so on." Local culture is self-perpetuating and reinforces positive proximity: in supporting each other, the makers and their friends have an overall pro-artisan ethos in which citizens and tourists can participate up and down the economic strata.

Olivia told me she likes how people in the art community say they "work on the side." This semihumorous recasting of one's livelihood also reveals the importance of culture in the community. Makers and artisans identify themselves by their craft first, their primary income source second. Artists exist in a pool of talent unrelated to any litmus test of "making a living" at it.

Art Menius calls the Weaver Street Market, the ArtsCenter, and the Cat's Cradle the "pillars" of downtown. Within this central circle of institutions are about ten indoor/outdoor restaurant bars; the glass-fronted radio station, WCOM; and Vespertine. There is also the Open Eye Café, which has all the markings of a good, positive-proximity building café: lots of tables and off-to-the-side corners in which to sit, a friendly staff, and a big bulletin board. It has music on the weekends, too. The Open Eye also adds to the cultural influences coming into town because it houses Carrboro Coffee Roasters, owned by Scott Conary. Like Carrboro's visiting performers, Scott comes in and out of town bringing stories of his travels. Scott's motto is "Coffee unites the world."

"I've got a ridiculous amount of information that I've learned from being on the ground," he said. He has a strong relationship with a coffee farmer in Honduras, for example, and he's been to Indonesia, Ethiopia, and anywhere else that grows coffee. He told me, "I think, 'How do I bring that back, how much do people want to know, and how do we connect that to what we do here, because we have a farming community, we have an agricultural community that's right outside of town?'"

It takes a certain kind of community to contain an enthusiastic, global-minded spirit like Scott, but the community was stimulating to him, and, perhaps more importantly, it welcomed him. He has always asked himself, "Do they want to connect to the world?" He wants to live in a place where his coffee could be a bridge to other cultures. He says, in answer to his own question, "Obviously we're still here."

Add to all these meeting places, maker places, and learning places the heavily trafficked green in front of the Weaver Street Market, which is really the central green of the town, and you have myriad ways in which new and old acquaintances can receive some daily enlightenment and connect their thoughts to the outer world. The geography itself helps the social scene grow. Carrboro has an excellent social circulation system. And yet it used to be known as the "other side of the tracks" from Chapel Hill. Carrboro was where you'd get your auto parts and not much else. It suffered after the close of many mills in the 1970s.

To get a sense of how and when Carrboro had transformed, Art told me I had to speak with former mayor Ellie Kinnaird before I left town. I sat down with Ellie, a whip-smart community thinker with a master's degree in violin, at the Weaver Street Market. She never meant to be mayor, but she was part of a small group, many of them artists, who anticipated that outside interests and their proxies might take over the town. These artist-citizens wanted to take the reins themselves. A few were running for town council, but one position on the slate was not taken.

Ellie said, "A bunch of us got together and asked everybody around the circle if they would run for mayor, and I was the only one without a really good excuse, so I said, 'Okay, but, you know, I'm not going to get elected.' So darned, of course, if they all didn't work their tails off, and I woke up one morning and said, what happened here?" She won. In fact, the whole slate won. She said she didn't have an agenda for the town, so "I just decided to have fun." She was a musician. She was married to an artist. Her friends were all part of the creative community.

Her very first act was to approve the Weaver Street Market in 1987, but soon after she turned her attention to the ArtsCenter, which was at death's door. She worked hard to save it, and she and her council succeeded. Under her tenure, both the library and the farmers' market opened as well. She heard that the Cat's Cradle was leaving Chapel Hill and looking for a new home. She spent a year convincing the owner to come to Carrboro.

She told me how the annual holiday parade got shaken up to become the festival that everyone loves today. "At one point this artist wrote me, Rick Hermanson. He had been to the Christmas parade and said it was the dullest thing he'd ever seen. And he said he had some ideas. So I just wrote him one line; I said, 'Go for it, Rick!' And he did. I've got these pictures somewhere, they're just extraordinary, a whole lot of artists and people who just wanted to have fun made these enormous Christmas floats."

She and her community of artists leaned toward enriching the arts, historic preservation, local commerce, and communication in general. Though she herself is not a painter, Carrboro was very much Ellie's canvas, and she welcomed all other creative souls to get in and "have fun."

APPLYING CREATIVITY TO A TOWN

There is evidence all around Carrboro of how this town's artistic spirit carries over into civic engagement. Local restaurants host fund-raisers for cultural stalwarts such as WCOM. Town meetings are well attended with civil, but dynamic, debate. And about five blocks from the Open Eye Café, on the periphery of downtown, is the PTA Thrift Shop, colorful and welcoming, as if it grew out of imaginations that allowed themselves to stretch beyond conventional limitations.

You might picture a sweet, little, secondhand store with baby onesies and a few lovingly chewed, secondhand books in the window, but this shop is a huge complex. Its one hundred twenty thousand-plus–square foot building houses not only the shop but also school services and a few other nonprofits and local businesses that mutually support each other. The PTA spearheaded construction of this sustainable compound. The PTA Thrift Shop sells clothes, electronics, and lots of household stuff, all clean and neatly arranged. There is another PTA store in Chapel Hill, and together they have contributed nearly three million dollars since 2000. The PTA Thrift Shop has been open since 1952, when it was called the Thrifty Store, and it's always growing (not for nothing: the Art Guild started the Thrifty Store to raise funds for art teachers).

I see a connection between the creation of so many things that benefit the community, such as bike paths, arts programs, the thrift store, the local radio station, and popular pageants, and the collective experience of culture. Why? Because there is a precedent of success through joining forces and because community members have experienced themselves as creative and enlightened, with an accumulated history of positive, even playful, time spent in each other's company. When I head over to the giant PTA Thrift Shop, I think of the connection between resources—things we can all contribute, whether manifested in bags of old clothing or volunteer time—and resourcefulness, the ideas we come up with to channel what we have to help our communities.

And then I think of creativity itself, which is often associated with the arts alone but really has a much wider definition. Here's one from *Merriam-Webster:* the ability to make new things or think of new ideas. Dictionary.com has an even more civic ring to its definition of creativity as the ability to transcend traditional ideas, rules, patterns, relationships, or the like, and to create meaningful new ideas, forms, methods, interpretations, and so on. Carrboro provides examples of self-reinforcing creativity, creative freedom, and creative problem-solving that stem from its cultural life.

OTHER VENUES, OTHER TOWNS

When you ask yourself where and how to grow culture in your community, the truth is that there are often a ton of spaces that can be used for the arts, often quite cheaply. In my twenty-plus years as a performing musician, I have played in a repurposed airplane hangar, a vintage clothing store, a diner, a boat dock, a few town halls, bookstores, countless churches, and, more and more often (pat yourselves on the back, North America), in beautifully renovated vaudeville theaters and opera houses. Natick, Massachusetts, turned its old firehouse into a multimedia, black box theater. In New England, I know of at least three old mill buildings in which space was cordoned off for coffeehouses.

And when the right space is not available, there are homes. When I first played at EJ's Café in Albuquerque (back when I had only cassettes to sell), I was lucky enough to have Victoria Johnson in the audience. When I released my first CD, she organized a concert in her backyard. Everyone who's put on a house concert is very anxious at first, and yet I've never had a bad one. With the right attitude, everyone is prepared to make a space work.

That said, I've also played in dozens of renovated, repurposed, and rehabbed old places not quite ready for prime time. They were really winging it. The conditions could be pretty uneven as these venues got up to speed. But their presenters persevered, and these venues are now the cornerstones of many communities.

When I opened for Joan Baez at the Tarrytown Music Hall (a few cities after Carrboro on our tour), about twenty miles north of New York City, we walked over a plywood board on the way backstage. The seats looked a little ratty. And I have a memory of some significant cracks in the walls. I remember thinking, "I don't think Joan digs this." But, of course, she was fine. Recently, I called Thom Wolke, the promoter who brought us to the Tarrytown Music Hall. He couldn't recollect the plywood board, but he acknowledged, "A lot of the seats were really old." As for the dressing room, "The floor had started to, I guess, rot—there was this horrendous carpeting down. So you'd walk across the dressing room, and it was kind of like walking across a really firm mattress."

In the end, it didn't matter. By playing at the theater, warts and all, we were getting the community to understand its value. Thom told me that other friends such as Tom Paxton and Judy Collins knew full well what they would encounter when they agreed to play there in the late 1980s, when it was really in disrepair. They knew they were helping a venerable concert hall find its way back, which the Tarrytown Music Hall surely did with an overhaul in 2003 or so. Today when I do a sound check there, I see an expanse of ruby-red,

velveteen seats set within the pillars and gold-filigreed balconies in a
fully renovated hall.

Tarrytown faltered after a major General Motors plant closed
there in the mid-1990s. Thom said he remembered sitting in a bar
across from the music hall and thinking you could see a tumbleweed
roll down Main Street, unimpeded by any traffic or any living soul. I
told him that when I was there with Joan in 1996, I got the impression from him that the town was just finishing a big renovation and
had run out of time when we arrived. Thom said, "Uh, I think I was
speaking to a dream." Neither Tarrytown nor Thom was ready until
the early 2000s for what would eventually happen in Tarrytown.

Success stories like Tarrytown's have made me feel particularly patient with other works in progress. I played in Skowhegan, Maine, at
its newly reopened opera house in 2008. The staff members asked me
to visit the restaurant down the hill for dinner because they were
trying to create a link between the theater and places for the audience to eat. Very smart. I went there before the show.

There was one thing the Skowhegan venue hadn't quite nailed
down yet. The staff had not yet insulated or heated the dressing room.
It was a December gig, but I was okay with this. Why? Whenever
someone is starting a new venue, I'm willing to do things like walk on
rotting floors, look past the decay, and freeze my ass off because, like
Joan and Judy and Tom, I support the mix of community goodwill and
public, private, and nonprofit funding that gets an old, abandoned
theater back on its feet. It's hard, it's admirable, and I love watching
how towns grow after they've taken on the mammoth, cooperative
task of running an art venue. It's like the town is letting a genie out
of a bottle, a genie that flamboyantly grants wishes (if your wish is for
a better town) and sprinkles magic dust in the air.

These venues also welcome local theater productions (I've played
in front of sets for *Huckleberry Finn*, *Waiting for Godot*, *Annie*, and one
production—*Our Town?*—where tissue-paper snowflakes floated
down from time to time throughout my set). They also host dance

troupes, political debates, movies, sing-alongs, and, consequently, countless ways for a community to gather and speak in an atmosphere of art and beauty.

Culture as a Magnet for Philanthropy

Although Carrboro's cultural tide generally rose, with an arts center that started as an art collective and grew into what it is today, other towns and cities have had individual benefactors who have contributed the lion's share of the original capital. When there is a venue for fine arts and/or performance—be it a community center, performance venue, or combination of the two—accompanied by a critical mass of community interest, there is often a moment when a local philanthropist gets involved.

I'm not talking about magical thinking that "attracts wealth." I mean that if an old theater is getting back on its feet by showing classic films every Friday, a wealthy film buff might look at the friendly volunteers and tattered seats and decide that this is a place where he or she can make a difference. A generous person will open a checkbook for a cause no matter what, but when a town demonstrates some form of positive proximity, some kind of civic pride, it's more likely that a philanthropist's money will go to a local project rather than (or in addition to) a national organization or political campaign. I've met many philanthropists like this because they often like to meet artists.

These donors have bestowed great gifts upon their communities, but I have seen the value of their contribution going both ways. I believe the venues are good for them personally. Instead of being isolated in the rarified air of a mansion on the hill, watching movies in private screening rooms, and going to big cities for cultural events, these philanthropists' commitment to local theaters has invested them, personally, in the places they live. I meet their spouses, and I meet their kids. I often get a sense that their interactions with the theaters are their primary relationship with their towns.

Sometimes whole communities have a higher income bracket than most. A cultural venue is an excellent method of distributing wealth in a way that benefits the whole community. I was one of the first performers at the newly renovated Avalon Theater in Easton, Maryland, in 1997. The Avalon is a jewel-box version of a grand opera house, ornate and compact with a small balcony. Not only had local philanthropists brought the theater back but also they'd done it down to the last detail, onstage and off. Ellen Vatne poured her energy into the theater and into making sure things went smoothly for the first musical acts. The board put me up in the historic Tidewater Inn, across the street, which had seen better days. Go to the website of the Tidewater today. It's gorgeous. It didn't look like that in 1997.

The next time I returned to Easton, there was a show at a small art gallery in conjunction with my performance so people could go see the paintings, have dinner, and stay for the show. I had always assumed Easton became more prosperous after the Avalon came along. I was wrong. The community had always been financially flush. The community commons became more prosperous after the Avalon came back.

On my third visit, there were helpful maps around town for visitors. Two unpretentious cafés with great coffee opened, one called the Red Hen, a great two-roomer (though now closed). Easton now has a well-known plein air (outdoor) painting contest in which painters spend three hours throughout the town working on their canvases. You can't have that kind of event without all the moving parts of businesses, civic-minded citizens, galleries, and municipal government working together. So Easton didn't necessarily become wealthier because of the Avalon, but the community spaces and the community conversation were richer thanks to the efforts of Ellen and the hardworking board of the Avalon.

Open Mikes

I've also seen towns, wealthy and not so wealthy, experience their creative contours by having an open mike, a weekly or monthly event at which anyone can sign up to sing or recite a few poems. Once I played after a woman who talked about the joys of cleaning and loading her shotgun. I followed with a song about my favorite hippie babysitter. Open mikes draw in some interesting eccentrics and draw out the talents of otherwise laced-up citizens, thereby providing a good way to widen a town's social perimeter and deepen its knowledge of who lives there.

My first open mike, at the Naked City Coffeehouse in Cambridge, Massachusetts, really lived up to its name in the early 1990s. We were letting it all hang out. Chris Dunn, a latter-day hippie with the beauty of a serene priest in an El Greco painting, was the emcee. His mellowness was both the key to the feeling in the room and the disguise of his greatest gift to us: he found a way to support and affirm every single act that came onstage. In retrospect, I know that took some effort.

Horrendous love-song singing duo? Chris always introduced them with great enthusiasm, as if we'd all been waiting for their return to the stage. Mumbling poets and slightly flat show-tune belters were equally valued. I was too afraid to even perform the first time I was there, but Chris was so accommodating, I got up the nerve the next week. When I finished, and the people were clapping, he asked if I'd written my own songs, and when I said "Yes," he nodded and said, "Cool."

That was all the encouragement I needed. I was in. The open mikes were where I honed my craft on the way to becoming a full-time artist. I was appreciated, as were the guy with the half-spoken, ranting protest songs; another who read his heartbreakingly vulnerable poetry; and then this other guy who was just a phenomenon. He shouted folk songs such as "The Lady Came from Baltimore." He strummed his guitar out of rhythm. When he sang it wasn't in the same key as the guitar, because the guitar wasn't in any key at all. But we loved him because he meant every word he sang/shouted. One day he showed up with two people in suits. It turned out they were his caseworkers. After he performed, he sat between them and said, "I told you they liked me."

We thought maybe Brother Blue, a wise storyteller, had the genius possessed by those whose sanity might be deemed marginal. He was an enthusiastic listener and recounter of every kind of story. Brilliant? Yes. Lived in his car? Maybe. We didn't realize until later that he was a Yale-educated actor, pastor, and husband of a Harvard professor. Brother Blue was doing fine; he was just ministering to us in our own vernacular when needed.

In our open mike community, our strengths and rough edges were witnessed with kindness, and our strong, strange feelings often found common cause with those of others. In other words, we were loved for the very things that made us so odd. Perhaps, on some long, dark night of the soul, some of us would have had a psychotic break or at least a rupture. The open mike provided an antidote to the loneliness and alienation of many creative thinkers.

You could say a cultural space that gathers up the energies of eclectic souls is a nice thing, but there is a valuable element of positive proximity at work here at the fringes of society. Sometimes it takes a weird person to help another weird person or a group of them. When these somewhat weird people from open mikes went out into the world, they were fearless of other people's liminality (to use a Harvard word). Their day jobs were often at nonprofits that worked with a spectrum of mental illnesses, addictions, or just lostness.

My compatriots also did things such as working with low-income children already caught up in the iniquities their parents faced. Some open mike participants rounded up meals and served them for Food Not Bombs. They worked for little or no money in secondhand bookshops and record stores. I actually saw a folk-singing friend pull off his raincoat and give it to a homeless person. Others sat deep in conversation with people usually in conversation with themselves on park benches. At open mikes, people had been accepted, and they were paying it forward. At my best, not my worst, I was one of these people.

We weren't crazy; we were just attuned to diverse frequencies. I call participatory arts such as open mikes (but also including open visual arts events) the spice rack of the community. If a town is like a big kitchen, you never know when you're going to need cumin, tarragon, or allspice. You rarely do, but you do. The open mike was the spice rack of Cambridge, full of people who contributed to a town of citizens who didn't necessarily go to Harvard or the Massachusetts Institute of Technology. My creative friends added to the local color, and they helped each other, but beyond our loose clique they also got out into the nooks and crannies, in this case onto the backroads of a wealthy, educated community, and into the world of its lesser-known, sometimes struggling citizens. As far as I'm concerned, participatory events such as weekly open mikes keep the spice rack stocked and in order.

Starting a writing or drawing group, a song circle, or an artists' collective can also be a way to see ourselves as creative people and to value the parts of our towns and cities attuned to our creativity. As I saw in Carrboro, both in the ArtsCenter's growing mission and in the mutually respectful community of artisans, the recognition of culture and creativity as a way of life became central to the identity of the town. "I think that the essence of Carrboro is that the townspeople believe . . . they own the town," Ellie Kinnaird told me.

They believe they own the town. That's a big deal. It can take a long time for a town to get to this understanding of itself. It takes effort to believe that your town is you, and vice versa. It takes some experience. It takes the personal understanding that as a citizen, it's your right to speak, to express yourself. In Carrboro, you're welcome to voice, paint, sculpt, compose, and versify yourself into the overall community conversation. And a healthy sense of ownership in the community means that there are people who welcome dynamic problem-solving, too. As Ellie said, "There's a nice collision between that idea and the planning that goes into it. It has to be carefully done. The gumption, rhetoric, enthusiasm, you need that, and then the people who will talk it through. That coming together is the magic."

Urban theorist Richard Florida has generated books, lectures, and a whole consulting company around ways to identify, court, and keep the "creative class," a term he coined, in one's city, arguing that this class is the financial engine of a city. In defense of the creative class as not just an elite bunch of entitled hipsters who have honed computer programming and cocktail conversation skills in various private institutions, Florida has said he believes that everyone is inherently creative and that every city does better when the creativity of all citizens is valued and tapped. He tasks himself with finding indexes that show where to find the creative class.

Like Florida, I seek out the inroads and impacts of creativity in towns and cities where I play, but whereas he measures the success of the creatives by their contribution to the postindustrial coffers of towns and cities, I gauge the presence of creativity by how it lives in the commons. How creatively does a town express its identity? How playful are its celebrations? How inclusive? How do problems get solved? I have seen that in its broad and imaginative range of expression, Carrboro's collaborations are sophisticated, useful, and inherently creative, and I submit that both the preponderance of cultural participation and the exposure to art invite new voices and a general sense of access to community problem-solving.

In Carrboro, citizens don't just value inclusivity; they rally around it. They are not just tolerant; they welcome the world and world-traveling citizens. And they aren't just dreamers; they are just as much hands-on makers of million-dollar PTA fund-raising shops, poetry slams, and free clinics as they are fashioners of giant puppets and costumes for their annual holiday parade.

Art Menius told me that Carrboro is, in fact, applying to secure a National Endowment for the Arts Our Town grant and that the town is very close to adopting a new motto, best recited by Art, who says in his honey-rich, North Carolina drawl, "It's Carrboro. Feel Free." The Carrboro I know is certainly living up to this proposed motto. Its denizens seem to embody what Richard Florida advocates: the collective embrace of their creative potential. A cultural culture.

6

Finger Lakes, New York: Food

ONCE UPON A TIME, a blizzard swept across a vast region of towns and cities. It silenced the streets, it buried the mailboxes, and it seemed to stop time itself, dropping in dense white curtains for two days and two nights. Finally, on the third day, the people pushed their doors open with effort, shook their heads, and wondered if they'd ever seen so much snow in their lifetimes.

I lived in one of these towns. My parents enlisted us, their three daughters, to help them tunnel out from this epic snowfall. There was nothing else to do but start shoveling. There would be no moving of vehicles, no getting to work. You couldn't even make a snow angel. You'd lie down and disappear. But when I stood on a six-foot snowbank, surveying all that whiteness and the tops of hats and clouds of breath from heavy exertion all along my street, I heard my parents talk incredulously about a faraway place that had gotten even more snow. It was called western New York. To this little girl in 1978, this distant land sounded like the tundra. Who would live there? Perhaps you were exiled there, as at a Siberian prison camp.

As I grew older, I recognized that many well-made but ordinary things came from this western New York; measuring cups from

Corning Glass and instamatic cameras from Eastman Kodak in Rochester. Typewriters from Smith-Corona. So that's what happened there. People made good, durable things, then they shoveled snow for a couple of hours, in every season, and then they went to sleep under many quilts and blankets. I heard there were cabbage farms and apple orchards, but I couldn't understand how even these hardy crops could survive. When I saw *Fiddler on the Roof*, I saw the struggles of hardscrabble, cold, village life and I thought of western New York.

I grew up and became a traveling folk singer. In 1994, I got a gig in Ithaca. I loved the creaky floors in big, old Victorian houses and the sleepy Main Streets, and I found myself writing a song called "Southern California Wants to Be Western New York," sensing a charm that could offset the snow and even induce envy in less settled regions. Of Southern California, I wrote,

> It wants to have a family business in sheet metal or power tools,
> It wants to have a diner where the coffee tastes like diesel fuel,
> And it wants to find the glory of a town they say has hit the skids,
> And it wants to have a snow day that will turn its parents into kids,
> And it's embarrassed, but it's lusting after
> A SUNY student with mousy brown hair
> Who is taking out the compost, making coffee in long underwear.

And then in 2005, as many manufacturing businesses were closing shop, I went back to Ithaca for a gig and went to the farmers' market the next day. I saw a different place, the new western New York, one actually there for decades but now on full display. I held up a head of broccoli, telling a friend it was so deeply green it was blue. I saw medals from international wine festivals draped on bottles of white wine, the bottles themselves shot through with late summer light. Sailboats passed behind the sellers at the market. This was a western New York with towns such as Trumansberg, Geneva, and Mecklenburg, and there were beautiful roads connecting them all.

This region in western New York illustrates the ways in which food can connect and strengthen communities and shows how a cluster of towns and cities can build what I call an agrosphere, almost spilling over with opportunities for positive proximity. To me it is particularly poignant that in this land of snow and American industry, a new consciousness and identity have emerged like a field of flowers in the spring.

WELCOME TO THE AGROSPHERE

What is an agrosphere? Technically it's called a foodshed. The agrosphere is my term for the patchwork of gardens, farms, food production sites, and places where local food is consumed. It includes all the agrarian-based activity that happens on a stretch of landscape.

"Agrospheric consciousness" is my catchall phrase for the sense of that agrosphere: the seasonal experience of what grows around you, the history, the wood fences and stone walls, the barns, the food markets, and, of course, the food itself.

Something happens when we pay attention to our local food and how we build at least some of our towns' identities through it. We become unique. We experience a sense of self-reliance and even abundance, a nice counterpoint to feeling subject to the vicissitudes of the larger economy. We affirm our farming traditions and families, which exist everywhere. Our vocabularies for local life become infused with nuanced colors and references to specific heirlooms that only grow in certain places.

Where I live, we have conversations with older Italian American men who pass our garden in the Hudson Valley of New York. "Are those purple Cherokees?" Yes. "Those Amish paste tomatoes are the best ones." Yes. "And how are those San Marzano tomatoes going? Badly? That's right, because they only grow *in San Marzano.*" They laugh and shake their heads at us. You want San Marzanos? Go live in Italy. We share a soil composition, and growing tomatoes reinforces our common ground.

Our food can also define us, both in its variety and in its equally informative limitations. In my early career, when I was feeling up-rooted by touring, my boyfriend at the time took me to a farm in western Massachusetts. We got a fifty-pound sack of butternut squash and had them in almost every dinner throughout the winter. He said we did this because we were New Englanders. We ate squash and root vegetables, and we were grateful for them, just as we were grateful for the honor of chopping our wood and digging ourselves out of snowbanks.

Everywhere I go now, when I tour, I have an opportunity to expe-rience an agrospheric consciousness, whether it's from walking past giant salmon and crabs laid out on gravelly ice in Seattle, seeing the chili pepper ristras in Albuquerque markets, finding farm-stand peaches in Atlanta, or seeking out the Portuguese clam chowder in Providence, Rhode Island. In regions where many grown things be-come a wide variety of eaten things, this consciousness can run very deep and connect us in a number of valuable ways.

Encouraging this sense of the foodshed, or agrosphere, can be as simple as pouring syrup into maple-leaf-shaped bottles and putting on a sticker that says "Local." Automatically, our minds connect to a landscape, and we envision where and how food grows all around us. And so we go to the Finger Lakes to find out how their agrosphere has grown, crop upon crop, story upon story, to become a food region, a food culture, a food economy, and a hotbed of positive proximity.

The Finger Lakes lie at the heart of western New York in an area shaped almost like a heart. Its farming and wine-growing region en-compasses seven glacier-formed lakes. To me the Finger Lakes don't look like fingers, exactly. It's more like a cat clawed long gouges down a map of New York and revealed a bright blue wall behind it.

The downside of choosing the Finger Lakes region as an example of positive proximity built and sustained by food is that other towns might find its successes daunting. The food economy is intricate, deeply rooted, creative, bountiful, and accompanied by a social counterpart that blossoms equally with color, depth, and richness. The upside is that western New York is not exactly what we'd associate with an easy growing climate; if its residents can do it, so can most others. The way in which Finger Lakes communities have created and held on to a food and farming culture both mirrors and generates a self-determining, robust, high quality of life, and from that many regions can learn.

I'm not a foodie. I'm an ordinary citizen and eater. But in some ways, not being an expert helped me see the social networks of the Finger Lakes with more clarity. Instead of collecting recipes to take home, I wanted to take the best town-building ideas from this region to share with towns and cities everywhere.

Kathleen Foley, an Ithaca College and Cornell University grad with a doctorate in urban planning, is a buddy of mine here in downstate New York, where I live. She'd grown up with her five sisters, one brother, and not a lot of money near a small town called Odessa in one of New York's poorest counties. She confirmed that the Finger Lakes communities had transformed themselves through their food culture. Growing up, she'd watched that regional identity shift from manufacturing to food and wine. Many of her family and friends who live there now are part of the food economy, so she kindly organized a group of interviews and came along with me for the weekend of a lifetime.

On the car ride up, Kathleen explained the history of the area. By the late twentieth century only a few seedlings gave any indication that this could be a thriving garden of food-based community. There was very little food tourism in the 1970s, save for the buses that came up for wine tastings at big operations that produced mostly sweet wines like Catawba. In the early 1990s, Kathleen worked at one of the first and only establishments to bring food and tourism together. It was called Captain Bill's Seneca Lake Cruises, and it was a grueling way to put herself through college. The workers would clean the boat in the morning, then start their shifts—brunches, dinners, cocktails—then clear the dishes and start again early the next day.

During her time at this tourist establishment, Kathleen watched the way wineries were beginning to pair even their sweet wines with local food for tastings, and the wines were getting better and better. Winemakers such as Konstantin Frank, on Keuka Lake, and Herman Weimer, on Seneca Lake, followed their instincts about the potential of the Finger Lakes' soil and climate and came over from Europe, later joined by other European winemakers, and also by young Americans, all trying to do something far more ambitious than what the bigger vineyards had done.

Meanwhile, on the food front, old family farms such as the Belkers continued to keep their heads above water. And on top of that, another great farming boom came along in the 1970s thanks to the really cheap land and nearby universities. The Finger Lakes region attracted some major hippies. A century before, the women's suffrage movement started in Seneca Falls. Transcendentalists and spiritualists had felt the magic in the area. In Palmyra, Joseph Smith had his first calling on a journey that became Mormonism.

And now a new post-Woodstock, visionary movement sprang up: groups of back-to-the-land hippies created communes such as Eco-Village, just outside of Ithaca, seeking a pure, egalitarian food and farming environment. The Moosewood Collective, responsible for the landmark *Moosewood Cookbook*, which brought vegetarian cooking to the masses, started there, too. Have you ever had back-to-the-land fantasies? These baby boomers made it a reality.

So that sets the stage: European winemakers, hippie collectives, and old family farms. There are also Amish and Mennonite farming communities. One more critical element: all of the region's colleges, especially Cornell, which was a land grant institution and major center of agricultural research from it origins, smoothed the transition from the industrial economy to the one in motion today. These were the lucky ingredients of an agrospheric evolution.

Today Finger Lakes area residents are reaping the rewards of agricultural diversity. There are more than a hundred wineries and every kind of farm and orchard. The hippies, vintners, and farmers have done well. So have the restaurateurs, farmers' markets, and artisanal food processors and distributors who followed. These days, nationally, the whole concept of local food, farm-to-table restaurants, farmers' markets, and community-supported agriculture (CSA) shares has caught up with the Finger Lakes region, which itself continues to take the next step into breweries, distilleries, pickling, juicing, and famous farm-to-table establishments. Every region has a way to grow food crops into a food culture, but the Finger Lakes communities show us what it looks like when that culture has been growing stronger and stronger over five decades.

THE POWER OF STORY

One of the most important factors that allows local food to become, as Kathleen put it, "more than an economy—a lifestyle" is that the Finger Lakes region is filled with people who know the importance of a good food story, and many of them know how to tell one. Telling these stories reinforces their loyalty to the area and creates a wonderful welcome sign for the rest of us.

Kathleen and I arrived in Ithaca, home of Cornell University and Ithaca College (and the farmers' market whose broccoli was almost blue). There we met her cousin Janet McCue, who would be our tour guide. A writer who specializes in essays that combine food, travel, and outdoor life, Janet had just retired from her day job as a library administrator at Cornell. Her neat, shoulder-length, gray hair and smart glasses told one story, but she's a lot like Kathleen. She's a member of a tight, matriarchal, Irish clan with shocking, funny family tales that come out at certain dinner parties. She's a storyteller on all fronts, irreverent when necessary, and she is a champion narrator of food stories.

Our first stop was the DeWitt Café, where she introduced us to Michael Welch, editor of *Edible Finger Lakes* magazine, one of more than twenty *Edible* magazines throughout the United States. The curious thing, Michael told me right off the bat, was that when he first started the magazine in 2008, he approached people in the food economy about advertising, and when they said "Yes," they added, "because we want to support you."

Michael responded by asking, "Wait, wouldn't an ad support the people who placed the ad?" They said, in a word, "No." The magazine would help the whole region. The message Michael got was, "Your storytelling needs our financial support. We all win when you make us look good." And Michael was just the man for the job. A former personal chef for people who wanted the best local produce available, he was a fan and follower of the *Edible* magazine in New York City, and when his wife got a job in the Finger Lakes area, Michael came up for a few days of reconnaissance, at the end of which he said, "We'll never run out of stories." He'd hit the agrospheric jackpot.

Michael said that he's been approached by people who tell him the stories in his magazine make them feel cool. The coolest, not just most economically viable, identity to be discovered right now is in the food and wine businesses. The stories I heard all weekend were about people pushing the edges of the envelope of the food economy, experimenting with kimchee, ice wine, ice cider, and cucumber popsicles. *Edible Finger Lakes* is always there to capture them in a flattering light.

In celebrating the food economy and continually engendering local pride about it, its stories draw in both visitors and innovators. What starts with a picture of a cow next to a couple of old milk pails becomes eclectic, colorful forays into elderberry syrup and maple liqueur. The magazines themselves are an incredible repository of the food scene, old and new.

Janet, who writes for *Edible*, too, gave me a big stack of issues that I looked through as she and Kathleen went into a local butchery called the Piggery. While I was leafing through the magazines, my book research kept getting sidetracked by all the stories, pictures, and even the ads. I found myself creating an itinerary for my family:

Day One:

Start with Corning Museum of Glass.

Go to late afternoon Damiani Wine Cellars wine and chocolate tasting.

Dinner at Red Dove in Geneva . . . no, dinner at Red Tail Ridge Winery. Well, one of them.

Day Two:

Breakfast at farmers' market. Or make a special trip to Wide Awake Bakery for wood-fired, oven-baked bread.

Walk around Ithaca.

Go up to dairy farm on Keuka Lake, or maybe the ice cream place at Cornell.

Walk along the shores of Seneca Lake . . . no, kayak on Seneca Lake? Bike around?

Lunch at Glen Mountain Market Bakery and Deli in Watkins Glen, *then* dairy farm, and dinner at the Hallgrens' restaurant, no . . . what about . . .

What's this wine sail? Where's that waterfall?

I love planning trips for my family, but this was driving me nuts. Two things I knew were that I wanted to come back here and that we could fill at least three whole days.

Aside from *Edible Finger Lakes*, there are websites, companies that sponsor tourist itineraries and food trails, and other publications dedicated to a cohesive, collective story; not a single kind of fruit but a fruit basket; not one field but striking juxtapositions of orchards, vineyards, pastures, and purveyors.

Many of the stories involve fermentation of one kind or another. A region has a definite edge in telling a good food story when there is some form of fermentation involved, be it beer, bread, hard cider, or wine. The Finger Lakes region has all of them. The reason is not that most of these fermented things can inebriate you but that they all involve a certain kind of careful, sustained process and relationships among growers, producers, and sellers. These relationships make for exciting stories of hard-earned victories (complete with medals!) and epic defeats. If the farming story is a Robert Frost poem, the fermentation story is an Icelandic saga that can draw you in and keep you rooting for its many protagonists.

Evan Dawson, an author and popular broadcaster in Rochester, wrote a completely engrossing book called *Summer in a Glass*, about different wineries in the region. Dawson describes harvesttime, when people cautiously walk around with something called Brix meters, which test the sugar content of grapes. He then writes about the grape stomping; the anxious conversations about bacteria, good and bad; the winning wine years; the wine-tasting parties and galas; and, best of all, the personalities in the wine community. To read his book is to have chronic fear-of-missing-out syndrome. I felt so connected to these winemakers that when Lisa Hallgren contacted me and offered to talk about her work, my heart was racing. *The* Lisa Hallgren of Ravines Wine Cellar on Keuka Lake?!

Dawson had followed Lisa's husband, Morton Hallgren, around during one harvest. The winemaker was waiting until the last minute to pick the grapes, risking that they would rot or turn to raisins. Had he ever miscalculated? Yes, once he had, and he had lost half his crop, but the difference between a ripe grape and the ripest grape was the difference between a good and an excellent wine, and the Hallgrens' vineyard is internationally recognized for the quality of its dry Riesling.

The winemakers, the wine enthusiasts, and the wines themselves have rich narratives. One of the character traits European winemakers brought to New York was an understanding of *terroir*, the taste of the soil, water, and wind in every sip of wine. The *terroir* of the wine, to these New York winemakers, didn't just include the natural elements; it was also the personal history, the touch-and-go adventures with new varietals, the celebrations with other enthusiasts, and the grafting of vines and expertise from older establishments, such as the beloved Fox Run Winery, with the new vineyards run by enterprising former employees and the excitement of collectively garnering the attention of wine publications and festivals throughout the world.

When we visited Sheldrake Point Winery, I saw the best fermentation stories have to offer. This wine country is filled with natural beauty, and each landscape resonates with the life stories of winemakers as tangled up in each other's histories as grapevines in a cheerfully untended arbor. And only one story I heard, about a guy who woke up after a party with permanent marker designs drawn all over his shaved head, involved intoxication.

Visiting a winery is a way to see and hear the narrative of the region. The tasting rooms at Sheldrake Point have picture windows facing Seneca Lake and others looking up into the expansive vineyard. On the way to the tables, an illuminated wall showcases fifty of their wines along with awards from three different continents. Sheldrake Point clearly stands out in the wine world, but the vintners place their victories in a Finger Lakes context. The rooms also have maps of the region and charts to describe different wines along with books about the history and food of the Finger Lakes area. This vineyard identifies itself as part of a particular region, like a Loire Valley or a Burgundy.

Head winemaker Dave Breeden and assistant Julia Hoyte sat us down and poured a reserve, dry Riesling made with the most carefully selected grapes. It doesn't hurt the fairy tale feeling of these vineyard stories that the wine itself has a semiprecious-jewel tone. We just stared at it a little before we started sipping it. Then we had a moment of silence to appreciate this exquisite, complicated wine.

While the wine was making its own statement, Dave talked about other people in the region, his mentors, colleagues, and mentees: for almost all the master winemakers, there was an initial, long apprenticeship, then a time of buying other growers' grapes while they established their own vineyards or found the best winery fit, and then an implicit promise to support others going through their own career journey. Dave wasn't even consciously telling us a food story; talking about wine just naturally took that narrative form.

And it was not a linear story but one with interesting subplots and side characters. Dave told me about some hard-cider makers he knew who were part of a new wave in the area. He was going to help them. Dave had attended the famous wine tastings of Peter Bell at his Fox Run Winery. Bell would pour a number of wines, anonymously placed in paper bags, and solicit feedback. It was a friendly system for which Bell had created a pedagogy of rating wines that was illuminating and constructive to all participants. That continues today. Dave said, "We meet together, and we taste each other's stuff, in progress, blind, so it can be critiqued, and you can get somebody else's palette's opinion of what you're doing and how it might be fixed and if it needs to be fixed, and we also have a commercial tasting so we can broaden our palettes and learn about other regions."

Dave was trying to figure out how he could start a similar paper-bag tasting with the hard-cider makers, instilling the same spirit of amicable, well-structured critiques. In the Finger Lakes region he has found what he calls both "community within a discipline" and the "intersection of disciplines." When different businesses choose to interconnect their stories, as it were, people in specific professions do better as well.

So the food story has spread in the Finger Lakes area through print media, photography, cross-promotion, cross-communication between food growers and winemakers, maps on walls, open farms, and especially members of the food community themselves. While *Edible Finger Lakes* offers us outsiders pictures of saturated purple wine grapes and adorable goats under rusty farm signs, the people who make and grow the food are finding ways to knit an overall narrative of community, beauty, and the continuity of this culture to be lived and passed on to the next generation.

SCHOOL-TO-FARM RELATIONSHIPS

The Finger Lakes region has an impressive range of institutions that connect the organizational dots as well as the narrative ones, and their work is crucial to the region's prosperity. They look out for the nuts and bolts (seeds and shovels?) of the food operation. Although all regions have agrarian support networks such as 4-H, the Finger Lakes area has had the extra boost of Cornell's agricultural college and its school of hotel management and hospitality, going all the way back to the nineteenth century.

In 1923, Cornell brought the Geneva Experiment Station (that's what everyone calls it; the name is actually the New York State Agricultural Experiment Station) under its umbrella and developed apples such as the Cortland and Macoun and varieties of grapes that could be pressed into award-winning wines. These innovations became important parts of the economy, and now they are the engine of the economy.

States such as Wisconsin, Oregon, and Maine have also been investing in test kitchens, farm-to-fork conferences, and food tourism. They're supporting growers and creating new markets, and now in Oregon, local food (arguably led by its wine) is its biggest industry. New York state government put a quarter of a million dollars into food tourism around 2011, and the investment was estimated to have brought in a return of ten million dollars. In the Finger Lakes area, the dominance of the food economy is a hard fact.

Eastman Kodak will not be returning. Walmart and its ilk will never provide stable employment. The boom economies of energy exploration might seem more "real" than an extensive interconnected community of food and beverage makers, but any "one-stop shop" of a single corporation or an energy extraction bonanza is ultimately less stable than a mutually reinforcing, geographically unique, and irreplaceable range of businesses.

The Finger Lakes region provides a model for what a new, and real, economy can look like. A perspicacious array of school programs aids its multitiered economy. In response to the growth of wineries, farms, and food tourism, community colleges offer degrees in winery management, hospitality, and other specific fields.

Families in the region can find a role in the food economy and, therefore, in the food culture and its networks. Positive proximity doesn't just mean that a few wealthy people enjoy the dividends of a highly developed agrosphere. Thanks to the colleges and universities, among other institutions, there are many points of access to the employment and enjoyment of the food economy. Justin Boyette, co-owner of the Hector Wine Company, talked about how, when he was starting out, he saw students from local colleges bringing their parents, lifelong residents, into wineries for the first time. Thanks to these college programs, not only does the food economy get more valuable infrastructure but also there are more people participating in what is clearly the economic future of western New York.

The decline of manufacturing doesn't have to mean the automatic default of working at Walmart or McDonald's while watching the goat-bearded foodies, connected to each other through expensive liberal arts colleges and/or start-up funds from their parents, gallivant along in the food world. In this food economy, you can find your way in and work your way up.

That said, the local colleges are also good places to figure out if the food economy is right for you before the long hours and sacrifices of farming life become a more high-stakes reality. Among the many degrees it offers in food growing and winemaking, in addition to its graduate school in hospitality, Cornell has its own cows and the Cornell Dairy Bar at the College of Agriculture and Life Sciences. This makes sense because New York is the third-highest milk-producing state after California and Wisconsin. And, considering that dairy farming itself is probably often more difficult than rewarding, the Dairy Bar is offering paths to make the whole enterprise more lucrative and maybe more fun, letting the undergrads name some of the twenty flavors of ice cream it produces, including "Sweet Cornell," described as "sweet corn with a hint of salted caramel."

In addition to schools, there are paid apprenticeships at wineries and breweries. Food tourism allows for a low- to high-end service economy as opposed to the stagnant economic mobility associated with staffing fast-food chains. The educational investment in farming and tourism is strong in the Finger Lakes region.

HUMAN BRIDGES

In any strong, self-defined social community with an economic back-bone that comes from decentralized commerce, some individuals go above and beyond to bridge socioeconomic gaps and actively help all boats to rise. It so happens that the Fingers Lakes citizens do another smart thing to grow their overall prosperity and positive proximity: they treasure these hardworking individuals.

Monica Roth is one of the directors at Cornell Cooperative Extension (CCE), an outreach department of Cornell University working with farmers and others in the community. CCE had always been helpful when it came to counseling about nontoxic *Bacillus thuringiensis* (BT) for cabbage worms and the heat resistance of romaine over loose-leaf lettuce, but at a certain point farmers and food makers asked for someone to help them tell their story and grow their markets as well. That's where Monica Roth came in. Everyone I met said that Monica had been instrumental to his or her business.

Monica is trim and no-nonsense. When I met her, there was only one hint of her getting out in the local scene she had helped to build. She was wearing a lovely, royal blue, chenille scarf made by a local weaver. Otherwise, her outfit looked all-weather and all-purpose, equally prepared for a budget meeting or an earnest consultation in the field.

Monica helped start things. The growers in the region wanted assistance with marketing, networking, and finding outlets for selling their products. Monica was a critical organizer for Finger Lakes Culinary Bounty, a clearinghouse of education, with special events, conferences, maps, guides to what was in season, and "member spotlights" that told the stories of individual growers. The organization's website does a great job of curating a region of orchards, vineyards, restaurants, and farmers, urging people to look for the Finger Lakes Culinary Bounty sticker. And it is everywhere.

Monica also helped create the Trumansburg farmers' market because she knew that people are attracted to markets not just by what they sell but by the social scene around them. Like Ithaca's famous farmers' market, Trumansburg has its own freestanding wood shelters. The market takes place from 4:00 to 7:00 p.m., so you can come with your kids and stay for dinner. It's a market where the food story can become part of the larger story of people's lives. She is also helping to connect the farming world through and beyond its products. The farmers' market requests that the owners and managers of the farms show up, for instance, because, as Finger Lakes Culinary Bounty's website said, "They are your neighbors."

Monica seems to be fluent in the language of collaboration. Monica met me twice, once in the CCE conference room and then at the Ithaca winter farmers' market, where she introduced me to several others in the field. Celia Clark, owner of Celia's Ice Pops, was doing her shift as a traffic director out in the driveway. One of the reasons Celia began her business was that she arrived during a year in which two late ice storms had damaged the first fruits of the season. The next year, she used scarred produce from similar storms for her first ice pops, wanting to be part of the unique agricultural scene while also helping farmers offload their less attractive fruit and vegetables. Fueled by enthusiasm, goodwill, and a strong instinct that she was in the right place at the right time, Celia was willing to chance the ice pop business. But when it was time to grow it, there was CCE. "I totally had to rely on CCE," she said. "Well, Monica!"

Dennis Hartland is the co-owner of Little Tree Orchard, which offers pick-your-own apples as well as cider, applesauce, and vinegar. "Monica is the woman," he says. "She can never retire." He is more a compatriot than a recipient of her expertise, which creates a nice sense of farm-and-school collaboration. Dennis came to the Finger Lakes region with the wave of young people in the early 1970s. He's one of those hippies. He looks like the actor Treat Williams with a little extra farm tan and longer hair. As the 1970s progressed, he got more involved with the orchard, which he now owns with his wife. "We have fifty-six acres, thirty-five acres of apples, ten thousand trees, and we do have time to enjoy ourselves and manage to have some fun," Dennis told me. They also host two festivals, both of which raise money for local causes.

Someone suggested he could make more money if he charged admission for the pick-your-own farm on top of the apples. Dennis said, "Admission? Why would I do that?" Like Monica, Dennis looks at the ways in which things are connected in the region. He wishes the farmers could put their heads together to make food more affordable. And yet when I asked Dennis about all this new farm-to-table food tourism and international wine culture, some of which catered to an upscale crowd, he acknowledged that the basic attention to the concept of "local food" was definitely helping farmers, among other local businesses, and he appreciated it.

Kathleen came out from the vendors' tables and recognized him. She knew Little Tree Orchard from when she was a kid and said she couldn't wait to bring her own kids. "You do that," Dennis said. See? Why would you charge admission when the most important thing to do is introduce the next generation of kids to the agrospheric consciousness? For all the economic ups and downs of the agrarian life, Dennis has never lost the thread of why he lives it, and he values the efforts of keeping the overall farming community strong as well.

Another name came up often during my visit to the region. This was a person who had been in it for the vision, not the money, and again, the community had been smart enough to embrace him like a folk legend, their own Johnny Appleseed. He was a tireless, generous, guardian angel hippy named Gary Redmond, who was, in the words of Michael from *Edible Finger Lakes*, "the ultimate foodie and the ultimate DIYer." He started a company called Regional Access in 1989, technically a distribution warehouse. But Gary went beyond the beyond, connecting all kinds of people and distributing farmers' food in all directions to caterers, restaurants, and even markets down in New York City. Michael said, "He filled the gaps. He got farmers in one poor county making canola oil from rapeseed. There's a reason that Stefan Senders has a bread called Gary's Bread. Gary was instrumental in convincing Stefan that we needed an artisanal baker here, using local grain, local flour, and making beautiful bread."

Stefan runs a well-loved bakery called Wide Awake, which also has a bread CSA (yes, a bread CSA, and everybody belongs to it). Stefan, too, saw Gary as a visionary: "He said, 'I'm going to connect with *anybody* who's producing top-quality local food, and I will *find* a market for it,' and the way he did it was completely bad business. People would come to him and say, 'I am beginning to grow mushrooms,' and he would say, 'I will *buy* every mushroom you make.' You know, this is transformative." Stefan said that farmers had this huge distribution problem off their plate, knowing that their supply would have a demand.

Gary would find a market or he would absorb their risk. Stefan continued, "And then he would buy out everything, and then he would go around to restaurants and sell it. And he would go to restaurants and say, 'What do you need? What do you want? I will *find* it. And he would go to people and say, 'How 'bout you try this?' and 'How 'bout you try this?'" And when Gary couldn't go somewhere himself, he would send emissaries to places such as Maine. "He said, 'I'm going to give you all a bunch of money. I want you to go up there, I want you to go eat, I want you to talk to people, and I want you to come back and tell me what's going on.' We're not talking like a slick business guy, he was like a total, total soul hippy, beautiful guy."

Stefan said Gary didn't actually convince him to start a bakery, but "he loved bread. As soon as we started talking about a bakery, he said, 'You want my building? I'll distribute it. Come over, we'll talk about it.'" Three days later, Gary Redmond died. But he is one of the souls that still inhabits the wood-fired bakeries, latter-day orchards, and now-famous restaurants throughout the farmland. Stefan said, "Every food person in the Finger Lakes owes their existence to Gary Redmond. If I'm exaggerating, it's only a little bit. Twenty years ago, he saw that the foodshed concept was the future."

What Gary did was transformative because he was looking at both an entirely new economy and a new model of economy building. Gary, apparently at the cost of making his own millions, invested his time and his heart into creating multilateral prosperity for an entire network of people.

CONNECTING FOOD TOURISM
AND OTHER TOURISM

In addition to the people who have made it their life's work to connect every corner and facet of the food economy, Finger Lakes citizens and institutions have connected another set of dots, another smart way to build positive proximity and low-impact tourism: the food economy flows into a less economically driven connection to the landscape. As I learned from trying to chart my own family's itinerary, in the Finger Lakes they don't just want you to eat and run. As well as having stuff to eat, there is stuff to do, places to explore, and ways to move around them.

You can usually tell that someone has lived in the Finger Lakes region by seeing an "Ithaca Is Gorges" bumper sticker that stays affixed to her car for a decade or two after she's left. Because of the way the glaciers formed the lakes and hills, it is a land of steep ravines as well as towering waterfalls, often surrounding lakes and state forests.

Janet McCue (tour guide, writer, and instant friend) has a food-and-travel blog that, for one, includes a six-day hiking/walking trip that starts and ends with her favorite restaurants and cafés. Janet lives in Mecklenburg, but in a way she could also be an ideal tourist. She's curious, appreciative, and interested in going where the food is made instead of seeking the resort that brings it to her. She likes to work for her supper. She wants to see the Finger Lakes communities in all their glory. The food culture of the area invites us to be like Janet, to see how these wineries and restaurants fit into the landscape of wilderness trails and unfolding history.

Traditionally there were always people coming to the lakes and trails. Kathleen said she rarely wore shoes in the summer. She described how she learned to walk on the slippery lake rocks versus the rocks and trails in the woods. As far as tourism beyond the region went, there was a Grand Prix racetrack in Watkins Glen and tourist shops that just had "a lot of kitschy kinds of stuff," she said, such as T-shirts and keychains. So, lakes, sweet wine, racetrack, keychains. The track now has NASCAR races, and there is more synergy between the food and the trails.

Despite the fact that some people on wine-tour buses "throw away their beer cans on the way to the tasting room," as one grower told me, most come to spend money on food and wine experiences, also called food tourism, accompanied by the low-cost tourism of hiking and biking. One attraction, the Corning Museum of Glass, recognized that it wasn't the biggest draw to the region anymore, so it pulled in elements of the food culture to add value to its appeal. People rave about how the museum is best seen over a couple of days, so it's perfect that they encourage visitors to branch out into local restaurants and wineries as well.

In general, Finger Lakes towns are also finding ways to build their economies to the scale and ethos of a food-tourism economy. Ithaca (already a very green city) is in the midst of building some mid- to high-end hotels, but in keeping with the environmental and labor-conscious food movement that has blossomed down its country roads, they will be Leadership in Energy and Environmental Design (LEED) certified (attentive to saving energy and resources) and just as bent on sending visitors out into the countryside as they are at attracting them.

In Geneva, home of Hobart and William Smith College, food and wine have given the town a chance to expand its already existing appeal to visitors as well as noncollege residents. The town didn't have its own hotel until about 1996. Now it has several hotels. I heard about all of this when I played at Smith Opera House, and the staff brought us dinner from the Red Dove. To them, dinner from the Red Dove, a restaurant that works hard to connect with regional growers, was a big perk of playing there. They also served us wine from Fox Run and locally made chocolate for dessert, introducing us to their world, not just the opera house stage.

One of the volunteers said that Geneva had come a long way in the past twenty years. When I asked how, he said, "We found the lake." In truth, Geneva always encouraged people to visit Seneca Lake. This town was one of the first to protect its lakefront for recreation. But when wine tourism found it, Geneva recognized itself not just as a very nice college town on a lake but also as part of a food culture that involved shopping, eating, and touring. It already had the Geneva Experiment Station and was part of a very amicable food web that included nearby Red Jacket Orchards, a big operation regarded as a good neighbor by smaller, artisan, food-making businesses.

But the food economy/culture allowed Geneva to get in on all the excitement around the wineries, breweries, cider mills, and distilleries that line the shores of Seneca Lake, including ones that host big, weekend-long weddings like Castel Grisch does, along with others such as Herman J. Weimer Winery, whose winemakers return from distant countries holding up their fistfuls of medals. Thus Geneva's street banners, which show boats with billowing sails, bring us to the lake itself, but they also signify a trade route that leads us to all of the town's exotic, albeit mud-booted, neighbors.

By interconnecting the land, water, and farming fields with the waterfalls, sailboats, and historic manses of the region, the Finger Lakes towns make the most of their food and wine reputations and offer an identity and a prosperity that extend beyond the food economy. The tourists are not the only ones who get to experience the food economy as the portal into other aspects of the region. The residents do, too, and that's another reason to grow a food culture (and economy, if you can swing it). Local food constantly references a region back to itself—to its roots, its landscape, and its good fortune. Local beauty, often embodied in local food, is accessible beauty.

LOCAL FOOD'S BRIDGES AND STUMBLING BLOCKS

Local food can be a shared harvest, literally and metaphorically, not just an exclusive world of farmers' markets (sometimes nicknamed "farmers' markups") and expensive farm-to-table restaurants that source every ingredient down to the last baby pea. But that's easier said than done; the expense of growing organic food and just the sheer snobbery that can go with it will easily deepen any chasm of negative proximity in a town, bringing up economic, philosophical, and even generational differences as flags for division and distrust.

We've all seen examples of how expensive, "natural" food can create social boundaries. Everyone who reads the news will want it. For example, which of the following have crop pesticides been linked to in recent years?

1. Cancer
2. Parkinson's disease
3. Multiple sclerosis
4. Extinction of native bees

The answer, of course, is all of the above. So some people who can afford it will go to a local natural food chain and simply spend more for organic food, but for most people that option is just as implausible as Marie Antoinette's advice, "Let them eat cake."

The Finger Lakes region does not have all the answers to questions about how to provide food at once affordable and healthy. But I got to see ways in which this economy, a *true* food economy, creates bridges, not boundaries, along with regard and concern for all neighbors.

First off, although there is a corner of the market with products for connoisseurs by connoisseurs, definitely out of reach for most middle-income families, the production is labor intensive, and consumption is based on appreciating the specialized work. When people pay a hundred dollars for a bottle of wine, that money is spread out across at least ten living-wage jobs, from founding winemaker to grape harvester. As Justin Boyette at the Hector winery points out, maybe because these professionals remember their dues-paying, nail-biting employment origins, they are now committed to making farming and fermenting livelihoods sustainable. All of his employees make a living wage and have benefits.

Meanwhile, Monica Roth and everyone at CCE are ready to dispense advice to anyone who wants to grow a garden, can and freeze food, and cook healthier meals, as do many of the people who live in the region. When your bounty is food, inherent in that sense of abundance is a desire to share it.

My friend Eric Rector, former president of Maine Organic Farmers and Gardeners Association, told me that there are more organic gardeners now (which means more competition) with steadily improving technologies. Farmers' markets can often now offer prices competitive with those of supermarkets, and there is legislation in Maine for food-assistance charge cards (replacing the more cumbersome food stamps) to get automatic discounts. And there's a push to add farmers' markets to bus routes as a way to encourage more people to check them out.

If you're like me, you've passed empty lots in cities and wondered how much soil remediation and positive proximity it would take to create a community garden, bypassing the wallet altogether and letting food itself feed our cities. Marty Johnson understood the potential of community gardening for building social networks and food security when he created Isles in 1987. He knew the importance of building stability in urban centers, but he didn't want to impose a specific agenda on struggling New Jersey cities.

Because he came to Princeton University on a full scholarship as an undergrad, Marty's interest in urban planning and community development had an extra layer of awareness. He remembered how his mom had packed him a sandwich as he set out for college that first year, unsure if her son would be fed as well as educated. Real food security includes the stability of access and a sense of agency in obtaining food, not the ongoing search for help or a handout.

Marty wanted to create food security, but he also wanted to "meet cities where they were," he told me. Gardening tools, seeds, and expertise were all low-impact ways to introduce himself to cities such as Trenton, where Isles is located. Citizens could choose what to grow and, by extension, choose how to grow as food hubs and as communities in general. People could work side by side and develop their urban plans according to what they experienced at eye level.

The food element was important to these cities. "Food deserts" are places that have an overlap of no cars and no access to fresh produce. But Marty always knew that gardens were more than gardens. If you ever wonder if you can dig into an unused or misused patch of ground, chances are that you can. And from the modest beginnings of seeds and dirt, organic positive proximity can grow. Marty set about building relationships that started with growing food, and today there are programs that train young house builders, assist first-time home-buyers, and help with testing for lead.

Another thing you might wonder is why we don't have more fruit and vegetable plants, as opposed to nonedible ones, growing in public spaces. There is an extra amount of management involved, but I often wonder how easily towns could fulfill the motto of my friends Deb and Rik up at Seeds of Solidarity in western Massachusetts: "Grow Food Everywhere."

On a tip from an audience member, I found a Pittsburgh-based organization called the Fruit Tree Planting Foundation and spoke with President Cem Akin about the orchards the group had planted, mostly in public spaces. Although the stated goal of the foundation is to grow eighteen billion fruit trees throughout the world, it assists food programs at home and abroad with many targeted projects aimed at increasing access to produce. It works with schools, small towns, Native American tribes, and even households to plant trees in almost every state. Some orchards are grown exclusively for food pantries.

Whereas Marty Johnson spoke with me first about seeds, shovels, and plant beds, Cem wanted to discuss the unique and mystical qualities of growing food in general. "Simply put, fruit trees are truly magical," he said. The advantages of trees themselves and the fruit they grow are manifold. There are the shade and the beauty, and there is something in the way all the generations can participate in the planting and the gathering space orchards provide. But then there is that experience of "being able to just reach up and pick the fruit, to have something that's actually healthy and nutritious in the diet."

At some point, all this crisscrossing of community benefits becomes hard to explain in any linear fashion. Cem says, "The communities really value the orchards that we donate and help with the installation and the training on the horticultural end of it." But, he continues, "there's this intangible side to fruit trees that—it's a little hard bit hard to explain this if you haven't been in one of the projects or been around folks who are working with orchards and fruit trees—but the 'clean air and the harvest' part of it is easy to quantify, and the 'intangible' is what keeps us coming back."

Local, organic food has some distance to go to offset its prices and its reputation of aloof piety. Let us all be a part of that by demystifying our gardens, sponsoring local food gatherings, and supporting local organic farms (if we can) as a way to drive down prices for all. Or you can seek out Marty in Trenton or Cem just about anywhere. When I spoke with him he was heading off to Uganda and invited me to join him.

THE FARMERS' FORMAL— BRINGING IT ALL TOGETHER

In the Finger Lakes region, the interconnected and, yes, intangible magic of a hardworking agrosphere culminated at the annual Farmer's Formal, for which Janet scored us four invitations. The event, created by Stefan Senders at Wide Awake Bakery, pulls the preciousness out of "local food" and demonstrates ways in which food can actually attract simple, collaborative, good spirit and everyday elegance. It shows how a shared food culture can connect us to where we live and why we live there.

I felt excited but guarded when I was invited to this well-known event. How formal? Long, expensive dress formal? Would this be one of those fancy galas where people of means pull out their checkbooks to boost the progress of a local food economy?

Michael Welch suggested that Kathleen and I "wear something we'd made ourselves." That was my first clue. Janet was going to wear a copper-colored skirt she'd gotten at a clothing swap. Another clue. I went with a dress I had *not* bought in Paris.

This Farmer's Formal was not a fund-raiser. It was Stefan's night of recognition. It was an event that bore witness. We parked along a country road and walked past a long line of cars with their dents and Bernie Sanders bumper stickers, then through a light film of mud on the driveway, navigating with our phone lights around silty, water-filled potholes. And then we walked into a room, Wide Awake Bakery itself, that was everything I hoped it would be, lines of tiny lights strung along the ceiling, wines chilling in the bread mixer, and friendly young women with no makeup in gold lamé disco dresses, circa 1978, taking our coats. About sixty guests sat down at four long tables. On every table were platters of root vegetables and cheese, loaves of nut-and-seed bread, and baskets of freshly baked French bread to be dipped in various tapenades. There were candles floating in mason jars, and every table had about six bottles of wine or hard cider.

Stefan and his friends at Wide Awake had gone to the trouble of making an almost entirely locally sourced menu in January. Every element of the event was homemade. The long, plywood tables were easily dismantled. And overhead were strings of gold-dipped beech tree leaves made by Stefan's daughter, Charlotte, that day. I'm pretty sure I'm the only person whose dress was bought retail (ten dollars at a New York City street fair). Charlotte wore an aquamarine, taffeta gown, and another young woman wore a Tarzana, one-shouldered, leopard-skin-patterned dress with sequins at the neckline. Outside was a long table of jewel-toned lids to remind people to pick up the pots they'd lent for the occasion. Stefan thanked the pot-lenders in his toast later that night.

Down the table from us was Bill, who had built the wood oven where all the bread and tonight's dinner were baked. Stefan had asked Bill to build the wood oven. Bill had never built one. So what did Bill do? In the spirit of this decidedly noneffete, adventurous food economy, he learned how to build one, and then he built it.

Tor, who grew the grains for Stefan's bread with similarly intrepid enthusiasm, was at another table. More than half of the guests seemed to be under thirty, and most of them grew or produced food for a living. They looked neither trust-fund subsidized nor hopelessly downtrodden. They looked happy. And I was happy watching all of these young, healthy people laughing and flirting with each other. Local food supports a real community here, middle income, young, and old, not a rich person's playground. Perhaps because so much must be taught by doing things side by side, the intergenerational bonds seemed particularly strong here as well. The people working at the event tonight seemed equal parts at ease with their roles and wanting to please their popular boss.

Stefan, with his close-cropped brown hair and wire-rimmed glasses, looked like a fastidious keeper of details, but he had come in around the time of the hippie waves, buying "a house and half an acre on a graduate student's stipend" at Cornell. He was busy but never not smiling because he was clearly in his element. This was just a little more of it than usual. After about twenty minutes, he clinked a glass and asked us to pass our platters up to the front of the tables, where they would "magically disappear" and be replaced by the dinner course. And could we also put down the two pieces of wood they were passing around and place the big platters on top of them? True to Stefan's word, the platters and plates were whisked away by the young men in their suits and women in their vintage dresses.

The whole meal was excellent, of course. When the dinner course was over, Stefan clinked his glass again, and we went through the same fast-clearing routine. Then he gave the toast that crystallized the whole evening. It was time to thank everyone who had participated in the evening: "Finch Farm, Stick and Stone Farm, Three Stone Farm, Crooked Carrot, Graft Wine and Cider, Blackbeard Farm, Blue Heron Farm, Revival Book Arts, South Hill Cider, Plowbreak Farm, Oechsner Farm, Farmers Ground, Center Brook Farm, Black Diamond Farm, First Stone School, Hammerstone School, Youth Farm, Full Plate Farm, Sweetland . . ." There were more than twenty farms. This was followed by a long list of individuals. The toast was an opportunity to give thanks to the collective efforts of this community. It was hard to know precisely how much or how little people had brought to the event, but I gathered that the toast was a thank-you for being part of Stefan's community throughout the year.

This event was all about participation, ingenuity, and simple, yet very moving, displays of creativity. I went outside for a breath of air and noticed the woodpile, stacked like a tall beehive. Stefan had thanked the wood stacker.

LIVES CONNECTED BY
ACTUAL ROADS AND FIELDS

There is tangibility to a social network like this. There are concrete things to discuss when we talk about food in our regions, even without the accompanying economy that the Finger Lakes communities have created. There is a discussion to be had about the proportions of salt and vinegar in pickling, there are transactions that involve transporting heavy crops, and there is a geography that connects and reconnects the food culture and economy every day.

To get ingredients for her ice pops, Celia Clark travels all over the region, often working with Red Jacket Orchards in Geneva, and other times driving to Amish farms nearby because the Amish would otherwise have to pay drivers (they don't drive cars) to bring produce to her. It's a beautiful drive, and "it reminds me to slooooow down," said Celia.

Lisa Hallgren, who runs the Ravinous Kitchen alongside the Ravines Wine Cellar with her husband, Morton, told me about the trips she makes to find specific ingredients for this "wineccentric farm-to-table eatery," as the restaurant describes itself. She aims to keep the quality of the food on a par with its prizewinning wines. This takes her on backroads all around Keuka Lake, looking for the best of what every farm has to offer, such as the elderberries that she uses in her desserts, grown on a Mennonite farm.

The food economy is a food community, in which being "local" is a way of life beyond the sticker on an apple at a store (not to disparage the sticker; it counts). To participate in the food economy is to invest in the community by physically knowing every part of it. Face-to-face, crate-hauling, keg-lifting, mutual support is essential to everyone's survival. This local food industry is socially, professionally, and financially linked. Yes, there are plenty of people who don't have jobs in this economy, but there is a large number, possibly a critical mass, who do, and they get to appreciate a breadth of positive proximity that jumps the groove of potential social divisions.

The Finger Lakes area is this maze of little, country roads criss-crossing and looping around each body of water like roots spreading out from an old tree. Within this maze I saw the social circles refining and reinventing the food culture with sheer youthful excitement (at all ages). Beyond the people traveling around the farms with their vats and crates and checkbooks, there were social events that gathered around, and continually grew from, their common medium, food. And these gatherings were taking place all the time. Whatever transactions were connecting people out on the land were continuing around their tables.

A strange thing could happen over a dinner with strangers, whether it was the Farmer's Formal or the equally memorable five-hour, five-course dinner hosted by Christian Thirion and another member of the Foley clan, Joyce, with Justin Boyette, Kathleen, and Janet the next night. At their best, these events evolved toward a sense of trust and mutual esteem, in which eight or ten people achieved a sense of common understanding about something bigger than they were. At all these dinners in western New York, the feeling of familiarity extended to all the places that provided ingredients for the table. As these guests were encountering each other and celebrating their common foodshed, every evening spent thus added yet another connection—an agrospheric one—to the already industriously interconnected region they called home.

And that's what I saw in the Finger Lakes region. Food and wine were both the means and the ends when it came to how citizens experienced themselves in a community. The means of supporting themselves and each other in the food economy—interconnected stories; triumphs and disasters; recognition of each other's hard work; well-conceived connections among food culture, tourism, and family life—were also the ends when it came to mutual trust, the strength of friendships, the awareness of who their neighbors were, and the pay-it-forward commitment to newcomers.

How strong is the positive proximity of this food culture and economy? The ultimate proof came when I saw how cheerfully willing they were to go to jail for the land, water, and livelihoods they so passionately shared. That's always a telling sign.

In 2013, the online version of the regional paper, the *Observer-Review*, reported on a protest against Inergy (now called Crestwood), an energy company that came to the Finger Lakes area with a plan to store millions of gallons of liquid propane gas in the old salt mines near Seneca Lake. Photographs showed citizens standing with their signs in early March. It was snowing. Twelve people were arrested at this protest. More than three hundred people have been arrested to date, many of whom come from the local food and wine industries.

These citizens, who have worked for decades to understand the microfilaments of their soil and the microclimates of their hills, will be damned if they're going to let a controversial energy company store liquid propane near their lake. They know that salt is not stable. They know what a spill would do to the ecosystem of the lake, affecting every single business next to it. The colleges with whom so many food growers and winemakers have worked have provided studies to back their skepticism about Crestwood's claims. The food economy comes into play here because extensive support networks have allowed hundreds of people to have an intimate relationship with the land and with each other.

We all have an opportunity to know our terrain, and each other, in this way, as growers, buyers, and appreciators. Our food can connect our landscape, our years, our relationships, and our daily lives. Our agrospheric consciousness can lead us, as finely aging communities, to understand and appreciate our *terroir*. In the Finger Lakes region, the agrosphere, the long view of the past and future, and the course of daily lives are one and the same.

Part Three

Translation

TRANSLATION IS THE MAGIC ingredient that makes successful towns and cities happen. Translation is how we spell ourselves out to each other and the world. A willingness to share our skills, our stories, and ourselves with each other marks the difference between towns that feel like actual places and those with people who jump in and out of cars all day, shopping at impersonal franchises and filling their ears with radio/Internet content that alternates between celebrity fairy tales and isolation-reinforcing crime reports.

The objectives of successful translation are twofold. One is to announce ourselves to the world, and the other is to have diverse access points into our world. When people truly arrive at some sort of communication, putting themselves forward and welcoming others in, we have positive proximity circulating and growing.

STRUCTURAL TRANSLATION

Structural translation is how a community is assembled and wired, whether by communication networks, by connecting sidewalks, or by signs that show us the way.

I will leave most of the structural translation to urban planners and theorists, who explain the ways in which we arrange ourselves and move, physically and socially, through our communities. It's as if there's an invisible design logic that mobilizes citizens in ways they don't even realize. Urban economics professor David Fiorenza, for instance, told me that at the center crossroad of a town, you should have strong, emblematic businesses on all four corners (he shook his head at Phoenixville's having businesses on three corners of its town center but only a parking lot on the fourth). Other experts explain the importance of accessible sidewalks and parking lots (not to mention the importance of limiting parking lots if you want to encourage public transportation), which help towns translate themselves in a confident, citizen-friendly way.

One aspect of translation of which I've been acutely aware, as a traveler, is the state of signage in every place I've visited. Signs that welcome and signs that wayfind (a recently minted urban planning verb that means "help us find our way") tell a lot about a city. I've often told people, especially in my town, that for a town to get on the map, to be a place with a sense of place, one nonfancy yet essential form of translation it should use is simply clear signage. When I played at German House, in Rochester, New York, I found a big kiosk with a map of local businesses; paragraphs about the region's history, flora, and fauna; and a guide to walking paths. I loved that thing. Good, clear, comprehensive signage is not only helpful and comforting to a traveler but also shows that a city is high on itself, proud of what it has to offer. "We are Rochester. We welcome you to discover how cool we are."

Rochester is now part of a trend. When cities have embarked on various identity-building projects, they have also taken the trouble to create their signs accordingly, incorporating information about history, geography, culture, and commerce into their prominently positioned kiosk and maps.

LOCAL MEDIA

Local media can also provide cultural wayfinding, a sense of place, and a confirmation of all the good that can come of positive proximity, from profiles of local artists to announcements about community events and activities.

I know something about local media from my work. I've been to countless radio and TV stations and done thousands of interviews. I've come to see how newspapers and radio stations locate themselves within the circulatory system of translation. Audience members will tell me they heard my interview, or ticket sales will spike after an article comes out. People might call in to radio shows even when the programs are not call-in shows. I also know local media from being a curious traveler. When I encounter radio stations with local programming, I can pick up on the personalities and priorities of a region. The WAMC radio network in upstate New York, for instance, has a daily, political "Round Table" led by area journalists; a book show that welcomes bookstore owners to talk about their favorite new books; and programming that covers gardening, regional medical services, local cuisine, and . . . more gardening.

Wisconsin Public Radio has book readings, food shows, and health shows run by local experts. Christy Williams Dunton played me into Moab, Utah, on KZMU with an acoustic music show and mentioned that she'd also be doing some astrological readings in a little while. Radio programmers get people excited about their local restaurants, performances, stores, and events. They also validate that the community exists and often give a shout-out to individual citizens.

Local newspapers are another example of successful structural translation. Free weekly papers are like a lighting system for illuminating the community landscape. They can also be successful boosters. I know the word "booster" isn't very journalistic, but I think it's perfectly valid for a newspaper to promote its region by highlighting the sense of achievement town residents rightly feel when they successfully pull off productions and events, even flawed ones (and who isn't flawed?). When I lived in Somerville, Massachusetts, the *Boston Phoenix* would savage every theater production that wasn't traveling up from New York City or produced out of Harvard's American Repertory Theater.

That paper scoffed at regional theater. A local playwright, director, cast of actors, and fleet of designers would rehearse for weeks, missing dinner, missing work, and frustrating their significant others, only to be decimated by theater critics. Local theater never had a chance to take hold and grow. Would it have hurt to have recognized what went well or encouraged audiences to support their local thespians? You'll hear this controversial, heartfelt statement from me: papers that give a little lift to local theaters, galleries, and music venues allow them to exist, mature, and ultimately thrive. And if you can't find anything nice to say . . . okay, say it, but don't be "too cool for school" and trash an entire gallery show, local band, or local production.

Our music scene had both an excellent journalist and a valuable advocate. Scott Alarik, writer for the *Boston Globe*, used to show up at open mikes and quietly assess the new talent. He'd offer words of encouragement, which meant the world to all of us. And Scott also told me once that whenever he saw some potential in an opening act, even if the musician were still green, he would make sure to write something positive that the artist could lift out and put in a press package to help him or her get gigs. On top of that, there were three radio stations that played local acoustic music and invited us in for interviews. Out of about thirty regulars in the open mike scene of which I was a part, seven of us became full-time, performing musicians. Meanwhile, unlike Minneapolis, Seattle, San Francisco, and Chicago, cities whose media fostered local theater, the Boston theater scene never became a feeder for any national stage.

The local media translated Boston's musicians to the city, and we were embraced. The *Globe*, and sometimes the *Phoenix*, made local musicians, including jazz artists, classical composers, and alternative artists like Throwing Muses, exciting. They framed us as culturally relevant, letting people "get in on the ground floor" with us, and many local artists ultimately became part of the national scene. We thrived, and the city thrived.

When a town finds a way to locate itself in the world and connect all the parts of itself into that somewhat shape-shifting, biomorphic, collective phenomenon called an identity, members of that community can take on some of that identity themselves, find a role in it, and discover that they are better able to function and grow there. Local media can help us find each other and ourselves in the scene and highlight our progress.

MUTUAL TRANSLATION

Mutual translation comes in the form of valuable partnerships. Sometimes entities in a town become power centers unto themselves. They can get a little isolated, in fact. They get stronger when they partner with each other, be it a big business with a town, a college with a town, or any combination of powers therein.

INDIVIDUAL TRANSLATION

There is a category of people who, when towns are smart enough to embrace them, disproportionately help their communities find their character and potential. I call these people "conscious bridgers." They get a charge out of making connections, and they are the gold of their communities. When towns put all of these components together, from hammering good signs into the ground to getting intergenerational conversations started, there is a feeling of hometown pride and worldly welcome. You can feel it in the air. I'll leave it to you to decide how comfortable you feel with translating yourself into your community, but I guarantee that if you're reading this book, you are interested in finding a way into and improving the commons.

Towns with good translation have what I call the ethos of translation. It's an ethos that moves in a self-reinforcing, upward spiral. A strong identity and harmoniously flowing channels of communication mean that an impressive number of people walk out their doors in the morning feeling appreciated and understood by their communities. They, in turn, feel motivated to find ways to connect people to people, people to resources, and the whole community to a state of greater health and wealth. In towns with high positive proximity, people want to participate. And why wouldn't they when they feel grateful for all that exists at the commons, when they have skills that are valued and valuable, and when they respect the people with whom they live and work (even when they don't always like them)?

7

Middletown, Connecticut: Partnerships

Bubble: that's the word people use when they talk about where Wesleyan University students live. They live in a bubble. When I was a student there, I was resigned to accepting this status, too.

Communities benefit from a flow between a college campus and a town. When I was at Wesleyan, there was a schism. We could have bridged it better and been better for it.

Part of the problem was that our college town was hurting in the 1980s, as many industrial towns were. From the look of the downtown, it was hard to imagine where we fit. When sociology professor Rob Rosenthal was taking another professor and me around in 2016, he pointed to a "Dickensian-looking building," a church at the north end of Main Street, and said there used to be five manufacturing businesses just beyond it. On this day there was just empty sky. In the early part of the twentieth century, there would be five thousand people out on the streets. There are more people out now than there were when I was in college, but Middletown is not having a second heyday, not yet. In the 1980s, Middletown's Main Street, the widest and longest in Connecticut, had the challenge of finding people and businesses to fill the hundreds of storefronts. The rise of shopping malls had pounded down those businesses and most of the downtown life that went with them.

It was hard to understand what was happening in Middletown for those of us who weren't from transitional, manufacturing towns. Most Wesleyan students came from suburbs where the postindustrial output was abstract: investment products, legal products, medical services, and the like.

Aside from this problematic divide with the town, Wesleyan provided us students a great education. It was an artsy, progressive school. You could do anything. I directed a Czechoslovakian play and stage-managed a Balinese-dance love story. When I was in *Marat/Sade*, a play set in a mental institution, we explored the dynamics of power and insanity by dutifully losing our minds. For one revue, I wrote a wistful, parody folk song called "If We Could All Have Sex Together," and after that performance, I had many suitors. There was a heady feeling of artistic freedom.

On a parallel track with all of this kaleidoscopic theater, there were the Wesleyan courses that encouraged us to find our place on the planet to be responsible and accountable citizens. I learned about global warming ahead of the curve in a class called "The Human Prospect." I was flipping off the light switches in every unused room a decade before my friends were. Most students took "Towards a Socialist America" in their first year. Rumor had it that anyone who took this class got an FBI file. Each group had a special focus, and one delightful, brilliant professor, Dick Vann, had a section about sexual politics. His group of students was nicknamed the "Dick Vann Dykes."

You could immerse yourself in every kind of social experiment, but the assumption was that the adventures would be limited to the campus. You could be in four bands, direct a show in a bathroom, protest trustee meetings (and get arrested by campus police), or choreograph a dance on the roof of a theater building. All of this could be done inside the "bubble."

But who wants to believe that he or she lives in a bubble? For students encouraged to expand their minds and experiences to be real adults, not coddled children, the desire to pop the bubble was strong. Likewise, a college that had acres of open lawns, playing fields, concerts, endowments, state-of-the-art facilities, and a population from all over the world had a lot of valuable social capital to offer the town.

Wesleyan sits on the top of a hill, and Middletown's Main Street is about four blocks away near the bottom of the hill, so the question of how students could get "off the hill" was both physical and existential. How we engaged in service to the town only reinforced our separateness. We knew we weren't in a college town with preppy clothing stores and ice cream shops. Nonetheless, the way we tried to do "good" things, volunteering at the soup kitchen and in the mental hospitals, meant that we weren't seeing the whole town, which included many citizens with college degrees, lifestyles, and jobs like the ones we would have someday.

Nor did we get a clearer impression of the town when we'd receive very official-looking bulletins every few weeks about housing break-ins, as if our security shield had been pierced. In truth, the break-ins were not frequent, nor were they dangerous. I had friends who lived in apartments right next to low-income housing on William Street. Once they came home to find an intruder in the middle of a heist, but they didn't call the police. The thief was eleven years old, and he was raiding their refrigerator.

We had limited contact with downtown. Sure, down on Main Street, you would go to Bob's and get a Bob's T-shirt, the standard-issue uniform for us (along with the crew team T-shirt: Wescrew). Sometimes you went to Pelton's Drugstore to rent a prosthetic leg for a performance art piece. A few times a semester you went to

O'Rourke's for its awesome brunch. And of course there were nightly trips to one Dunkin' Donuts or another. We were in New England, after all.

But there was one instructive exception, an establishment that brought us to Main Street and managed to hold our interest. La Boca, a Mexican restaurant, was a melting pot of students, professors, and people from town. Students worked there, professors' kids worked there, and a lot of people who worked part-time at Wesleyan worked there, too. Bands from Wesleyan and town, some made up of a mix of the two, played there all the time. And everyone went there to eat. When I went, I always felt like I was closer to the real world, one I could imagine living in, more like an adult. I wished that I felt that way more often. When I was hanging out there with my best friend, Laurel, who was a server, I'd always think about Mark Masselli, a Wesleyan professor's son and community activist who'd challenged us to find the "town" in our college town.

During my first week of school, I went to a rally and heard Mark speak to the students. He talked about painting houses in a low-income neighborhood where one of the residents asked what he was doing. Mark replied that he wanted to help out in the community, and the resident said, "You're really doing something with your education."

Mark was issuing a call to action: Wesleyan students would learn about injustice and inequality in the world. We would protest against apartheid in South Africa and the US-funded insurrection in Nicaragua, but we would always have to ask ourselves: Students or not, how were we going to be citizens of *this* community? I heard this as a call to serve the community, but it was more than that. It was a question of how to be in a town. It was the way I felt at La Boca when I didn't just feel like a cloistered student from up on the hill.

BRIDGING THE DIVIDE

Today the distance between the campus and Main Street, less than a quarter mile, still seems far, but it's shorter than it was during my time there. I visited Middletown to understand how it had changed and how the changes in the town and on the campus had been mutually beneficial.

On the top floor of the five-story Community Health Center (CHC), on the north end of Main Street, I talked with none other than Mark Masselli and Jen Alexander, a Wesleyan graduate who married Mark in the early 1990s. From this high up, I watched the lavender light descending over railway bridges on the Connecticut River and remembered all the moments when I'd thought my college town more beautiful than it was credited with being.

Jen was just as I remembered her, as animated as if she were still an undergrad. Mark, too, looked about the same as he did in 1985. His ponytail was gray now, and maybe a little neater. What I didn't know, back when he was talking to us through that bad sound system, was that in 1971, he had cofounded CHC, now in two hundred fifty locations throughout Connecticut, with programs in twenty other states to provide care to underserved and underinsured citizens.

Both Jen and Mark are extensively involved in the life of Middletown, and this includes a connection to Wesleyan. Mark and Jen were awarded honorary degrees (Mark had dropped out in 1971). They both feel that the less "otherness" between Wesleyan and Middletown, the better, but where there is undoubtedly a sense of separation, they have been insightful about when and where to build bridges between the two.

Jen told me that when a Wesleyan administrator approached her circa 2007 and asked what she thought Wesleyan could do for Middletown, she said, "Wesleyan needs to be really good at being Wesleyan. We want Wesleyan to thrive and be its best self. And also just *live* here. Middletown is not where you go to do your charities."

She talked about a time when there was a hearing for a new liquor store in town. It would be across the street from the CHC building, right next to the affordable-housing complex and the Green Street Art Center. As advocates of healthy lifestyles and neighborhoods that reflect them, Mark and Jen were opposed to the liquor store. Also among the opposition were people from Wesleyan who didn't speak up because they didn't want to "overstep" by weighing in, so they didn't. Frustrated, Jen wanted to remind them that they were part of the conversation. The college was part of the town. "It matters to you; it matters to all of *us*."

She went to Wesleyan at the same time I was there, in the late 1980s. She never saw Middletown as a charity case or as just a network of streets and buildings that happened to surround her campus. Quite the contrary, she fell in love with Main Street. She came from a New Jersey suburb with "one cul-de-sac after another" and no town center, close to New York City, where everyone would go to do things. In Middletown, she liked the way the adults would go to Main Street at night. The architecture was still there, so the bones were there. Jen has been committed to the downtown ever since she first saw it.

After graduation, when it came to getting involved with the town, she didn't look to Wesleyan for support. She did what she thought would make Middletown a better town for herself. "I'm a strong believer in organizing around your own interests," she told me. As she and Mark were raising their four kids, she kept noticing how Wesleyan faculty friends in the playgroups she organized would eventually leave for college towns such as Ann Arbor and Santa Cruz. It was a "perpetual exodus."

Jen said to herself, "I've got to make Middletown harder to leave." That was the beginning of Kid City, the children's museum she founded in 1998. Like Mark, who was growing CHC in all directions, she followed her instincts and worked diligently to create a completely original and now beloved museum that draws on the talents of local visual artists and musicians and receives one hundred thousand visitors a year. Mark said, proudly, "The most frequent sound at Kid City is crying." That's the big joke there. The kids have to be pried from the exit doors. Parents from out of town talk about going an hour out of their way on family trips just to visit.

Jen pointed out that Mark, too, started out organizing around his interests. The people he noticed who needed better access to health care were often young, many of them friends. They were all people he knew. Jen added that creating the things you want to have in your community is a secret to longevity. Susan Allison started the Buttonwood Tree, a small and popular coffeehouse, with her husband, Steve, because "she needed an intellectual community where musicians and poets would gather." Buttonwood has been around for more than two decades.

Apart from summing up one of the best citizen-based planning concepts I've found, that it's most effective to organize around your own interests, Jen was doing what she told the Wesleyan administrator to do. The best way to "help" everyone, she found, was to create Middletown as the best version of itself she could envision.

Middletown has many enviable community institutions that could inspire any college student, not just those at Wesleyan. There's nothing like CHC. One project it initiated was Vinny's Jump and Jive, a stand-alone center that offers every kind of dancing, such as hip-hop, ballroom, salsa, and Zumba classes. People come in from the Netherlands and India to study CHC and its community projects. And I've rarely seen a place so original and community based as Kid City.

Jen is a little annoyed by the whole town-gown question. Pratt and Whitney, one of the largest aircraft-engine manufacturing firms in the world, employs thousands of people in Middletown, and yet there's no burning Pratt and Whitney–town question, she points out. But I think she is more frustrated that Wesleyan students haven't sought out the charms of Middletown in the way she did.

In the early 1990s, Jen admits, before Kid City, Buttonwood Tree, and other projects had begun, things had gotten pretty bleak. "Mark counted twenty-six vacancies from church to church" at either end of Main Street. Wesleyan students were surveyed about what they liked and didn't like, and their top three dislikes had to do with their college town. To make things worse, some changes at that time had the effect of separating university and town life, guided by market forces and budgeting decisions such as pulling four hundred units of student housing from Main Street and offering fewer mortgage incentives for faculty to buy houses in Middletown.

Both of these moves put more of a hermetic seal on the campus. Jen remembered when there was a core of professors who lived within walking distance from the school, and students would walk their dogs and babysit their kids. Jen ate dinner at professors' houses once or twice a semester. "All those people sent their kids to the schools here, all those people cared if somebody tore down an old house."

Cathy Lechowicz, director of the Jewett Center for Community Partnerships, addressed this question simply and head-on, leading tours through town when students first arrived at school. Now some orientation events happen in First Church, on Main Street, instead of on campus. Mark thinks this kind of introduction would work even better at the beginning of sophomore year, when it doesn't have to be mixed with the newness of being a college student, but these tours are a good start for basic wayfinding.

There are also some places that mix town and college populations. One popular institution has town members offering most of the expertise, and that is radio station WESU, which made a move out of the Clark Dormitory about a decade ago to a space above Broad Street Books, near Main Street.

The way to start working there is to intern with other programmers, often people from Middletown, and there are many all-station meetings. Adrien DeFontaine, my research assistant, worked there and was on the board for three years. He told me that Ben Michael, the station manager, worked to foster relationships between students and residents. "In that time, I came to befriend a number of Middletown residents who shaped my college experience. It's a wonderful thing, and something I wish Wesleyan would encourage further for its students."

Adrien believes that Wesleyan's general relationship with Middletown should be stronger. Like me, he received those public-safety bulletins about break-ins. In fact, they came more frequently than when I was a student, and it pained him that these postings might be the only way students would define Middletown's identity. He said emphatically that more face-to-face relationships between students and other Middletown residents would easily pop the bubble of misconceptions (yes, he used the word "bubble," too).

SERVICE LEARNING THAT SERVES EVERYONE

As I emphasized at the beginning of this book, shared spaces are important. The crucial ones for a college in a town combine everything from shared services to shared café tables for the two populations. La Boca's success, when I was a student, was in its employment mix of students and town residents, the social opportunities for resident professors and students to hang out, and a music scene where people played in each other's bands. At WESU, mentoring, leadership, and programming rely on a constant exchange between Wesleyan and Middletown radio programmers.

Opportunities to introduce the town to the students, whether initiated by citizens or emerging organically from shared spaces, are important to seek out. Cathy's initiative to show students around orients students to understanding that, far from living in a bubble, they have come to reside in a place of history, beauty, and strong community. On top of that, I encourage people attending college, or sending their kids there, to have some curiosity about the town they are entering, not just the campus.

Ultimately, the college itself, in its administrative policies, can encourage ways for students to "know that they live here," as Jen said. If college administrators believe it's important for students to see themselves as part of a larger community, there are ways to create a flow between the college green and the town commons. Yes, one of the ways to be in a community is to "serve" it, but in a way that reflects the desire to serve one's future community or the world at large, as many Wesleyan students wish to do.

In 1987, my housemate Grace Lee told me there was a new profes-sor on campus, and the students were talking. "He looks like Robert De Niro, he wrote a rock opera, and he's a really good professor," she said. "Everyone loves him." Sociology professor Rob Rosenthal made a name for himself as soon as he walked on campus. In 1998, almost ten years after I'd left Wesleyan, he invited me up to do an interview for his book *Playing for Change*, which I now use as the core text for the class I teach at Wesleyan.

For all his popularity, he was neither a narcissist nor a firebrand. He was kind, he was funny, and he was a listener. He was a radical in the sense that he was always looking at the roots of social injus-tice and the roots of social change. He became a resident who sent his kids to the Middletown public schools. His wife, Sunny, started working at the Middletown Public Library. So Rob was a radical who knew the importance of committing oneself to living in a community.

In 1999, Rob started several things at once. Students had been asking for a service-learning program modeled on those that other schools were starting, which coupled work in the community (not just "service," despite the name) with classes that contextualized what students were learning. In 2003, at the urging of Rob and Direc-tor of Community Relations Frank Kuan, the umbrella Center for Community Partnerships (CCP) brought together students, faculty, and administrators under one roof. It was important to Rob and his colleagues to create a space in which there could be more synergy among students, professors, provosts, and everyone in between. The university had always had its administrative ambassadors who knew the mayor and city council and how the town worked. Now professors and students would know them, too. Likewise, as students and classes brought new projects into the pipeline, there was an opportunity for the administration to watch them and learn.

The center would be a unified "portal," as Rob called it, for students who wanted to connect with Middletown. CCP offered many different ways of "finding" the town, through teaching, coaching, WESU, and data-driven study. Its building served as a brick-and-mortar version of a multifunctional wayfinding tool.

Another dividend of having all of these departments together was that people from the community also had a "one-stop shop" when they wanted to bring ideas and questions to the campus, sometimes discovering each other at the monthly meetings, another networking advantage.

In 2004, all of these combined forces moved over into the Allbritton Center for the Study of Public Life (ACSPL), already home of the town-focused Center for Quantitative Analysis, which often uses Middletown as the model for its data-driven studies. And then they added the Patricelli Center for Social Entrepreneurship. Rob is now the head of the Allbritton Center, and that is why he is also my boss (I teach a course called "Music Movements in a Capitalist Democracy" at the ACSPL).

There is a positive confluence between the ACSPL, the place where, if you want to plug in to the town, Rob said, "you come here and we work it out," and the spirit in which Rob, Cathy (the director who gives tours of Middletown to incoming students), and Michaela Kingsley run the Patricelli Center.

The spirit, in short, is respectful and collegial. Rob sent me a pre-publication draft of his cowritten paper, "Centering the Center," which defines the work at the ACSPL. The paper describes the approach its leadership takes in proceeding with community work: "We move forward inch by inch, error by error, success by success, seeking to stay centered. There are no universal principles, perhaps, but there are guidelines that seem worthy: genuine reciprocity, building trust, and openness on all sides to learn and adjust as we move along." They recognize everyone's contribution toward mutual benefit in order to avoid "service" being perceived as condescension.

These leaders understand that a college is bound to have more money and warm bodies to mobilize than the agencies with which they engage. The paper's cowriters emphasize their "respect for our community partners who persist year after year in pursuing social justice without many of the resources or the safety net that the university provides." There is recognition of the community partners who have worked "under often difficult conditions, and the opportunities they thus provide to us and our students to learn how they've accomplished what they have using comparatively restricted resources." And where do the students fit? "Reciprocity requires that we in turn offer something of value, in most cases people power, youthful energy, and sometimes forms of specialized expertise that they might otherwise be unable to access."

What Jen Alexander could understandably have heard as awkwardly incorrect in the question "What can Wesleyan do for Middletown?" the CCP endeavors to dispel. To Rob, there is no distinction between what helps Middletown and what helps students. Like the Center for Quantitative Analysis, the service-learning classes have a lot to do with amassing information in a town, and that can energize the students. The data have to do with actual streets and citizens as opposed to distant cities or countries.

When he spoke about service learning to my class, Rob pointed out, "Most of the things we think, the theories we have, are shared between two people, the student and the professor." With service learning, he said, "You can actually look and see, 'Does it work?'" He encouraged my students to check out the service-learning classes not because they would be "giving back" but because they would likely find these classes truly exciting.

Service-learning classes go into the town and do things such as surveys, histories, and data collection. If you can think of any other entity that can pay this kind of detail-oriented, institutionally supported attention to the community, I'd be amazed. This is the kind of thing college students can do. Rob teaches a community-research seminar. Anthropology and American Studies professor J. Kehau-lani Kauanui taught a course in association with the county histor-ical society called "Decolonizing Indigenous Middletown," in which the students used every tool in Wesleyan's toolbox, methodically going through archives and collecting oral histories, to track down Middletown's precolonial history, resulting in, among other things, an impressive overhaul of the Wikipedia page on the Wangunk tribe in the area.

The ACSPL also provides the advantage of a campus meeting place for students engaged with programs in the town. Had there been a central building where we could go to find a Middletown con-nection and a group of people with common interests, we students back in my time could have made more interesting connections and had a greater sense of Middletown as a whole.

And perhaps by having more conversations about our larger town, we could have also known how to get away, occasionally, from the campus "village" in which we lived, predominantly populated by cit-izens from the ages of eighteen to twenty-two and (as with most pri-vate colleges) full of drugs, entitlement, naiveté, romantic infidelity, academic insecurity, and competitiveness. Wesleyan was, as my friend Doug MacKenzie said, a "cult of fascination." You put your beautiful painting of a tree on the wall? We're going to staple toast to the wall to challenge your hierarchical definition of art and self-expression. You wear all black with fantastically bright red lipstick? Well, I do the same, but with orange lipstick, questioning the very notion of cos-metic beauty, and I'm also a man. Wesleyan was an exhausting, and strangely rarified, treadmill of fascination.

When I was a student, venturing out into Middletown was more of an isolated act in 1986, when every Wednesday I took my cheap guitar and song sheets down to the Middletown Health Care Center and played Sing-Along-with-Dar for heavily medicated patients and a bemused staff. One of the requisites of being in the play *Marat/Sade* was that we had to volunteer at one of Middletown's four mental hospitals (Wesleyan was often called "the fifth"). I loved going there. Other cast members were very affected by their experiences, too. Spencer Reece, now an award-winning poet and Episcopal minister, volunteered in the state hospital. One day he returned and said, "I used to have a measure of self-pity. Now I have none."

FINDING COMMON GROUND

But it was only in my senior year, when I emerged out of a cave of depression, that I heard about what other people had been doing. Had we, the literacy mentors, Big Brothers and Sisters, garden growers, and sing-along leaders, known about each other, we could have discussed what we saw and arrived at a clearer, more interesting understanding of our complicated town. I'm sure more collaboration would have helped everyone, on and off campus. It could have shifted our attitude. There is a difference between "helping" and actually building a relationship with a population of people outside the campus, even a service-based relationship. We were ready for the relationship.

The ACSPL is a point of synergy for Wesleyan and Middletown. The parallel point of convergence in Middletown is the big and busy Green Street Teaching and Learning Center, on the north end of Main Street. The center, a handsome, sturdy, former schoolhouse, was the result of a three-way partnership among Wesleyan, the city (which donated the building), and the town's North End Action Team (NEAT). Many of the renovations and half of the annual budget (it used to be more) come from Wesleyan. When Michael Bennet was president of Wesleyan, and the CCP was well under way, the service-learning program had an opportunity for a big grant to do an ongoing project in Middletown. What did the town want? NEAT and other citizens wanted a community center.

President Bennet became deeply engaged with this and many other projects in town. He had grown up near Middletown, and Jen Alexander told me that when he arrived at the nadir of downtown life, he shook his head and said that when he was growing up, Middletown "was where your mother took you to buy a nice jacket."

As the president of Wesleyan, he wanted to help the town but not so it would experience itself as the beneficiary of a wealthy college. He wanted to return Middletown to what it had been. "That was really inspirational," Jen said, "for a lot of people in the downtown to feel not like Wesleyan was saying, 'You really need our help.' It was just like, 'This is not us.'"

The stars aligned for this community center to model a true partnership. The center offers a friendly, open-ended environment, like a laboratory for many skill sets Wesleyan students can develop. It is a community space with every kind of learner, a great training ground for every kind of teacher. Executive Director Sara McSorley took me around to see the two dance spaces (one of which becomes a black box theater when it needs to), the "wet" and "dry" art rooms, the general classrooms, and a recording studio complete with a huge console and isolation booths. Wesleyan doesn't have an education major anymore, so this is the go-to place to participate in teaching young students.

Also, because the community center is a physical address with ongoing programs, Wesleyan students get to have a continuous relationship with the families who come in, and, by proxy, they see the workings of the town. Sara, in the midst of wearing all her hats at the center, told me she also notices how Wesleyan students gain a broader perspective of town life. "They can understand how zoning works and how people can struggle to pay their electricity bills."

If there is a desire on the part of students to "help," they are helping as any community members would want to help an underserved neighborhood in their town, not as students at an elite college who want to bestow their beneficence on a needy town as a whole. Green Street is in a low-income part of Middletown that does need more than a little love. Many of its students have working parents who can't afford expensive after-school programs. But through its doors also come people with a diversity of incomes and lifestyles from the town. Sara believes that by having these relationships, Wesleyan students can see family life up close, enabling those from more economically homogeneous towns to "get past the bubble of where they came from."

OTHER HUMAN LINKS

Faculty members can also help to bridge the gap between the campus and the town. There was an on-campus restaurant called Downey House before I got to Wesleyan. Students and professors went there, and it was natural for them to sit together. That's where young adults, recently children, with their parents still paying for everything from toilet paper to car insurance, got to explore the social terrain of adulthood by finding out about their professors' spouses and dogs and children.

People who work at a college can link students to the town. If a student said she wanted to start a secondhand clothing store in a church basement, a faculty resident would know whether the Presbyterian or Methodist church was the place to go. He or she could tell you where to find a hammer, or an acupuncturist, or an open mike that wasn't just populated by your friends. Students who go to school for two-thirds of the year don't have the continuity or long memory of their professors.

Professors and staff who work on a campus can help soften the edge between the suspended reality of a campus and the future life beyond it, thus blurring the line between dorms and other domiciles. Our professors acted as stewards of "real life." They were attuned to our desire to connect our vision of the world with our real lives in it, so they were particularly careful not to inject our idealistic plans with cynicism. When we sat at a candlelit table for drinks with theater professor Fritz DeBoer at La Boca, we told him we wanted to start a theater company. He didn't dismiss the idea. He pondered it.

"Have kids," he said. "Without a theater company, having children is unutterably boring. But," he paused to further assemble his thoughts, "without kids, a theater company would be inexpressibly lonely." We sat with this wisdom for a minute. He was speaking to us as future parents and professionals. Then Fritz straightened up and said in a different tone of voice that whatever we started, we should fund it by getting a liquor license as the first order of business. Fritz himself was a beautiful dreamer, but he knew there was some important wisdom to impart about the real world.

OTHER TOWNS, OTHER GOWNS

In my travels, I've encountered surprisingly few town-gown relationships that truly achieved positive proximity. Some coexist peacefully but don't have a sense of symbiosis. Wesleyan and Middletown are not the only ones to have grappled with finding a mutually beneficial relationship. The ones who have tried to create more flow between the two are instructive exceptions.

Skidmore College has become invested in its town, Saratoga Springs, New York, by studying it. I found out about this when Jessa Blades had me as a captive audience in 2012. She was doing my makeup for a TV show. She'd gone to Skidmore College, and I said I'd stopped for breakfast at Uncommon Grounds Café, and how I loved the stores on Broadway. She told me that economics and business school professors had actually brought these local businesses into their classrooms and studied their business plans. This was like service learning at Wesleyan with a focus on local commerce.

I don't know if that is why I get such a sense of harmony between town and gown in Saratoga Springs. When I told the mother of a Skidmore student about this relationship between the college and the community, she nodded and said, "That explains why the mayor of Saratoga Springs addressed the students and their parents on graduation weekend."

Skidmore and Saratoga Springs have a mutual investment in each other. Professors created the venue that allowed for a relationship between town and gown and for the town to benefit from the imported income from the campus. Saratoga Race Course is booming with tourists in the summer, and as that activity tapers down, the school year begins. With the boon of outside dollars flowing in, it's still important for towns to find ways of serving students' and tourists' needs without getting subsumed by their appetites. One way to foster more than just a cold, transaction-based relationship is to create an avenue for students' interest and curiosity, even if they're not in Saratoga Springs full-time. In this case, the avenue is Broadway; students know the town they live in, and, by learning how much their support of local businesses affects the town, they have an automatic sense of stewardship and connection.

In Blacksburg, Virginia, home of Virginia Tech, there are huge stone pillars on either side of a ten-foot-high gate that clearly delineates the entrance to the campus. But the town is no less attractive or desirable a destination than the campus. It is full of beautiful old houses, and although some shops sell swag for the college, they're not T-shirt warehouses. The store windows look to attract homecoming alumni. They are working hard in Blacksburg to make sure they don't slide into the service economy of "T-shirts and two dollar beers" described by a promoter in State College, Pennsylvania, another wonderful city that has grown itself up for adults.

In the case of Blacksburg, there has been a physical translation of connection between campus and town: a stretch of road and sidewalk just outside the stone gates was torn up and replaced by an open pedestrian plaza that softened the stark divide the large pillars and iron gates presented. The campus now feels like it's spilling into the town.

And notably, both the towns of State College and Blacksburg have renovated performance spaces near, but not on, the campuses, just as Middletown did, putting cultural life into the towns instead of relying wholly on the colleges for enlightenment and entertainment.

There is synergy at work in these towns: faculty and alumni residents can experience the towns as their homes, modeling and translating grown-up life for students, while the colleges themselves bring their scholarly interests and "youthful energy" into the town, not to mention things like bookstores and affordable restaurants, which I am always grateful to find when I play in college towns.

Institutions of learning can become isolated and seem aloof, but when the powers that be find ways to help burst the bubble and point out mutually beneficial partnerships, positive proximity can grow with added self-awareness and self-reliance. When colleges recognize that their "gowns" are only one garment in a wardrobe, the reputation of the "college town" can be realized: a healthy, locally prosperous downtown supported and well loved by a population that brings in new technology, new ideas, multimedia arts, and lecturers from around the world. And where one entity is lagging at some moment in time, there can be a respectful shoring up of support from the stronger member of the partnership. That can mean a campus lending support to a town, but it can also mean a town bringing resources to a campus at a critical juncture.

Fighting State and County Capitalitis

"We are cool, and we know it, and our people know it!" That's what the capitol complex in Madison, Wisconsin, seems to exclaim every time I've played in that city. The giant statehouse stands in the middle of the city like a beacon. All traffic flows in relation to this center point. Around it is a heavily used plaza, with a mile of farmers' market and craft stalls set up on Saturday mornings, and there is a ring of restaurants and cafés all around the plaza. Madison is not afflicted with what I call capitalitis, where the nexus of government is somehow bereft of civic vibrancy. Perhaps it's no surprise, then, that in 2011, when Governor Scott Walker was trying to limit the power of the unions in Wisconsin, there were rallies outside the capitol building that made national news. The people knew it was their building. It was easy to reach and a well-trafficked part of Madison's life.

All too often, capitals lack the active engagement that Wisconsin's has. The main symptoms of capitalitis are a sense of disinterest and even despondency in the residents toward an entity that should be seen as representing them, namely state government. The capitol campus in these cities seems more like a glorified bunker than a hive of democracy. Sometimes this impression spreads to the legislators who actually walk the marble halls of capitol buildings.

I spoke with Laura Rose and Kae Warnock of the National Conference of State Legislatures (NCSL). They were surprised I saw capitol buildings in this way. Kae told me that after you get inside the Harrisburg Capitol Building, for instance (and every citizen has the right to do so), "it's one of the most elegant capitol buildings you'll ever go into. It has been perfectly restored. The stairs have a gorgeous, sculpted, gilded railing. There's a frieze in the ceiling. It's like going into a fine art gallery in Paris."

All I could think of was how demoralizing it must be for legislators in Harrisburg, Pennsylvania, to walk past detritus and police tape to get to work in the morning. The capitol area has something of a crime problem. It must be almost as hard as walking up all those capitol building stairs in Albany, New York, with black clouds of corruption allegations over one's head all the time.

There's a problematic metaphor here. We have capitol buildings with gilded railings inside and syringes littered outside. Laura and Kae were not delighted by my observation. They saw the life of these buildings. They saw the ways in which citizens were welcomed inside. But I hold firm to my belief that capitals can feel like black holes in their states and counties and that state governments can go much further to engender a sense of access and pride in the areas that surround them. A more enlivened relationship between a capitol complex and a capital city can help the reputation of that city and maybe even state government. Without government-citizen partnerships, capital cities are in big trouble.

This is an issue of translation. Proper introductions must be made, and relationships must grow to a sustainable level. An elected government is supposed to be representative of its people. Many state politicians, individually, translate what they do very well. Almost every state official I've met wants to be an ambassador for her or his job. They define public service. I met one corrupt one. She knows nothing about government, doesn't want to, constantly struggles to cover up her ignorance, and, of course, keeps getting elected. In my twenty years of meeting public officials, I'm glad to say, she is the exception.

The feng shui of government buildings and properties tends to work against these elected representatives. Yes, the capitol buildings are almost universally beautiful. Capitol buildings are built to be grand and impressive. Many of them feature the "dome and cupola" design of the Capitol in Washington, DC. The majesty of capitol buildings ennobles the achievements of a deliberative, participatory government. They are secular, antihierarchical temples of democracy. No capitol building looks like a cathedral or a castle (okay, there's Hartford, and Albany's looks a little like a French chateau).

But the grandeur of the buildings disguises the troubling fact that they contain a small population, mainly confined indoors, only during session and office hours, five days a week. The capital district becomes a dead zone for many hours of the day and night. In about ten states, the main buildings are basically empty for up to nine months of the year. That's a lot of badly used public land, not to mention strange symbolism.

On top of wasting valuable space, these massive buildings tend to hide our officials from us and us from them. If we're not around our governments, they can't see us and our smiling, hopeful, citizen faces.

I fear that they just see our tired profiles during their morning commutes, then come up from a parking lot to a lawn that has a couple of newly discarded beer cans and cigarette butts.

Let's take the whole sad situation apart:

1. Capitol buildings are huge, as are the courthouses that surround them, with many doors, most of which are locked save for the main entrance, often at the top of many stairs. So many stairs! And, of course, after you're in and greeted by armed guards, there is usually only one purpose: a state government that only operates during business hours.

2. Because government is basically a nine-to-five job (unless legislators lock themselves into their buildings, which they've done in times of tense negotiations), the buildings lie fallow most of the time. Not only that, there are often five- or ten-block-wide auxiliary buildings across the street, such as courthouses and general assembly buildings, also open for only nine or ten hours at a stretch on weekdays. Marty Johnson, director of Isles in Trenton, New Jersey, told me that Trenton's capital footprint takes up about a third of the city (two square miles out of the city's seven), when you include the legislature and court buildings. This means a huge, temporary population and about twelve hours a day of dark buildings and grounds. He said this plan has "damaged" the city even though it was meant to bring jobs.

3. Beyond the acreage of government buildings, with their restricted hours of operation, restaurants and cafés tend to avoid the property's periphery, further extending its isolation.

4. Capitol building grounds are often thoughtfully landscaped. In Topeka, Kansas, for instance, there is a well-tended, expansive green that takes up an acre or two. But without life outside the grounds to complement the offering of grass and benches—without food trucks, restaurants, museums, theaters, and cafés—the capitol "parks" become just more underused space no matter how many rows of tulips and marigolds are planted.

Have you ever reposed on the grounds of your state capitol property, or taken a hike or a picnic? If you have, it's because your government has come up with ways to limit or offset capitalitis. Wonderful examples abound. There is a welcoming, semiwooded park around the Salt Lake City state building. It can be done. Citizens can be lured into walking around their state property.

5. Let's take a look at how legislators fare in these capital spaces. Legislators might exude charisma during election time, but after they're in office, well, do you feel excited by the phrase *state government?* For most of us civilians, state governance is seen as a mountain of tedious, though necessary, small bills that get passed after months of endless jockeying. And many of these bills are impossible to understand or follow. Sometimes there is an equally unknowable, parallel maze of petty corruption.

Add to that the transience that elected office brings, with new people rotating in and out every two to four years. Then there's the lack of variety of food and coffee places, the absence of nightlife after work, and the evidence of drug use in the park outside the temple of democracy. As I said, I've mainly encountered motivated, enthusiastic legislators, but these variables do not make for the happiest workers. And let's not forget that many elected officials take a pay cut for the honor of serving us.

These acres of central real estate are supposed to represent the vital workings of the state. They are filled with highly intelligent people who influence how we, in our daily lives, will interact with our communities via our schools, roads, hospitals, and communication systems. These representatives should be exciting—isn't it they who legislate sex, drugs, and rock-and-roll?

In Madison, the central location of the capitol building has allowed it to be not only the venue of rallies but also the location of sustained, public action. In the months that followed the protests against Governor Walker, there were noontime singing rallies outside the building every weekday. I was invited to one and went in the spring of 2012. They gave me a songbook with adapted lyrics to well-known songs such as "Which Side Are You On":

> Don't believe the governor
> Don't listen to his lies
> Working folks don't have a chance
> Unless we organize!
> Which side are you on, boys, which side are you on?
> Which side are you on, girls? Which side are you on?

The day I participated, there were about a hundred people at the singing rally. They were joined by about twenty postal workers who had come down from up north.

Governor Walker's administration arrested members of the Solidarity Chorus for their assembly on state property. But they did not stop. They kept assembling, and they kept it up for years. I'll never forget singing Anne Feeney's "Have You Been to Jail for Justice?" When we got to the line "Have you been to jail for justice? I want to shake your hand," I looked over at a tall man with muttonchop sideburns who led the singing, and another short, wiry man who played fiddle. Both were lawyers. Before singing the last verse, they leaned over and shook hands. They were each awaiting their own trials for protesting.

Transforming grounds into multifunctioning, real parks is one way capitol buildings can endeavor to invite in the public. Hartford, Connecticut's popular Bushnell Park, for instance, extends right into the capitol property. Hartford still suffers from capitalitis, but there has been revitalization, called Riverfront Recapture, along the Connecticut River, and a genuine effort is being made to connect the state government with the new life stretching up from the waterfront.

Denver is also trying hard to build immunity against capitalitis. For example, there are always food trucks around the capitol perimeter, which has culminated in a day per week with extra trucks called Food Truck Tuesdays.

Hannah Ackerman is the volunteer coordinator at Swallow Hill Music, a community music center in Denver that extends its tendrils of education, community jams, and performances into the community. Hannah keeps a close eye on how things work in the city. She told me about what they've been trying to accomplish at the capitol building. Civic Center Park is the forty-acre property to its west. She points out, "It's Denver, so there's always some kind of music event happening." Not only are there concerts but also Denver has a Cinco de Mayo celebration, the decades-old People's Fair, one of the biggest Pridefest celebrations in the country in June, and the Black Arts Festival in July, all of which arguably inject inclusivity into the government and connect government with daily life. The backdrop of all of these events is, after all, the gold dome of the capitol. Hannah also pointed out that the main branch of the Denver Public Library and the Denver Art Museum are directly adjacent to the grounds, as are many smaller, private museums with which Swallow Hill has partnered.

On the flip side, Denver's Civic Center Park also hosts many citizens who cannot otherwise find shelter, that is, homeless people. The United States has a problem to solve when it comes to homelessness. Perhaps, in the case of people sleeping on the capitol grounds in full view of legislators, it is fitting that the problems are there to be confronted as well.

Laura and Kae of the NCSL are big supporters of what legislatures can bring to civic life. Laura had lived in Madison and was quick to point out the ways in which Wisconsin has bucked what I consider the capitalitis trend. I assured her I'd seen what was happening in Madison with my own eyes. They told me about other exceptions. In Augusta, Maine, legislators don't have private offices, so they're just walking around in the main part of the building, presumably accessible at all times. I've been to Augusta. The capitol building is grand, but it is an island in a sea of municipal buildings and busy through streets. I wonder how people get the memo that legislators are so accessible to them. Down at the Roundhouse, in Santa Fe, New Mexico, artisans, particularly Native American silversmiths, come in at all times to sell things in and around the capitol building, which has a centuries-old plaza (a Mexican tradition long before New Mexico became a state) and no lawn, meaning there's less distance between citizens and the state building.

There are also about twenty mock legislatures called Silver-Haired Legislatures that meet in state capitol buildings throughout the United States. They are usually comprised of retired citizens, and they meet to discuss and debate, inside the legislative chamber, issues that often become their policy points after they've had an opportunity to explore and shape their arguments. Not only do they create policy but also their work together motivates them to get into the capitol buildings when they are in session.

As with the people in Middletown, Connecticut, who have made the best of the town-gown partnership by dismissing any sense of a "wall" between the two, members of the Silver-Haired Legislatures have familiarity with legislative space and process, and with that sense of access comes more transparency. Likewise, Model United Nations and student courts also meet in their capitol buildings.

Montpelier, Vermont, has a plan that all state capitals could consider. Food is grown on the grounds of the capital to be given to local food pantries. And why not? It's not like the grounds are crawling with people. If you work in state government, do a quick study (just look out a high office window) to see how many people actually stroll on your grounds. If it's less than thirty a day, you can replace lawns with lettuce, especially if you're Frankfort, Kentucky, whose state leaf is lettuce and whose past resident John Bibb developed Bibb lettuce.

Imagine what could happen if all that capitol space could be used in more creative ways for the public good. Taxpayers are already paying for the heating, cooling, and property upkeep. I have visited some twenty-two state capitols, and I'm always amazed by their potential. Annapolis, Maryland's is right in the middle of town but only meets for half the year. In Topeka, Kansas, the property taken up by its palatial building, coupled with an expansive lawn, is often completely empty.

Richmond, Virginia, is in the middle of many revitalization projects. I hope the city will continue finding ways to integrate its massive capitol grounds and buildings with its interesting waterfront and all the new nightlife that's popping up. Just making a pitch there, Richmond.

Charleston, West Virginia's complex includes the state cultural center, which houses the radio show *Mountain Stage*. The staff members, including host Larry Grosz, include some of the state's proudest ambassadors. Whenever you play on the show, you're invited to the Empty Glass afterward to jam with members of the house band into the wee hours. They want you to remember their mountain state with fondness (and we do!). They literally fill up the capitol complex with their music.

Capitalitis doesn't just apply to state capitals. County seats, too, often seem to lack a daily citizen presence. I'd advocate dog runs, tot parks, and outdoor cafés for all grounds, state and county, to bring people closer to government. Thoughtful design can invite citizens in. And that feeling of welcome is important. These are the halls of democracy.

Laura and Kae of NCSL work in capitals all over the country and spent more than an hour talking me through the innovative programs many of these places offer. They themselves are at ease in capitol buildings. They are enthusiastic believers that capitol grounds hold the democratic promise they were built to represent, even though Laura admits, "In Hartford, they told me, 'Don't go through the park at night.'"

Kae points out that most of these buildings were designed when the country was very young. Democracy itself was a departure from European monarchies, and the capitol building "was going to help the people to govern themselves for the first time instead of having a king tell them what to do." The architecture celebrated the achievement of self-governance. "They chose to make them very regal so that there was an element of magic as people went into those beautiful buildings and sat in the gallery and watched what happened, where people would debate on their behalf in order to make change."

Houses of Faith

Religious congregations can have very strong bonds. In facing the ontological questions (ontology is basically the study of what it's all about) of mortality and morality, members of faith groups offer each other the consolation and recognition of a common search that sometimes finds a common answer. By nature, most religions focus on communication over commerce and often provide services to their congregants and people in need, from soup kitchens to clothing swaps. In Moab, the Episcopal church was the first home of the multicultural center, recognizing that the substantial Hispanic and often non-English-speaking population in town was living on the margins of the community.

Faith groups can argue that with the role conscience plays in all houses of worship, they can address issues of disenfranchisement, illness, disability, and economic hardships very effectively, and sometimes exclusively, within their own communities. There is an internal store of social capital they can build to very secure levels. An Episcopalian delivers soup to an Episcopalian with a twisted ankle, led both by scripture and by the fact that other Episcopalians delivered soup to her after a heart operation. Harvard sociology professor Robert Putnam would call this "bonding social capital," which strengthens the sense of community coffers within a self-identified group.

When houses of faith find ways to communicate with each other beyond the church walls, congregants have a tremendous opportunity to make the most of what Putnam calls "bridging social capital." This happens when a new and possibly unexpected bridge is built, as when an Orthodox Jewish man, for instance, might discover that his Episcopalian neighbor loves growing roses as much as he does. After a few conversations, he'll cross a line of mutual guardedness, and even prejudice and misunderstanding, and bring soup to her when she's sick. And then when he meets another Episcopalian woman, also bringing soup, they get to talking, and he discovers that she's not so bad either. And then the three of them come up with a library fund-raiser that brings in people from a wide cross section of the community, including a whole network of associations from their separate faith groups, so the library event is a huge success, and so on.

In Beacon, New York, Rabbi Brent Spodek got to work with bridging and bonding as soon as he came to town. Beacon has a mix of ethnicities and first languages. By bringing together different houses of faith with their somewhat self-segregating congregations, the interfaith Bible studies he held with other religious leaders were some of the best ways to bridge the racial divide that towns often experience despite their best intentions.

The first conversation we have with people is often the hardest one to have. The discussion of what is meaningful to us, with the goal of mutual understanding, is a powerful starting point, as citizens of Beacon, seeking solutions for affordable housing and finding ways to shore up their schools, have found.

Right in my own hometown, Chappaqua, New York, members of the Interfaith Panel wrote a letter to zoning officials in support of a mosque being built. The letter seemed to say, "We're sure that your zoning concerns are devoid of any prejudice, but given the raging Islamophobia in our country right now, please know the regard we hold for our brethren of faith. We hope you resolve those pesky zoning issues soon so that our neighbors can build their mosque." The first one to sign was a rabbi, followed by four other religious leaders in town.

8

Gainesville, Florida: Conscious Bridgers

I've saved conscious bridgers, individuals who make a disproportionate contribution to positive proximity, for the end. To hang the life and future of a town on the work of a few individuals is precarious. Positive proximity is determined by a collective effort. There are mechanisms that help to build it and spatial configurations that grow it. We don't want one person doing all the work or one voice hogging the microphone.

But there are certain kinds of people from whom we can all learn how to be powerful community builders because they love to make connections everywhere they go. They weave together disparate fibers of a town's identity, open channels of communication, and turn up the volume on all that is fun and good in a town, often initiating those fun and good things on their own. There's no getting around it: these individuals are the main translators of their communities.

Sometimes these citizens don't even know that what they are doing involves an actual skill set, but it does. They are conscious bridgers, and I found a treasure trove of them in Gainesville, Florida.

Walking around Gainesville, you'd never guess that it's anything but a very nice, still affordable, somewhat conservative, college town.

The campus itself is so big that you'll see large groups of tanned students getting around on pastel motor scooters. The Gator Stadium is enormous, and a twenty-foot-high wall at one entrance announces, "THIS IS THE SWAMP."

The town has lovely cafés; a big sushi restaurant; and other cheap places with healthy food, organic coffee, and a casual, slightly sleepy feeling. It's a wonderful place to live, and that presents a big problem. Without the stake in the ground that says "We ARE this" and "We are NOT this," a cool town can attract some very mercenary attention. There are two or three very big proposed projects for which two real-estate development companies want to make the most amount of money with the least amount of feedback from the community. Despite the energy with which Gainesville citizens plunge into their interdisciplinary projects, there are still very few people who show up at public meetings. And in the meantime, there are divisions the developers can and do exploit.

Gainesville has its points of separation, which can be purposefully widened. The university has a life of its own, and sometimes coexists, rather than harmonizes, with the rest of the city. Both town and gown are such big entities that it can be hard to unify them in the pursuit of fruitful citywide collaborations.

As another potential point of division, the University of Florida's medical research department, which holds the highest number of medical patents in the United States, has plans in place for Innovation Square, where researchers will explore lucrative applications for their patents instead of seeing them make millions for others out of state. Seeing this off-campus megacomplex in the making, the social connectors of Gainesville ask: How do we integrate this into the city and provide opportunities for its surrounding community? They worry that too few of the planners are asking these questions.

Then there is the long road about ten blocks from the city center that symbolically divides black and white populations. Everyone I spoke with mentioned that road. Many, perhaps most, Gainesville citizens would like to bridge it. But the developer of another giant project has presented an "environmental concerns versus potential jobs" argument that widens socioeconomic divides as a way to splinter, and thereby weaken, dissent.

In my travels, I've learned that there are two things for which developers have a keen sense of smell: blight and momentum. It's smart to seek out blight because it means no one is looking, and you can do whatever you want. But Gainesville offers the latter seduction, momentum. Targeting momentum means finding areas where creative, innovative people have done all the work of bringing life and color to a place. In ten years, any investment will be doubled or tripled just because you showed up at the right time. Momentum development has nothing to do with increasing that life and color but only with capitalizing on it. Developers can smell the basil and parsley in your community herb garden from a thousand miles away.

But as I was ending my most recent visit to Gainesville, which started with a volunteer green-burial grave digging and ended with an experimental drum circle for teenagers (all part of an itinerary my friend Jenny put together for me with five days' notice), I passed under the Double Helix Bridge, a footbridge representing blue and red chromosomes that connect twisted strands of DNA. "This, to me, is Gainesville," I said. DNA is defined by its precisely connected strands. Each element is crucial, but the elegant genius of DNA is dependent on the relationships formed between each of the helixes. The code and expressions of identity are in the bridging.

The question is whether Gainesville can keep up with all the new connections, fast rate of change, and challenges that come from both inside and outside the city. Conscious bridgers will be crucial to the effort. Conscious bridgers are doers, but they also come with open palms and say, "We've got a problem to tackle. I solve problems all the time. I like to find solutions, often with limited resources." And at a certain point, they say, "And now I'm at a loss. You have the information. Your turn." And from this ingenious plea comes an unexpected response from the people who find the personal volition and resources to say, "I'll try." Ultimately, conscious bridgers bring out the bridge builders in all of us.

CONSCIOUS BRIDGERS HAVE YOU THINKING IN POSSIBILITIES

Perhaps you know a conscious bridger, perhaps you are one, or perhaps you have some of these traits and haven't understood the role they can play in connecting your town. As I described in Chapter 7, "bridging social capital" interweaves the strengths and weaknesses of different demographics so that positive proximity can be experienced more widely and confidently throughout a town or city. Conscious bridgers are always on the lookout for new alliances and connections.

Rabbi Brent, in Beacon, New York, with his interfaith Bible studies, is a conscious bridger. My artist friend Charlie Hunter, in Bellows Falls, Vermont, who came to town and painted new signs for local businesses, started a concert series and a festival and put his painting studio at the busy center of town for all to find him, is a conscious bridger. Monica Roth is a crucial conscious bridger in the Finger Lakes region. Barbara Cohen is such a passionate conscious bridger in Phoenixville, Pennsylvania, that she'll round up a posse of friends and track down actual bridges constructed of elements from Phoenix Iron and Steel.

THE VISIONARY

Nowhere did I find such a hotbed of conscious bridgers as in Gainesville, Florida. The person who led me there was Jenny Lee Baxley. Jenny's a green-eyed, blond, third-generation Floridian with an unaffected and joyful smile and almost childlike enthusiasm. She is a dance therapist, a field devoted to building bridges between mind, body, and emotions and to connecting creativity with healing. She is also a visionary when it comes to conscious bridging. Every interaction is an opportunity for connections. When I visited her, I got a full rundown on all the people she introduced me to: what they did for a living, their hobbies, how they related with the community, what they were working on, and anything they might have in common with me.

I already had a history with Jenny. Earlier, when she lived in St. Petersburg, Florida, Jenny had built a festival from scratch, and I played there. Jenny created and presented an entire city neighborhood event to benefit her arts organization, Creative Clay. Back in 2010, my manager had a feeling I should take a chance on this new festival, and he was right. Everything about it was as breezy and warm as the weather, including a big open stage in front of a blocked-off street and a packed audience that ranged from families with kids to couples raising their beer cans in salute.

Later, Jenny took me and my keyboard player, Bryn, out to dinner. Over a globe-shaped glass of wine, Jenny confessed that this was her first crack at concert production. Her neophyte status was a revelation that bordered on alarming. The day before I had come, the Indigo Girls had played there. They are hardly high-maintenance people, but their stage plot is complicated. No one had known the steep learning curve on which Jenny had been.

Jenny called on a wide range of people, cultural and municipal, to bring this concept out of her head and into the streets, Byzantine paperwork and all. "I found out that the fire department wouldn't allow a stage with the size and specs required by our headliners. I went to the fire chief and described our plight. I said, 'Look, I work in the arts. I wake up every morning and say, How much can I do with less? Because that's what I always have to do. I can't give you more money, and I want you to change this. I need you to do more with less.'" And they did. They found safe loopholes and adaptations.

In 2012 she and her family moved to Gainesville so that she could be a lecturer in a university program that is itself a bridge between two worlds, the Arts in Medicine Program at the University of

Florida. I intuited that Gainesville was a good fit for her despite my first impression of the city years before.

In 2009, I played a gig in Gainesville. I knew I was in a foot-ball-crazy, Florida college town, home of the Florida Gators. The venue, Common Ground, was a bar. There were pinball machines right next to the stage. I walked in and said, "Uh oh." I knew this kind of college-town gig. *Head down, get through it.* I was completely wrong. It was a stellar night. The audience listened and laughed, and, after the show, a few of them handed me copies of Gainesville's radical left-wing paper, the *Iguana*. They didn't hand me the paper surreptitiously; Gainesville experiences itself as a town of many viewpoints.

This wasn't just any college town. In subsequent visits, I met peo-ple who were using all the space, affordability, and resources of Gainesville to explore cross-disciplinary fields of work and study that ranged across the political spectrum and almost never had anything to do with football. Even before Jenny arrived, I could see that this was a perfect place to study which personality traits are strong in a conscious bridger and what kind of environment supports him or her.

The Arts in Medicine Program was established by Jill Sonke be-fore Jenny was invited to the faculty. Jill, a world traveler, published an article for the prestigious *British Medical Journal* describing arts and health connections used during the Ebola outbreak. Gainesville is one of the preeminent institutions in the country for bringing to-gether therapeutic worlds. The whole Arts in Medicine Program has created a mutually curious bridge between two disciplines. This is perhaps one of the reasons Jenny was in her element in Gainesville right from the start. Bridgers like to be where different worlds meet. That's where they flourish.

Jenny invited me to spend time at the teaching hospital at the heart of the Arts in Medicine experience. Arriving from the airport, I found the University of Florida Health Shands Hospital at the end of a long road under banners that read "For the Gator Good." Jenny greeted me as I got off the elevator and gave me a crash course on the people in the unit as we walked. She dropped me off at the lounge while she made sure everything was set with doctors and the patient I had come to visit. I was here to play a "tiny bed concert," a one-on-one performance. This one was for a sixteen-year-old girl awaiting a heart transplant. She had made a request for songs that had the word "heart" in them. Other musicians were wandering the halls, having just done their own concerts, and they joined me in the room. The girl was frail but not overwhelmed. She was used to being surrounded by friendly musical strangers. The guys accompanied me on guitar and mandolin.

Around us was the silent percussion of monitors. It was a social, creative scene in a high-stakes, specialized wing of the hospital for treating noncontagious but critical illnesses. Instead of wondering what we were doing here, we felt like this was exactly where we should be. Jenny and the doctors and nurses were collaborating along a healing continuum. Jenny and her colleagues were assiduously following medical protocols while directing musicians in and out of the rooms. Doctors and nurses worked in tandem to make sure everything went smoothly.

After our good-byes, Jenny brought me down to play at Cymplify—owned by Ken Block from the band Sister Hazel, and his wife, Tracy Montgomery-Block—where I did a benefit for the Arts in Medicine Program (a partial benefit because Jenny insisted on paying me). I wasn't surprised by the Sister Hazel association. This is a hardworking, touring band with a reputation among my fellow troubadours for kindness and fairness. Out on the road, the musicians are connectors, bridgers. How appropriate that Ken would bring that ethos back to his town.

It was a very lively crowd at the small club, on and off the stage. Everyone I met after the show said he or she was Jenny's friend. Even though she'd been here for less than three years (and had put this concert together with three weeks' notice), her connections were all over the social map. Jenny, busy raising two girls with her husband, Gabe, while also teaching, digging green graves, counseling veterans, learning how to make kimchee, and running tiny bed concerts (I'm sure I've left a few things out), is getting ready to put her ideas together in a book or a program.

The ambitious bridge she aspires to build is between artists and arts therapists. She believes there is an unnecessary waste of energy when, on the one hand, arts therapists believe they are less inherently creative for not pursuing art professionally and on the other when artists don't believe they can use their creativity to affect health. Worst of all, she has encountered artists who have disdainfully dismissed the work of arts therapists, such as music therapy or dance therapy, as if the application of the arts to therapy somehow diminishes the impact of the artistic or creative process itself.

Considering how much local artists love her and find themselves capable of doing good work in hospital units of seriously ill patients, I'd say Jenny's an effective advocate for her cause, and I believe that before she's done, her bridge will become the new normal in further connecting arts with arts in medicine. The distance between the two is just a construct, and a silly one at that. I say that as an artist who felt transformed by my own conversations with Jenny during the time I spent in the places she took me.

She was a little tearful when I said she was the perfect person to take us on this evolutionary path of reconciliation. I think she was emotional because, throughout our trip, she was busy thinking of other bridgers. There was always another person she wanted me to meet, often describing this or that person as "very dear, very thoughtful." Even when we went out for pizza, she jumped up and hugged Betsy Carlson, her yoga teacher, who came over to say hi. This teacher and archaeologist, Jenny explained, did things that were nothing short of transformative.

Jenny was unused to hearing, I could tell, that her own vision of the world was worthy of assembling people she knew from all over the city to offer their spaces, insights, and collaborative energies to bring her ideas to life whenever that time would come. And it will come. I am sure that her plan, really a paradigm shift, will be aided and abetted by the many friends and colleagues with whom she has worked in Gainesville.

I called Jenny a few months after the Cymplify gig and asked if she could introduce me to more people with whom she shared her interest in social bridging. The answer was an emphatic "Yes." This was a place, she had discovered, in which the people she met, just as I had predicted, were as interested in expanding imaginative frontiers as she was.

Let's look at the personality traits that make up these conscious bridgers—of the DNA builders, if you will.

THINKING INSIDE THE BOX IS GOOD

The first thing I noticed, to my surprise, was that conscious bridgers *don't* think outside the box. They accept the "box," but that doesn't mean they follow conventional norms once they're in there.

Chuck Levy doesn't look like a person with far-flung and sometimes seemingly chaotically connected interests. Chuck looks like the doctor he is, tall and neatly dressed, enthusiastic and warm but also measured and thoughtful. He has impressive job titles such as chief of Physical Medicine and Rehabilitation at the Malcolm Randall Veterans' Assistance (VA) Medical Center and codirector of psychology for the Center of Innovation on Disability and Rehabilitation Research, funded by VA Health Services.

I was quick to learn that Chuck is also a conscious bridger of the first order. He took us to a small, chapel-sized studio behind his house. The walls were filled with hanging banjos, guitars, mandolins, and violins. Jenny and I asked him to play, and he picked up a banjo from its stand and played a beautiful Appalachian ballad; he also coadministers the Suwannee Banjo Camp and codirects the Stephen Foster Old Time Music Camp.

Chuck has a passion for music that rivals his commitment to medicine. And he has spent more than a decade bridging the two worlds. "I've got this medical part and this musical part, and sometimes they meet," he said. One of the connections between the two was that he heard about the Arts in Medicine Program and, inspired by it, started playing music for some of his patients. Now he is the chair of the advisory board for the program.

Chuck's vision involves connecting very real forms of human capital in new ways. And he has a good enough track record that he is an esteemed member of the medical community, and he continues to get grants that incorporate different disciplines, not just music, into his job at the hospital. He knows this is his strength. One of the reasons he took his job in Gainesville was the permission the hospital gave him to explore his different worlds. He asked for 50 percent research time even if there was no specific grant to fund it. He explained that if he got the research time, he'd make a grant from it. And he has delivered on his promise.

Chuck thinks *inside* the box. In fact, he figures out exactly what's in the box and how it works. Then he sticks his hands inside the box and moves stuff around to make it work better. Sometimes that simply means matching resources with resources. Chuck saw that artists and arts therapists were available through the Arts in Medicine Program, and he knew that most veterans had emotional issues as well as physical problems, so why not make a visit with an arts or dance therapist a regular part of every medical visit?

Always on the watch for how technology can help solve the age-old problems of former soldiers, he is very interested in telehealth—online tracking and consulting with patients about their medical conditions. So he started to explore whether remote consultations with arts therapists might also be effective. Veterans' progress was tracked within the VA hospital, so there were ways to use the system for allowing patients to follow up with creative arts therapists and vice versa just as they would follow up with medical doctors.

He told me they'd just started pulling together data to gauge the effects of these arts therapist consultations. Nothing was conclusive yet, but he was encouraged by the evidence: the patients loved the arts therapy program. Chuck gave Jenny credit for much of the program's success. That's another thing I noticed about these bridgers. They are quick to acknowledge the contributions and talents of others. There is an inherent humility in the way they give others the limelight. Conscious bridgers' pride is in knowing when to call each player to the stage.

Part of thinking inside the box is recognizing and bringing out people's strengths. Whenever Chuck mentioned a new program he had invented, such as a virtual grocery store to help returning combat veterans navigate environments with many emotional variables, he listed the names of the people crucial to it. When he told me about a symposium he coordinated between American and African musicians called the Akonting-Banjo Collaborative (the akonting is a West African instrument), he named every single player who came over from Africa and every banjo player he brought in, stringing accolades after the name of each musician. "I'm not the smartest guy I know, I'm not the person who reads the most, I'm not the person who has all the details," he said. "I do seem to actively like to connect the different parts of stuff that I see with other parts."

Chuck is a great example of the somewhat elusive intelligence required for creative bridging. He is well versed in conventional rehabilitation practices, but he is also interested in new technology that can approach the needs of returning soldiers from a fresh, accessible angle. Veterans use Xbox controllers in the virtual grocery store, for instance, because most of them are familiar and comfortable with video games. In his musical world, Chuck loves banjos, but he is passionate about the way in which they connect with other cultures and histories. He has, in fact, recorded a CD called *Banjourneys*, with a website that provides information about all the instruments and songs he has chosen. And although he has a passion for both medicine and music, he is most excited about connecting them in the service of healing.

BRIDGING WITH FOOD

Anna Prizzia is another conscious bridger in Gainesville. When I met her she was in the midst of planning a dinner for a celebration at the Cotton Club Museum and Cultural Center in Gainesville. The museum was about to commemorate the Cotton Club and its historical role in the neighborhood. Back in the 1950s it had been part of the Chitlin' Circuit, where young performers such as James Brown and B. B. King got their start. Anna explained what would happen during the celebration of Emancipation Day on May 21.

Anna was participating on behalf of Forage Farm, which she had been running with her business partner, Melissa DeSa, for five years. Forage Farm's mission (or part of it—it's huge) was "protecting the story and the diversity of our food system." This meant "making sure people understand that the cultural heritage of our food and the genetic diversity of our food are important to the sustainability of our food system, as is water, as is healthy soil." Forage Farm has gathered and stored a variety of seeds, many of which refer back to the history of what's been grown over the centuries in Gainesville, including vegetables that would have accompanied those chitlins on the Chitlin' Circuit. These foods are part of the DNA of Gainesville.

This celebration would enable people in the community to experience the food heritage of the region and know firsthand the work Forage Farm does. It would also be a way to bridge the farm's work with a cultural community already uncovering a history of music and art. Anna said, "During the day they're going to have storytellers and a lot of similar events. We're going to do some tastings and some fun things that connect the dots between the black roots of music and the black roots of food in our culture, especially here in the Southeast."

"And then at night we're going to have a big banquet," Anna continued. "We're going to have a lot of the blues music, traditional bands, and storytelling from the African culture here in particular. And then serve a meal that's traditionally Senegalese but will look almost exactly the way southern comfort food looks, because it all came from West Africa."

Like Chuck, who found the connection between the banjo and African instruments, Anna appreciated the derivation of southeastern American from West African food. "People will get to eat jollof rice, and people will be eating red peas and rice, and people will be eating all these things that look very much like what they're used to eating as soul food, but they'll be eating a Senegalese feast, essentially," she explained.

Anna was planning to bring in more members of the community to strengthen these bridges, members of the university's African American Studies Department and other faculty, so that the community could have greater access to the university as well as all the programs Forage Farm offers. In a city like Gainesville, where the racial divide always threatens to get wider, this celebration day is a way for East and West Gainesville to find each other through food, music, history, and mutual appreciation, literally, of what is brought to the table.

Anna Prizzia's dream, as a step beyond Forage Farm and the celebration dinner, is to create a community center that's centered on food. "There would be a kitchen, and that would be literally the hub," she described it. There would be a space for eating and running programs as well. The kitchen could be used to can your own sauce if you had bushels of tomatoes, or to "cook for a big family reunion," or to test making your own line of foods, which, of course, could bring an opportunity for entrepreneurs to find a place in the local economy. The plan is to have planting and growing space outside, as well, for people to try new varieties. She holds the belief that "you pull a string, and all things are connected. All things spiral, and you create programs and events and workshops and classes and art and music and dance and theater and all of it, surrounding this idea that food is not just the literal nourishment of our body, but it has all these other connections."

Anna is looking for sites right now. One is on the road that defines the racial divide between East and West Gainesville, but developers might get there first. Nevertheless, I found myself telling Anna that I knew the community kitchen would happen and not only that, it would be a huge success. How did I know? Well, I'd already learned from the Finger Lakes region of New York that food-based projects, communities, and economies tend to build and "harvest" positive proximity. So there's that. But I'd also heard about how Anna has cultivated relationships across Gainesville by working on gardens at the university and showing up for city council meetings.

Also, beyond her call to Vivian Filer, director of the Cotton Club Museum and Cultural Center, to coordinate the museum's day of celebration, she has gone out of her way to find citizens, particularly older people of color, to carry on traditional cultures of cooking and making tonics and tinctures by enlisting them to teach workshops. She has built institutional support, but she has also recruited a range of valuable teachers outside the traditional academy. So I know that when she breaks ground on the community center, Anna will not only know what to build, she'll know what to plant, literally and figuratively, and she will honor all the diversity and biodiversity her community has to offer.

BRIDGING THROUGH ART

The Hippodrome Theater, Gainesville's community-based theater and education center, is a few blocks away from where Anna and I had our tea, and there I sat down with Gabby Byam, who started the We the People Theater, a very experiential, process- and communication-oriented theater for teenagers and preteens.

Gabby explained the first teen-based project to me. There were twelve kids in the program. "We went into the woods, and we did *Midsummer Night's Dream*. We started taking that piece and dissecting it and going, 'Well, what's at the root of it? What themes do we want to talk about? And then we wanted to kind of take that theme and what we felt was the idea of love. We thought that was one of the themes that came out, and we somehow got into the concept of what does that mean in terms of the community? Does the community thrive on love? Does it fall apart because it doesn't have it? So we started doing pieces that were just pop-up pieces."

All of this was very successful, but Gabby wanted to push out into another part of Gainesville with a new group of kids. She said, "I really would like to find a population that maybe couldn't afford [a theater program] and see what we can do with that population. Let's head over to the East Side. So we started doing stuff at Loften High School, and we started doing some outreach there, and we said, 'Oh, well, what if we had this kind of coordinating where we talked about these themes, and we had the Loften High School students work with some kids that were in residential facilities, and the students became kind of mentors to these kids?' And that program took off."

"Residential facility" means a place where kids are incarcerated for six to eight months. Gabby set up the Loften High School kids as mentors for these children. "And it was great because the students that I worked with at Loften weren't necessarily the academically excelling students, but they found this role as teachers and facilitators. They went in and ran workshops with these girls, who were just primed for it. They were really into it, so we did a lot of stuff about the idea of love."

Then there was another opportunity to work with boys from a residential facility for young sex offenders. They worked on Shakespeare's *A Comedy of Errors*, and the theme was identity. Gabby explained, "One of the things that really resonates with them, and with a lot of the young people who have been in trouble, is that 'these actions don't define me, but unfortunately sometimes in the eyes of other people they do.' So how do we have a conversation about that?

How do we start asking questions about that? So we did a restorative justice piece. It was really well received. We actually got to do it here in the cinema." Gabby was literally bringing people from the margins into the cultural center of Gainesville.

If, as Martin Luther King Jr. said, paraphrasing abolitionist minister Theodore Parker, "The arc of the moral universe is long, but it bends toward justice," the conscious bridgers I've met are interested in following that curve as far as it goes, finding opportunities for the whole community to gain more access to understanding, to healing, and in both the long and short term, to justice. They bring as many people as they can find on that arc, and then they stay the course.

Conscious Bridgers, Active Learners

And none of them are doing their work with any Pollyannaish desire to "help others." Bridgers experience each project as a learning opportunity in which they themselves can thrive. Out on a walk through Payne's Prairie Preserve State Park (which included about a dozen alligators lounging on the riverbanks), Jenny revealed the curiosity she and fellow conscious bridgers have about the world.

"At Forage Farm, we had this group of people learning how to make kimchee together. It's actually really easy, because it's Florida. You leave anything on the counter in salty water for three days, it's going to ferment." But then she describes how she was in a group that was getting all the basics down, making kimchee in different containers, stirring at the right time every day or so, and how they experimented using all sorts of different vegetables. "I love that, I love the not knowing things together and then learning how to do it."

For some people, not knowing things in public would be like having a naked-in-public dream. But for Jenny, the spark that comes when we move from collectively not knowing to knowing is something to celebrate. She's very happy to locate herself in the moment of learning. One of the few things for which she has disdain is condescension.

Jenny has courted these process-based experiences. She told me about a veteran with whom she loved working. He had trouble breathing and walking. She wrote poetry with him. He wrote a poem that he wanted to read at a veterans' commemorative event. Jenny facilitated the trip, helping him navigate the space in his wheelchair. But when it was time to read, he stood up, and then, to her amazement, he walked to the dais to read his poem. This was the moment a therapist hopes for, when all that not knowing together is transformed into words that turn pain into poetry. In this case, the poet's inspiration transcended his physical limitations, fusing physical and emotional healing.

All the conscious bridgers I've met have a similar interest in taking their skills into the field, risking a moment of public ignorance. Gabby invited me to watch a group of teenagers playing hand drums at the River Phoenix Center for Peacebuilding (RPCP). She wasn't sure this was going to fly, but from years of experience with teenagers in the theater, she knew it was worth a shot.

The next day, when I got to the RPCP building, an unassuming bungalow a few blocks from downtown, there was a circle of chairs for the teenagers, who had already shown up and chosen their drums. The teacher, a professional percussionist, was playing a little, and Gabby was talking with the kids, keeping everything casual and conversational. As the drumming started, I was impressed that they tried a lot of exercises, such as call and response, imitation, and building one big rhythm forest. It was unclear at first whether these kids were going to find that kinesthetic link between their inner chaos and the collective patterns of drumming.

But Gabby was there to absorb the discomfort, the awkward attempts, and even the acting out. One kid was clearly frustrated and at one point started drumming against the rhythm. Gabby didn't say a word. Everyone was here to figure something out, not to get something right. I also noticed that one boy was getting the hang of things. He was connecting, but he didn't look like he was ready to admit that he was converted. Gabby noticed what he was doing but she didn't say, "Check it out. Follow what he's doing!" These kids came from places where it wasn't always safe to be a standout student. And so they proceeded, openly and unevenly.

Gabby's job title, or one of them, is facilitator here at the RPCP, a community bridge-building organization founded by Heart Phoenix and Jeffrey Weisberg in 2011. Both Heart and Jeffrey had a long list of credentials that preceded the origins of the RPCP, but the organization itself is by nature exploratory and open to taking on new approaches in the field. Heart came to the organization with a long history in the peace and justice and feminist movements. Jeffrey came from a similar background and was a court mediator, a job description that had everything to do with finding ways to improve communication, not control the outcome of it.

Jeffrey worked as a mediator for violent children in the court system. The government ran out of funding to pay him, so he did it for free. But then the mediation program itself was terminated. That's when Jeffrey and Heart went to the assistant attorney general and offered some pilot mediation programs of their own. The assistant attorney general dismissed them out of hand, but Heart said they convinced her to have a little faith. "We just kept talking about what if, what if." So the assistant attorney general finally gave them a green light. Heart and Jeffrey are consummate bridgers.

Heart has a steadiness and intensity that you can see immediately. She has beautiful blue eyes and looks a little like the actor Joaquin Phoenix, which makes sense, because she is his mother. She took me through the chronology of creating the peace-building center, starting with the successful meeting with the assistant attorney general.

The pilot programs she and Jeffrey initiated were so successful that people started to come from other organizations to work with them. Finally it was time to become a formal nonprofit based in "solutionary" approaches. They named it the River Phoenix Center for Peace-building, for Heart's other son, who died in 1993, "because River was that way. As a young person he was like, 'Enough with the problems, what are we going to do about it? And then let's talk about that. Let's think about that.'"

They didn't have a clear picture of what the center would become, but they wanted to investigate best practices—in an ever-changing and multifaceted environment—of peace building and solution-based communication. "We said, 'Let's take what we know and bring it to a small community, a community where you can meet the city manager usually, and the mayor, and you can meet the people and meet the teachers and talk to the school board." And so they went to Gainesville, a city near their home.

In their case, Heart and Jeffrey didn't only bring an open-minded attitude of exploration with their skills. They also brought the space, the laboratory of solutionary skill building (and rebuilding). They provided the programs and the brick-and-mortar bungalow so that others could join in and grow it in new directions. The space they offered was crucial. After many years with people's movements, Heart observed, "One of the things that we know in terms of sustaining peace on the level that we're really talking about is there has to be some kind of structure in place where not only do you create the conditions for peace, but that there is a continuity that is available to the general public." So they put out their shingle and told people who they were and where they were.

They knew that with a few tenets in place, the rest of the process would unfold in time. This was a forum in which new ideas could be explored and incorporated. So much of what they have accomplished comes from holding that space where no one has all the answers. "There was somebody who said, 'We have some solutions that we're happy to share,' and everywhere we went it was to learn about who they are and what they do and appreciate what they do. When you value someone, even though they don't really feel the same way, they are so open. Their hearts are open. They're more apt to say, 'Well, that's interesting.' And at first it's like, 'Are you kidding me?' And then it's like, 'Wow.'" Clearly Heart, like Gabby and her expanding group of Gainesville students, was in it more for the "wow" than for the ego or for creating a formula that can be used in the same way again and again.

Heart was ready for the interactions in her life to truly shift her own conceptions. She said, "I cried the first time I talked to the sheriff. We went into the office to share some of what we were doing." Heart listened and watched and came to a realization. She remembered saying to the sheriff, "I never really gave it a thought what you do. I never gave it a thought that when there's a car wreck you're picking up the pieces. Your deputies are out picking up severed bodies, babies screaming, parents burning. I can't imagine what that is. You go to sleep at night, and you don't know what the next day is going to bring you."

Heart went on to search for ways of communicating that recognize trauma on both sides of the law. When she approached police officers in creating police-youth dialogues, she always made the point, "These are not bad kids. Something happened to them." But she's also reinforced in all communications that many officers have also experienced trauma, both preceding their life choices to join law enforcement and on the job.

It's hard to assess through data how well all of these acts of bridging are working. These bridgers have decades of experience and training, but they know formal gauges are sometimes insufficient. Considering how unique every situation is, when you bring an element of chance into each interaction, it's hard to go by known indicators of success. Gabby said, "I did a program here that was an at-risk outreach program that went into the schools. We did a lot of measuring and a lot of validating, and there was a lot of pretesting and post-testing, study groups, and putting things in boxes, and I always felt that was never really a great reflection, those post-tests or pretests."

She came to realize, "My test if a program was good was if I would see a kid at Publix, and if they said hello to me. Today I saw somebody, and they walked by me, and they were like, 'Loften High School,' and we're like, 'Yeah, what's up?' To have that connection still, I think that that's community, that's the idea of knowing, 'Oh yeah, I'm here, I remember you, and how are you doing?' and having that kind of old-timey thing that your mom and my mom and people's moms used to do back in the day checking on each other's kids. That's what it feels like for me." So that's Gabby's validation that things are going right: "When I work with the students, I see them again, and most often they talk to me."

There is bound to be a wide margin of error in making something new. In creating their programs and institutions, Jenny, Gabby, Heart, and Jeffrey had the right temperaments for applying what they had learned in their previous lives to the high-volatility environments in which they work now. They started by valuing the people they encountered, they moved with the situations presented to them, and they observed moments of profound connection as a way to track their work.

But perhaps the most sustaining quality of their commitment is that they truly seemed to enjoy all the things that enlightened them and surprised them from the "not knowing together." Their life path is to work for social justice, healing, and peace building. And they are also in it to learn.

BRIDGE OF POSSIBILITIES

After the people I'd met had, in their life's work, planted themselves in one place, not only could their plans come to fruition but also their projects became the foundation for new bridges in Gainesville. The tools in their toolboxes were their understanding of how people, institutions, and neighborhoods tick, and they used their savviness to work on community projects accordingly. They were also building trust and a track record. So when the next idea comes to them, doors open more quickly.

The latest project at the RPCP hooks in with the UN Sport for Development and Peace Program. Heart explains that the program is for kids perceived as "at risk" (she said, "All kids are at risk, by the way, but anyway, these particular kids they say are at risk"). "So we do a thing where they are doing sports—and now we're trying to just say physical activity—integrated with emotional learning." This involves all of the positive messages of sports as well as shifting away from some of the more bloodthirsty attitudes of some parents and coaches.

It's clearly a new world for the center, and it has initiated a strong element of the unknown. I can't imagine Heart playing one-on-one soccer or basketball with teenage boys (well maybe I can), but the center's allies are now spread among a wide cross section of Gainesville residents who know its leaders and trust them. Combined with the "structure" RPCP has traditionally provided, there will be new mentors and mediators from across disciplines to bring the sports and movement project to life.

For all of its rah-rah, sports-loving party-hardiness, complete with more than twenty fraternities and sororities along Fraternity Drive, the University of Florida has welcomed new thinkers and new ideas. The university is also a very multicultural institution, exploring ways to learn more about other countries and welcoming their international students. Nobody I spoke with said the university gates were flung wide open like a big playground, but there was a mutual curiosity in how to bridge a powerhouse college and outstanding research university with the terrain of new and more equitable social frontiers presented by the community.

Gainesville's size and location (relatively small and remote) might be considered a disadvantage, but I have found that small cities have the advantage of some extra space to spread out, and they're just far enough off the grid to incorporate intuitive, trial-and-error processes that can yield important discoveries.

FUTURE OF A CITY

How do we gauge the outcomes of conscious bridging in terms of the overall life of Gainesville? For one thing, I hear more about Gainesville from people like my friend Father John Dear, a Jesuit priest from California, who talked to me about the RPCP. John knew about its projects. He wasn't surprised I was already familiar with the center. He said more and more people are talking about it. To him, the work of this highly committed coalition of communicators could be a game changer for restorative justice.

Nonetheless, I'm still concerned for Gainesville's future. Unless it's integrated into the surrounding community, Innovation Square, for example, could become a disconnected cube instead of a link to the community or even a portal through which young students could see science and engineering translated into everyday inventions. And for all the bridging I see, there are still the challenges the two outside developers might bring to the distinct, yet fragile, fabric of identity Gainesville has woven over the past half century.

Time will tell. When Jenny and I met Heart Phoenix for lunch, the city manager and Ken from Sister Hazel walked in. Everyone knew each other. They all had each other's phone numbers, and I'm guessing that when it comes to Innovation Square, phone calls will be made, and the city manager will be receptive. He did, after all, design the DNA Bridge.

And then there is a viral video that came out in early 2016 that confirmed my hope for Gainesville and the work of its bridgers. In a tinderbox era, when we see one video after another of violent confrontations between African Americans and police officers, my back stiffened when a YouTube video of young kids and a police officer in Gainesville came up on my Facebook feed.

But I remembered some of the stories I'd heard from Heart. "Our main focus within the community is we do police-youth dialogues. They've been doing these for years." She said, "This happened way before Trayvon Martin. It's how to break down the judgment, the fear between cops and black kids. And so these dialogues are with black kids. They're specifically for black and brown kids, meeting with police. We have a five-hour training where there are twelve to fifteen cops and twelve to fifteen kids, and we bring them together, and we do some games, some kind of group building, have some laughs, and start really having some deep questions, deep situations, deep talk. Then we break for dinner, and each cop pairs with a kid, and they have forty-five minutes together, just interviewing each other, talking to each other. Once, it happened that actually a cop that arrested a particular kid got [paired up with him], and this was just random. He ended up being the mentor for this kid."

I thought about Heart, took a breath, and clicked the YouTube link. The first images of a dashboard-camera video showed a police officer, Daniel White, stepping out of his patrol car to address some teenagers playing basketball. He had been called to investigate a noise disturbance. As he strode toward the kids with a gun visibly holstered at his side, his gait had the same appearance as that of a video in which a simple interaction might quickly go awry.

But then he started to shoot hoops with the kids, and he played with them for a while. When he said he would "bring reinforcements next time," his language consciously echoed the menacing words we hear, the kind of "reinforcements" that can lead to confrontations. But because he was implying he would bring more teammates, these reinforcements were safely in the territory of play.

The second video started in a roomful of Gainesville police officers getting ready to go back to play with the kids. But they were also awaiting a special guest who arrived with such a large presence that the camera zoomed back to take in all seven feet one inch of him. "Wow, you're tall," one of the officers said. Shaquille O'Neal was there because he saw the first video and offered to come up and join the "reinforcements."

The next scene was of the kids shooting hoops as the police officers drove up in squad cars. Again, this arrival of multiple cars suggested a more ominous outcome. Officer White came out first, followed by about eight other officers, after which Shaq, who looked like he took up an entire car, stepped out and joined them. For the next hour or so, Shaq played with gentle aggressiveness, at one point picking up a kid to move him. He added a helpfully destabilizing element to the scene because everyone, including the officers, was in awe of him.

9

Bringing Positive Proximity to Your Town

How do we calculate the value of positive proximity? How do we quantify it? This is how I measure it: what I saw in Gainesville, with the police and the teenagers, was a living laboratory, an effort to realign conventional law enforcement toward community peacekeeping, a bridge at once as powerful and fragile as a strand of DNA in one of our healing, human, American cities. I calculate the strength of positive proximity by the things communities do that bring power and life to the commons even when they're hard to organize and sustain.

Other examples? Three hundred people showed up on a cold January night in Beacon, New York, to demand the resignation of a school superintendent who everyone agreed, after many conversations in all the spaces throughout Beacon, was driving the schools into the ground.

Over on the shores of the Finger Lakes, hundreds of people showed up, too, countless times, in snow and sleet, to protest the plans of a company that kept changing its language (and its name) to achieve its goal of storing liquid gas in precarious salt caves. The community's response to the company's ever-shifting narrative was not fatigue. It was more protesters, three hundred of whom got arrested making their point.

Phoenixville, Pennsylvania's cultural institutions are all expanding, and they are in dialogue, confidently so, with developers building apartments where the iron and steel buildings once stood. The citizens are abreast of the coming changes, and they are ready to, as Robin Groff in Moab said, "manage" it, not just arbitrarily embrace or reject what's coming.

Wesleyan University, increasing its commitment to an ongoing presence in Middletown, Connecticut, just signed a deal to have its main bookstore on Main Street, two blocks farther from the campus. The positive proximity built over two decades of mutually respectful partnerships will have a new address for mutual translation in the future.

The proof of positive proximity is also displayed in the ability of towns and cities to increase in complexity and in the number of points of access for their citizens while ultimately building a cohesive identity, though undoubtedly in a "loosey-goosey way," as Joe Knightley from Moab, Utah, would say. Widening the range of access to the community diversifies its voices, yet paradoxically, Carrboro, as a town, "knew" that citizens wanted food trucks and swiftly permitted them in one week. Phoenixville "knew" that the Firebird Festival should incorporate crafts, poetry, and choreography and not be a glorified beer festival, as an outside planner originally proposed. Strong positive proximity allows us to survey the terrain and "know" what the reserves of social capital are and proceed to understand what our towns can handle and what they can accomplish.

As a traveler I can sense positive proximity pretty quickly. Are there posters for strange, funky events, like the Frozen Dead Guy festival in Nederland, Colorado (complete with frozen wet T-shirt contests)? Are there signs at all? Are there helpful pedestrian bridges over highways (Minneapolis, Minnesota), over streams (Phoenixville, Pennsylvania), and over railroad tracks (Roanoke, Virginia) to physically connect every part of the city? Are there social bridges between people, such as dog walkers who say hello to each other and stores that put out free coffee?

I'm guessing you might have questions about your own town or city. How are you doing? How can you grow? Where do you begin? The way to start is to find something that interests you, such as the unique foods that grow where you are, the history of your town and its peoples, architecture that can be brought back to new life, or streams that are only a few discarded truck tires away from being a gathering place instead of an eyesore. Also, if you look around, you'll find people already committed to growing the positive proximity of your town. I guarantee there are some.

When we let our curiosity and interests, and a little trust, lead us outside our doors and onto the village green, we will flourish as citizens and so will our towns. We don't just feel good today or tomorrow when we become involved; we accumulate a sense of meaning. We will always have the challenge, individually, of facing every new day, but we can be guided by a trustworthy compass when we have a sense of who we are in relationship to where we live, when we know how to find out what's afoot and how we can have a role in it, when we live and breathe with a sense of positive proximity. When we get out of bed in the morning, if we have positive proximity, we don't have to go too far to figure out where the day might take us. We just have to make it to the mirror, where we recognize ourselves as citizens, or look out the window, where we see a world in which we belong.

Where to go from there, I suggest, is to bridge whenever possible. Find the retired citizens who might very well be standing at the periphery wondering where and how their time could be best spent. Enlist the schools, the library, the differently abled communities, and local businesses for the sake of coalition building, which will influence the success of other projects as they help build the foundation of your town. Yes, there might be that first "No," but give collaboration a chance. I have learned how to get past the threshold of "No." And if there's a wall just past the threshold, that can be a valuable sign your town isn't quite ready for what you have to offer. You might have to find a different way into the public square.

So first off, start with yourself, and second, bridge from there. I am reminded once again of the recommendation by Robin Groff in Moab to manage change. New technologies, ideas, and demographics will always be passing through your town. If you embrace change fatalistically, you might end up disliking its outcomes. Not every army coming up over the hill is a friendly one. But if you resist change wholesale, you might find yourself behind the times for no good reason, caught up in blame, resentment, and frustration.

How might your involvement in the community both allow more voices into the conversation and ease your own way into the future? Managing change can mean the active struggle to save beautiful, old buildings and preserve sacred groves of trees. It can also be a decision to raze a lead-paint-and-asbestos-riddled structure and start anew. It also means not thumbing your nose at tourists or new businesses. There are ways to invite tourists to appreciate who you are. There are standards that businesses should meet to fit the look and feel of the town. As citizens, you know better than I do what makes you special and how to balance your identity, and even drive it, by managing change.

Another question we can ask is, "How can I find and support the translators in my community?" Translation and conscious bridging can occasionally be challenging if they must be created out of thin air. Although every town can dig in to find its past, start an open mike, or build paths to its waterways and waterfalls, it's more difficult to recommend what to "do" to cultivate translators, be they the individuals who build on the strength of weak ties by connecting networks to networks or the outstanding conscious bridgers I've described. But we can identify them and define our relationships with them. We can find our own translation skills as well.

And what is my own personal story? I try to be a bridger, but the truth is I've often found it's hard to introduce myself to people. I am a public person. My work involves meeting new people for a week at a time (leading songwriting retreats) and even a night at a time (in about seventy-five performances a year). So why should I have any social anxiety at parent-teacher night at school, or at my kids' camps, when I encounter a new face? There's an unspoken barrier that keeps me from saying, "My name is Dar, like car with a 'd.' I'm Stephen and Taya's mom. I hear your son is a *Star Wars* aficionado . . ." (and so forth).

As I started to learn the importance of bridging social capital in communities, I started trying to introduce myself to people more. I experience a strange feeling of exposure and commitment when I do this. Will we start talking about something that I don't know about or that bores me? Does this person know who I am and dislike me? Do I have to hug her or him? These are irrational thoughts, and they are surprising for me. I am, no doubt, a *social* person, and I always have been. When I was in kindergarten, I had to get off the bus last, leaving me alone with the bus driver. He terrified me. So I talked to him. I asked his name and if he liked being a bus driver. His name was Lou, and he pleaded the fifth about his job. But now he had a name, and it wasn't Charles Manson (my sister had a copy of *Helter Skelter*).

There have been so many slogans, such as "Be the change you want to see in the world" and "Practice random acts of kindness," that prescribe individual strategies for making the world a better place. Even "Buy local" is something you simply do as an individual. All of these personal acts are valuable. But this is not a book about the power of one.

Translating ourselves, in an open and open-ended way, can be anxiety producing, and yet the habit of introducing ourselves to people around us can amount to a more solid, less fearful way of being in our communities. I would recommend, just from having met hundreds of shy volunteers at concerts over the years, that if you are uncomfortable about conversation, you can still bake, organize, or offer to find uniforms for a local sports team on which you or your children

play. We can all extend ourselves, even without words, and these individual expressions will add up.

Right now my town is wrestling with negative proximity, which
has put all of our translation skills to the test. Despite the presence of
all the funny, smart, accommodating citizens around me, not to mention the fact that we have every town-building asset I've discussed in
this book (a deep history, gorgeous scenery, and Hudson Valley food
tourism, to name a few), I got a real lesson in what can happen when
a large entity comes in to tear down any kind of unique, interactive
identity a town has started to assume.

A developer wanted to build an enormous complex on the outskirts of town, and the local newspaper embraced his cause, or seemed
to. I say "seemed to" because if I say the editors were all-out boosters
for the developer, I would be threatened with a lawsuit. Again.

There was an election in which both boosters and skeptics of the
development participated. After all the votes were in, not one schism
had been left unwidened: new citizens versus settled, Democrat versus Republican, older versus younger, and even pro-gun versus more
gun control. Worse than that, the paper advanced a narrative of division in general. People were saying they loved living here despite
being "divided."

The town seemed to be in tatters. Many citizens felt humiliated
and intimidated. The paper and/or its owner's spouse had threatened
lawsuits against at least five citizens. Residents of our town were
scared, demoralized, and anxious about legal threats. A friend who
runs a poetry series protested by not submitting a press release to the
paper but then feared retaliation against her nonprofit, her poetry
series, and her family. It was like that.

I was already writing this book, and I thought, "What would a
person who wanted to build positive proximity do in this situation?"
I looked for the broadest common denominators. I wanted to put together an event that was just fun, not targeted at anything particular
about our town. I thought of Rabbi Brent and the broad swath of

community members meeting across the bounds of their constituencies. I came up with the Beatles. Everyone loves the Beatles.

I proposed a Beatles sing-along in the parish hall of the church in the center of the village. Our town is filled with harmony-seeking musicians and artists. As soon as I put out the word, four musicians set up the rehearsals, another friend said he'd lend us his sound system, other friends offered to bake, and another said she'd take care of my kids at the event. Two months later we went into the parish hall. About two hundred people showed up, of all ages and with differing views on the development project. We put lyrics in PowerPoint and projected them on the wall. One teacher brought a basket full of shakers for the kids. About half the kids played and danced, while others ran around outside on the church lawn.

I saw the town I knew from ten years of living there. Old and young, new and settled, all political backgrounds, all of us happily leaning in to our collective experience. The event wasn't necessarily a driver of positive proximity. It was the reminder that we still had it.

The development is happening. We'll live with it, but what we can't live with is the sense that we are a "divided town." Perhaps we can start to act like Ellie Kinnaird, who, when she became mayor of Carrboro, "decided to have fun." Our town is like a treasure chest, or at least a costume chest.

Thinking about Phoenixville and the way in which acknowledging its retired citizens proved a boon to the whole community, and recognizing that our retired citizens had been particularly targeted in the paper's narrative of "division," some friends and I wanted them to know we valued them, so we organized a "remembering" event at the library. We randomly chose the year 1955. We invited people to come tell stories from that time that were fun and educational for our kids. We printed out ads and pictures from that year, when Play-Doh officially became a toy (instead of wall spackling) and McDonald's opened its doors. We made the Hershey official chocolate cake of 1955 (it was strangely awful:

I was the one who cooked it. Operator error?). We had an iPod mix of hit songs from the year, and an art teacher and his family made a fantastic foldout display of old 45 records. Their daughter, Rowan, researched and told us the events from that year and then proudly held up a picture of her grandmother, who was an Olympic skater later in the decade.

Nancy was the emcee and knew everyone. There were only twenty-five kids there with their parents, and about ten senior citizens, but we filled the room. For all our quaint window-dressing of the event, the stories themselves and the people who told them were the stars. Some people prepared stories and spoke; others just piped up.

Bob got up and said that when he was growing up, he had a relative on every street, given all the intermarriage between the large families in the region (many of which are still here). He said it was like a "big party," and he said, with emotion, that he wished the same for everyone in the room.

Another woman, who had recently had a stroke, sat and prompted her daughter to tell stories of her attendance at a one-room schoolhouse on a hill, where they sledded on their backpacks during lunch every day in the winter. She was able to say a few things herself. When one kid asked if a one-room schoolhouse felt small, she simply said, "It was wonderful."

The stories devolved beautifully into the years before and after 1955, with memories of the car dealerships, the soda fountain at the drugstore, and drag racing across the Hudson River when it was covered in ice. We learned from this event about what we would do next: ask more people to prepare stories. Invite high school classes. We will have another remembering event. The kids loved it.

SPEAKING OF OUR SENIOR COMMUNITY, we also have Chestnut Ridge, a senior housing complex of one hundred citizens on the outskirts of town. Many have no family in town. How could we get to know those who live there? We could have a big meeting, but given the acrimony in our community, I didn't foresee a meeting as helpful, and it certainly wouldn't be fun.

Luckily I got a tip from Dorothy, who cuts my hair. Someone told her about a child who had trick-or-treated at Chestnut Ridge the year before. A woman opened her door and said, sadly, that this was the first trick-or-treater she'd ever received. That is crazy. These are row houses, a safe enclave on Halloween.

Chestnut Ridge is only two streets away from Parrott Street, where homeowners compete with each other for the scariest display on their doorsteps, roofs, and lawns. It's a tradition that grows in originality and gruesomeness every year, and we all donate bags of candy for the hundreds of people who visit the living spectacle of zombies and re-mote-controlled spiders. What if we transformed Chestnut Ridge into a place for very young kids to go on Halloween?

I thought of my dad and all the different people he knew when he was trying to get a new library built in our town. I, too, am a parent, a neighbor, and a gardener. My mental wheels started turning. What if the PTA (I'm acquainted with its members) arranged for older kids (I know tons of them) to make decorations that transformed Chest-nut Ridge to "Spookytown" for two- to five-year-olds?

In the end, Julisa, the head of the PTA, and I met and scoped out the site. We could do this. Three groups signed up to make decora-tions: a Girl Scout troop, the private school where my daughter went to day camp, and Ms. Cendali's second graders at the public elemen-tary school.

I knew only one person at Chestnut Ridge, Barbara, but she signed up three other people who lived there to organize and talk it up. We were late in getting the press release in, and someone else dropped the ball on a poster. The Chestnut Ridge residents had seen only a letter from me asking them to be the preschool-kindergarten destina-tion for Halloween. Some were suspicious and others anxious. This could mean a lot of candy and a lot of mess. We assured them that we'd provide the candy and we would clean up the mess.

Someone posted an angry comment on Facebook, and for a minute I thought the paper would write an op-ed about my being a senior-scarer. Where were that press release and poster? The paper was always poised to drive a wedge into a plan, especially if my name was attached to it. I got an e-mail from a resident saying she thought trick-or-treating was a bad idea. People had mobility problems, she said. People didn't want trick-or-treaters. If the kids were afraid of Parrott Street, maybe they could go elsewhere or just stay home? In the last comment was the insinuation that real Cold Spring kids weren't afraid of Parrott Street. More division.

Taking measured breaths, I pressed on. I asked Jamal, who owns Angelina's Pizza, if he could make twenty pizzas in the late afternoon on Halloween, or if he'd be too busy. I explained what we were doing and the connection we were hoping to make in the process, and he nodded. He agreed that we could use a conscious bridge to the south end of town, where Chestnut Ridge is, where people could feel isolated. Without my asking, he offered me a steep discount, and my eyes welled up. Jamal got it.

Meanwhile, it turns out that our ambassadors had indeed explained the event to their Chestnut Ridge neighbors at knitting groups and on bus rides. My friend Kim made a poster in twenty minutes after I sent her an all-caps plea. Ivy swept in and said she'd been out of the loop. Could she help now? Perhaps she could write a press release?

I was on tour when Kathleen and Nancy passed out the decorations. I checked my phone every ten minutes. Nothing. Kathleen and Nancy were on the newspaper's enemies list, as it were. Were they run out of the complex? At 1:15 p.m., the texts came in. Most people had wanted the decorations. Kathleen and Nancy made some friends. It was a beautiful, warm day. Why was I so worried?

I'd already been to the apartments once, passing out the initial letter. I returned to distribute the massive load of candy my friend Molly had donated. The building manager was skeptical about the whole thing as he and I decided where we'd put the big inflatable pumpkin, donated by Sue and her husband from the hardware store, but he was game. Six friends came and helped me hang the biggest decorations. The History Museum, across the street, was already having a Halloween party and offered to host the pizza party after trick-or-treating was done.

At around 3:00 p.m. on Halloween, Toby and Steve came down to put out the bags of LED candles that my friend Hara had kept from her party the week before. By now more than twenty people had participated in this event. Everything was in place. And then it happened. One resident saw me pacing in my witch hat and said, "Relax!"

At the starting time, two doors opened in Building One. Rhoda and Patricia, who'd helped us spread the word, were bringing small tables out for the candy and chairs for themselves. Then their neighbors came out. In the building across the way, five other residents came out with their tables and chairs to welcome the young guests. Everywhere, people were peering out of their apartments. The seniors were ready.

And now, where were the guests? First there was a fairy. Then there was a ghost, then a butterfly, and then there were fifty kids streaming through the apartment buildings, some very shy, first-time trick-or-treaters. The residents kicked right into gear, graciously offering their candy.

It was a fun, intergenerational, low-pressure (for everyone but me) way for people to meet people. As soon as we were seated afterward and eating pizza, we agreed to do it again next year. Rhoda said, "But we have to get more inflatables. Kids loved that inflatable pumpkin." So we will figure out how to solicit big, inflatable, Halloween decorations from families that are downsizing. Rhoda's right. More inflatables. That was the only hitch.

All of these projects will, we hope, build our town's sense of positive collective identity and bring out all the people who like to facilitate connections. These projects express Robert Putnam's vision of bridging social capital. Sometimes bonding social capital only strengthens one group or another (and sometimes reinforces one group *over* another). I was looking for loose ties, new connections, and as many bridges as we could build.

THE STRONGEST TOWNS I have encountered have welcomed the contributions of their citizens. When Beth Macy, author of *Factory Man*, did a reading at one of my concerts, she concluded by saying, "People and communities prosper only when they celebrate a diverse range of equal voices." I want to continue trying to harness the energies of diverse demographics and help add new points of access. I am not the only one.

I've watched the citizens in a thousand towns find ways to bridge to each other and the world. Their histories engage people and illuminate the story of the present, their natural landscapes are well used and lovingly stewarded, their distinct cultures invigorate daily lives, and their local food becomes a currency of proud and good-hearted community exchange. These towns have accumulated a wealth of human capital because they found ways to value the input of their introverts, senior citizens, purple-haired teenagers, and green-thumbed gourmets. Spiky tempers and salty language are welcome.

I met a guy from New Paltz, New York, a town with strong, positive proximity and a robust natural, historical, and cultural identity. I asked if he'd enjoyed growing up there. He said it was *"awesome."* When we have built something extraordinary, a place where we have both hometown pride and a worldly welcome, our kids come back to tell us how well we did by them. Doesn't everyone want that?

I've noticed that people are saying they love our town without adding the caveat "but it's so divided." I didn't orchestrate even an eighth of the projects that knitted us back together. We have movies by the Hudson River, play readings at the train depot that was converted to a theater, and prime sledding at Winter Hill, which had been slated for residential development when a local philanthropist, Chris, rushed in and saved it. I have tried to follow the lead of my conscious bridger friends.

I'd like to think my town has become savvier about keeping out the ill winds of negative proximity. We look around at each other and see that change is coming. The question isn't whom to blame, it's "How will we manage this?" Bigger and bigger waves of tourists are coming in every weekend. Our public schools are improving, and wealthy young families are bound to notice and move here. How do we retain our character and avoid economic displacement? Positive proximity means we know we have only ourselves to decide how to face these changes.

When I was still feeling persistent social anxiety of division in my town, I came up with one final idea (for now), something that would be fun for me, at least. I started with self-interest and bridged from there. I want my next birthday to be a fund-raiser for the Episcopal church, at the center of town. It's a landmark; the Episcopal priest, Shane, is a gem and a conscious bridger; and the church rents out its big parish hall for events that build positive proximity. And it's really expensive to heat.

Some friends have already offered to make the cake, procure the lighting, bring baskets of costumes, and plan the music for this party, because I think it's going to be a high-production blowout. But I've also gained an unexpected asset, Lithgow, a tall gentleman with a great sense of humor who wears natty suits and argyle socks. He is also a fearless contender who ran for county legislator twice. He's been through more muck than just about any of us.

When I started talking about a fund-raiser, I found out Lithgow also had planned events at Danceteria in New York City back in the day. I knew him as an acquaintance, but I floated the idea to him in an e-mail. "Lithgow, the theme of the fund-raiser will be the great equalizer of all communities, and that, of course, is disco." He wrote back soon afterward with words of generous and unabated enthusiasm that resonated with my feeling of excitement for our town's future. He said, "I'd love to help you celebrate your birthday, and I do mean celebrate!"

Acknowledgments

Many thanks to Hal Movius and Kate Bennis, the power couple who introduced me to the dynamics of social capital, giving me a name for what I was seeing in American towns and cities. Also, Charlie Hunter, a good friend and talented painter, trained my eye to appreciate the way communities grow and thrive in our country.

A big thank-you to my patient husband, Michael Robinson, who listened, offered insights, and cooked, and listened some more, and to my wonderful kids, Stephen and Taya. Love and thanks as well to my in-law family, led by Carole Robinson.

Thanks to everyone I've worked with at Basic Books. Lara Heimert took my overflowing box of road stories and observations and gave it structure and a feeling of purpose, and Liz Stein edited out the nonessentials, guiding the best course for the book, as did Melissa Veronesi. My agent, Anthony Arnove, supportive from the start, brought me to Basic Books (and Cliff Chenfeld, you brought me to Anthony—thank you!).

It turns out that I've surrounded myself with people who understand how hard and rewarding civic engagement can be: US Representative Jamie Raskin read my pilot articles and helped me find a path; Kirsti Reeve read the chapters as they evolved and shepherded me through them. Toby Shimin offered me the perfect room of one's own as well as unbelievable support. Julie Burstein helped me record interviews and modeled the way one could weave stories into chapters. Tamar Avishai did the same. More thanks as well to Richard Shindell,

Patty Romanoff, Nerissa Nields, Anne Weiss, Eric von Beck, Paul Ratliff, Maggie Siff, Darren Kapelus, Julia Moskin, Patty Smythe, Lisa Wittner, Barbara Coe, Father John Dear, Melinda Adamz, Blair Woods, Alison and Eric Rector, Jian Ghomeshi, my managers Jessica Weitz and Barry Taylor (and to Camila Guerra-Garcia and Gabby Morsella), my booking agent Seth Rappaport, and Kathleen Denney.

I'm very grateful for the encouragement and guidance of brilliant urban theorists such as Jeff Speck, David Fiorenza, Jonathan Rose, and Douglas Jackson. I've also become a more attuned observer of urban planning thanks to books by Jeff Speck, Robert Putnam, Richard Florida, Peter Owen, and, of course, Jane Jacobs.

Thanks to all the kindred spirits at my songwriting retreats for their faith in creativity on every level, and to my fabulous Wesleyan students, past and present, especially my research assistant, Adrien DeFontaine.

I wish I could thank every single person I interviewed for this book for sharing his or her passion and stories with me. Mary Foote was the first person I called, and her generosity of spirit emboldened me to continue making calls.

Special thanks to my own town. From the school garden up on the hill to the literary readings down on the river, Philipstown bestows the gift of positive proximity, which I feel every day, especially from Stephanie Hawkins, Dave Merandy, Kathleen Foley, John Hedlund, Matt Francisco, Joe Patrick, Raquel Vidal, Michele and Rick Gedney, Tom Todoroff, Emily Moulton, Val Clark, Ivy Meeropol, Zanne Stewart, Suzi Tortora, Felice Ramella, Joe Meisel, Nancy Montgomery, Christine and Ray Bokhour, the Maasiks, Bo Corre, Leo Sachs, and about a hundred more. What I experience in my town is something I wish for everyone.

Index

Dar Williams is a renowned performing singer-songwriter based in the Hudson Valley who has sold millions of albums and toured around the world. Williams is also a well-known environmental and social justice advocate.